DENISE RILEY was born in Carlisle in 1948. She grew up in Gloucester where she attended a local girls' grammar school, going from there to read English Literature at Somerville College, Oxford. She transferred to reading Moral Sciences and Fine Arts at New Hall, Cambridge, and later took her D.Phil in Philosophy at Sussex University. Her jobs have included translating, working as a home tutor for the Inner London Education Authority and intermittent teaching and lecturing for adult education classes, colleges and universities in Britain and Australia. She has been a library assistant, and, most recently, has been doing a study, as a Research Fellow of North East London Polytechnic, of the Becontree Estate. Denise Riley is also a poet, and gives frequent readings: her work in poetry includes *Marxism for Infants* (1977), *No Fee* (1979), *Some Poems 1968–78* (1982) (with Wendy Mulford) and the forthcoming *Living a Life* (1983).

Her writing has included articles and reviews for *History Workshop Journal, Ideology and Consciousness, Feminist Review* and *Spare Rib*, and she has contributed to several books, among them *Women and Society* (also published by Virago), *No Turning Back: Voices from Women's Liberation* and *What is to be Done About the Family?* Her son was born in 1970, her daughter in 1976. She now lives in London and Cambridge, where she continues to try to balance the competing claims of earning a living whenever the chance presents itself, of being a single parent and of pursuing her own writing.

If you would like to know more about Virago books, write to us at 41 William IV Street, London WC2N 4DB for a full catalogue.

Please send a stamped addressed envelope

Book Tokens

**Give them
the pleasure of choosing**
Book Tokens can be bought
and exchanged at most
bookshops.

War in the Nursery

Theories of the Child and Mother

Denise Riley

Virago

Published by Virago Press Limited 1983
41 William IV Street, London WC2

Copyright © Denise Riley 1983

British Library Cataloguing in Publication Data
Riley, Denise
  War in the nursery.
  1. Child psychology   2. Mother and child
  I. Title
  155.4118   BF723.M55

ISBN 0-86068-273-0

Printed in Great Britain by litho
at the Anchor Press, Tiptree, Essex

Contents

Acknowledgements

I am extremely grateful to friends for their generosity with time, criticism and encouragements, especially where these have been extended to me over a number of years. In particular, for some or all of several kinds of help – for many discussions and exchanges that were invaluable to me; for reading through sections or the whole of this manuscript, making many comments and improvements and so saving me from worse errors; for offering to look after my children, for typing, or providing me with space in which to write; for pointing me in the direction of useful reading – I am indebted to Mary Bernard, Jane Caplan, John Churcher, Roy Edgley, John Forrester, Carol Kendrick, Sylvia Lawson, Colin MacCabe, Stephanie Macek, Jeffrey Minson, Ursula Owen, Susan Pennybacker, Jonathan Rée, Kate Soper, Deborah Thom, and Martin Thom.

Versions of parts of this book have appeared in periodicals as articles. With these I was greatly helped by members of their editorial collectives: Judy Keiner and Elizabeth Wilson with 'War in the Nursery', *Feminist Review* 2, 1979; Valerie Walkerdine with 'Developmental Psychology: Biology and Marxism', *Ideology and Consciousness*, 4, 1978; while amongst the editors of *History Workshop*, I owe a special debt to Sally Alexander, with 'The Free Mothers – Pronatalism and Working Women in Industry at the End of the Last War in Britain', *History Workshop*, 11, 1981.

I would also like to acknowledge the help of the librarians and archivists of the British Museum, the Trades Union Council Library, the Public Record Office, the University Library, Cambridge; and my particular thanks go to the Fawcett Library.

CHAPTER 1

Biology, Psychology and Gender in Socialist and Feminist Thinking

> *'Seek those images*
> *That constitute the wild*
> *The lion and the virgin*
> *The harlot and the child.'*
>
> W. B. Yeats, from 'Those Images',
> *Last Poems 1936–1939*

Biologism or culturalism as unhappy alternatives

In its editorial entitled 'War in the Nursery', the *British Medical Journal* for January 1944 commented, .

. . . in the years from two to five the battle between love and primitive impulse is at its height. . . . Winnicott, Bühler, Isaacs, Bowlby and others all note the turbulent characteristics of the age. . . . Destructive impulses let loose in the war may serve to fan the flame of aggression natural to the nursery age . . . the Age of Resistance may thus be prolonged to adult life in the form of bitterness, irresponsibility, or delinquency.

Such wartime psychology might produce a reaction of scepticism or even of derision now. But are there ways of deciding what, if anything, psychic struggles have to do with social struggles? Are psychic upheavals rooted in nature, or are they socially constructed – or are these bad explanatory choices to settle on? For what do we mean by the natural, the biological, the social?

The 'biological' here is not the formal object of the biological

1

sciences, but, rather, common-sense understandings of the natural, the bodily, and the corporeal, common and at the same time private to every human being. The 'social', too, I use in the loose sense of the unbounded imprecise communality of society which is everything except the individual: this usage ignores the fact that society and individual have more complicated relations than those of a sum and its parts.

Much speculation on these questions has faced an unhappy choice between two opposed but equally unpromising positions. One is a biologism which explains social and psychological life with reference to biological causes; the other is a culturalism which explains everything through the workings of 'society'. This second position looks, and in several ways is, more liberal, more 'political'; but while it rejects conservative views of biology, it also fails to do the necessary rethinking of this area, and so falls short again.

My aim in this book is to try to sort out some preconditions for an alternative to both these positions; an alternative which would allow an understanding of how the body – crucially, the gendered body – acts and is acted on in the world, instead of the gloomy choice between coming down on the side of the body *or* of the world.

This is hardly an original aim. But I have turned to it because some socialist and feminist persuasions continue to write off consideration of biology and psychology, and do so by two means. They use, on the one hand, the pejorative category of 'biologism' – the reduction of everything to the workings of a changeless biology – and, on the other hand, they make a supposedly progressive claim about the 'social construction' of most human behaviour. But neither of these positions can do much to illuminate the difficulties. For 'biologism' as a dismissive label ignores the fact that there really is biology, which must be conceived more clearly – while to put everything down instead to the effects of 'society' results in utterly discouraging vagueness and rarely tells us anything new.

The very components of 'the biological' require thought; we aren't working with some kind of brute reality here, which somehow has to be slotted into a resisting socialism. But nor, on the other hand, is it enough to entertain a culturalist thesis instead. In this, the first cousin of the social construction thesis, all is ascribed, the better to fly the ills of biologism, to the effects of 'culture', a culture understood in opposition to biology.

Such claims, for all their polemical uses as correctives to claims about brute nature, are apt to drown everything in the deep seas of the vaguely social. To assert the social and cultural construction of, for instance, femininity, heterosexuality or maternity, is an advance on putting them down to nature. It is also an arrival onto another unsteady ground.

Certainly these concerns are by no means the territorial imperatives of feminism and socialism alone; the difficulties of producing a more helpful, and true, account of the biological and social are tenacious in any theory of human development. But they are especially pressing for a political theory committed to systematic thought about gender. And puzzles – elaborated in the second chapter of this book – about the scope and the edges of the individual and the social are also inescapable for any kind of thinking about individuation, whether from the perspective of psychology or of political belief. I dwell on Marxist thought here, not because I assume it to be some watertight secure theory of and for socialism; but because it does set out to understand the relation between individual and social, posing this as a crucial problem from the start. Even if this question is never resolved, nevertheless Marx's writings offer the most vivid and suggestive statements about what's at stake.

The traditional indifference of Marxism to gender, however, has been rehearsed to the point of exhaustion. But while feminist work has done a tremendous amount to drag problems of fertility control, maternity and sexual choice away from the clutch of received opinion about the 'natural', we cannot subside contentedly at this point. Any feminist-influenced political philosophy would have to commit itself to a more profound re-examination of nature and culture than is given by reiterating the usual corrective to biologism, the claim for the 'social construction' of reality. For this only substitutes an unbounded sphere of social determination for that of biological determination. If we are to talk in the language of social constructions, then the construction of the very concepts of the social and the biological must also be elucidated.

The danger for feminism in overlooking this necessity is that of grinding to a premature halt in accounting for sexual difference – of only asserting it, or characterising it in a way which renders it timeless, and thus apt to be greeted by rhetoric about 'truly female nature' which only replicates that freezing in position. The tactical problem is in naming and specifying sexual difference where it has been ignored or misread; but without doing so in a way which guarantees it an eternal life of its own, a lonely trajectory across infinity which spreads out over the whole of being and the whole of society – as if the chance of one's gendered conception mercilessly guaranteed every subsequent facet of one's existence at all moments.

There is a truth in Freud's 'anatomy is destiny' which is unshakeable. Anatomy, *given everything as it is*, points us irresistibly along certain paths, to certain choices; and there is a terrible ambiguity built into the possibilities for feminism in the face of this. It is indeed essential to concentrate on inequities and miseries – and pleasures – stemming from gender as it is lived now. But that necessary weighting to the wrongs or consolations of the present may, despite its own intentions, distract from a transformed 'destiny' by sticking in a rhetoric of 'men' and 'women' as untiring actors of determined psychic-to-social roles. It's in the light of this risk that 'sexual politics' are, despite this exciting coupling of 'sexual' and 'politics', less likely to be productive of the truly revolutionary than the more pedestrian-sounding areas of social and family policies.

Certainly the feminist barracking of 'biological urges', of what is 'natural' for women, is proper enough. But such accounts frequently paper over profound conceptual cracks, and their fragility then appears to prove the seemingly inescapable power of 'the biological' all over again. An incomplete challenge here is worse than none at all. For the return of a familiar conception of biology and nature 'after all' carries the world-weary conviction of what we always knew but did not, for our own ideological reasons, want to have to admit – as if biologism had proved, in the end, to be a piece of realism we had better grow up and accept.

The structural weakness behind these cracks lies in the reductive nature of both the biologistic and the culturalist theses. Yet versions of these two forms of reductionism feed straight into the very construction of psychology. And once the workings of psychology are questioned, it is hardly plausible to pin all one's hopes instead on psychoanalysis as a virginal territory of purer science, able to speak for all manifestations of the soul in the world. There is a vast area, denoted by the psychological and the biological, which the classical theory of the unconscious cannot encompass. It is this area which needs close scrutiny; for the existing attempts at synthesising a Marxist Freudianism have not really touched on this difficulty, and confusion and loss have resulted from the omission.

And it is this failure which is in part – but only in part – an explanation for the extraordinarily eclectic tone of current responses to psychoanalysis on the Left, and especially among feminists. It is as if British feminism – to assume, for once, such a unitary creature – has adopted a shoulder-shrugging, take-it-or-leave-it stance, so that an allegiance to psychoanalytic thinking is left to the idiosyncracies of private taste. It is barely possible to map the gamut of socialist, Marxist, liberal, feminist reactions to Freudian theory, let alone to the outcroppings of psychotherapeutic forms. But such an elaborate cartography makes one despair of the huge amounts of working over of ideas of society, nature and culture needed to trace them all.

The effects of this eclecticism – inevitable and benign though they may be in some ways – are, I think, bad in others. An indifference to what constitutes the biological, and what the social and cultural, can easily slip into an indifference to what is meant by sexuality – which, it is generally agreed, has components of all these. And when this indifference escapes any direct challenge, either from those who espouse psychoanalytic theory, or from those who practise different psychotherapies, then the outcome is a curious silence about the sources and the weaknesses of the noun 'sexuality'. This may seem an extraordinary remark, given the proliferation of debates about the sexual from many feminist and leftist groupings. But what 'sexuality' itself might be goes surprisingly unqueried, while many column inches tacitly equate it with sexual behaviour, as if all that we needed were a newly progressive set of practices; a *Joy of Sex* for feminism and socialism. But this often programmatic referring to

5

the sexual can serve to shore up wastes of human sadness. For the polemical shifting of sexual zones and acts, in which some become more 'progressive' than others, ignores the whole question of what – if anything – is referred to by 'sexuality'. This fundamental question is evaded by a concentration on behaviour alone; and is only obscured when 'sexual behaviour' and 'sexuality' are treated as identical.

———————————

Much of what follows is descriptive: a case study of misunderstandings about gender and work, and its repercussions for both theories and practices to do with the care of children. I have made use of the history of psychology – which carries a particular view of the child as an admixture of the biological and the social – as well as of the history of social policies on childcare at a peculiarly intense moment, the end of the last world war in Britain. I have concentrated on Kleinian psychoanalysis, on psychologies influenced by the analytic theories of Melanie Klein, and on the spread of postwar 'Bowlbyism'. This refers to a set of suppositions taking some of their authority from the psychologist John Bowlby; especially from his theory of maternal deprivation, according to which any separation of the young child from its mother results in psychic damage for the child.

My use of 'psychology' is limited. Often it is a shorthand for a local if deeply influential piece of British child psychology in the 1940s and 1950s. The names of better-known developmental psychologists – most obviously, Piaget – do not appear; and certainly aspects of Bowlby's work have received strenuous criticism from some psychologists, a few of whom would prefer to see him relegated to the securer dungeons of 'psychoanalysis'.

It might be objected that the psychology I have written about is poor stuff: that there would have been more point in concentrating on Freud than on popularised Bowlby. To that, I can only offer the justification I gave once to a friend who asked me why I spent my time 'pursuing the history of second-rate ideas'. My aim all along has been to understand the nature of 'popularising'; it is this which has an impact in the world, and this which has to be examined if the entanglements of psychology with social policies are to be unravelled. It is not pure psychoanalytic theory which has been most visible; it has been Bowlby's work with its particular characterising of maternity, the family, emotions, institutions, zoology.

When British writers have denounced 'psychoanalysis', it has sometimes been an idea of Bowlby which has acted as the irritant – a just annoyance with the effects of Bowlbyist utterances on the provision of childcare in this country. For Kleinian-influenced work, which included Bowlby's, was the most disseminated; it was Winnicott's cheerfully commonsensical broadcasts to parents which came from the wartime radio, and not the sad analytic charm of Freud's *Mourning and Melancholia*. This is all the more reason for taking notice of applied Klein, as well as of Freud.

Moreover, a concentration on only 'the best' of psychoanalytic theory can, particularly in its effects on socialist and feminist thinking, give rise to an unfortunate division of labour. Psychoanalysis as a study leaves other forms of psychotherapy untouched, so that into those forms notions of an unbounded psychic 'energy' are all too free to pour; and an 'academic' attention to, say, Lacan, becomes an irreconcilable counterpoint to 'practical' psychotherapies. To say this isn't to yearn instead after some unattainable holism of thought, in which cool theoreticians and warm hearts might generously embrace. But it is to issue a plea for close attention to be turned also to the wider effects of psychology's assumptions. However dispiriting the study of the sociopsychoanalytic literature may be, it must still be undertaken. It cannot be relegated either to the hinterland of a culture located somewhere behind the front line of politics, or to the unsorted wastepaper basket of 'ideology'.

The later sections of this book argue that invocations of motherhood at this period effectively rendered invisible the needs of those working women with children. Without looking at this emphasis on the artificially isolated figure of the mother, conceived in a strikingly restricted way, it's not possible to grasp the long reaches of a psychology which relied on a nonemployed mother at its heart. And without reference to postwar social-democratic, labour movement, and feminist political thinking, it's not possible to make sense of the apparent quiescence which met this psychology.

For it seems that women workers after the war were accepted, to a limited degree; but women as mothers were taken to be wholly different beings, assumed to be always outside production, pursuing a distinct 'creative' task of childrearing. This violent separation between the class of women workers which could be embellished with the tag of democratic comradeship, and the class of mothers had elements in common with the tenets of child psychology: one of my aims is to raise the question of the nature of this overlapping, and its influences. For the immediate postwar period was a stretch of years in which a form of writing and talking, weary in its generalisations, cut across both psychology and social democracy to address an unshaded and characterless Mother, of its own making, at home. This continued irrespective of the practical truth that more and more women with children did go out to work. But an unexcited common sense buoyed everything up: in the popular sociologies of the 1950s, 'we all know' that children need their mothers at all moments; and child psychology, ostensibly drawing on the 'experiences of war', was scientifically reiterating 'what everyone already knows'.

But what is there to do as a corrective to all this, beyond putting an idealistic request to psychology to be more alert to its own history? It is urgent to find productive ways of questioning the interplay of biology and society, gender and work; for while this interplay was particularly convoluted at the period this book dwells on, it continues, in different incarnations, to produce political uncertainties and private strain now. How could such questioning be most usefully conceived?

In part, it is a difficulty of method: of how never to overlook or to mistake gender in its manifestations; but also of how *not* to bear it in mind in such a way that it must always hang like a veil to filter every glimpse of the world; as if we perceived all of it in advance; as if being women or being men produced, out of that division itself, exhaustively decisive lives. In brief, the challenge for feminism is to be fully attentive to every effect of gender – and, by means of that close attention, also to know where gender might end.

Ideology as a means of analysis: its difficulties

We need a fresh sense of the biological and the social, if we are to understand social-sexual differences – those differences, apparent or real, which stem from gender as it is lived. Such an understanding is essential for any socialist and feminist ethic. But what such an ethic might be is a raw and open question; there is a need, in the often painful gap between the body politic and the individual body, for an idea of a socialised biology. This would speak to problems adumbrated in slogans like 'the right to choose', 'the right to sexual self-determination', 'control of one's own body' – the language of campaigns concerning abortion and contraception, welfare and population policies, or asserting sexual categories. The idea of a socialised biology would also join broader questions about human capacities and wants, growth, illness, ageing; and, instead of holding these at the margins of socialism, would set them at the centre of its ethical nerve. At the same time, I want to illustrate ways in which the history of psychology has in fact worked against this kind of development, sometimes by acting as an inadequate representation of socialised biology.

Why should the nature of biology and psychology continue to present such difficulties? These speak officially for the life of the body and the mind. It is dangerous to abandon them wholly to the professional attentions of human biologists, psychologists, demographers, medical sociologists, and sexologists, on the grounds that all these are hopelessly in the grip of conscious or unwitting reaction, are 'ideological'.

But this dismissive category of the ideological itself marks a more generally dangerous tendency: too great a reliance on the concept of ideology. This can often operate as a tool which weakens the hand of its user, instead of cutting through the material it is applied to. Frequently treated as a device for negotiating the obscure gaps between politics and psychology, between biology and society, as well as generally constituting some account of the persistence of disabling ideas and their grip on the world, 'ideology' has been severely overstrained. Its invocation often serves to deepen the confusion it aims to alleviate. Socialist and feminist tendencies in particular have engaged with ideology as a key issue, but not much light has been shed on what it is, and whether there is indeed a single 'it'. 'Ideology in general' has been proposed either as a form of systematic misrecognition, produced by the opacity of social surfaces; or as embodied in institutions – school, church, family – which act by means of it (ideology) to secure state powers; or simply as a throng of illusions which flies hither and thither to settle in a dulling cloud over our perceptions of the world.

All of these general senses of ideology have their difficulties; understanding the workings of particular ideologies is an equally bedevilled undertaking where the conceptual means are too slight to bear the weight placed on them. For instance, 'ideology' is some-times used to characterise a look of harmony between beliefs and their climates. People often observe that 'it is no accident that' a particular conviction should flourish or decay in an appropriate social climate; but this produces impressionistic natural history, rather than any true analysis. When psychology's relations with politics are called into question, the notion of popularisation is often pulled in as if it were itself a theory of ideology. But this notion artificially distinguishes the originating psychology from what then becomes viewed as the contaminated field of its effects. It sounds as if the gap between psychological theory and its effects is being explained by the phenomenon of popularisation. But it is only being redescribed. It is as if there were quite separate and distinct entities of psychology, popularised psychology, and politics, with the second of these running like a strange messenger of ideology between the other two.

A main preoccupation of these chapters is psychology as a his-torical actor. This is where it's tempting to glide into claiming a 'coherence' between psychology and a sociopolitical climate; and indeed there is a surface here of an apparently impenetrable hard gloss. But it's no help just to attribute 'coherence' to a moment of history, psychology, politics, since what is at stake is the nature and production of this 'coherence', and whether it may be a mirage. And what are the components of a vagueness like a 'sociopolitical climate'? Can we trust the materials of history to break it down into something more precise? The nostalgia-misted history of wartime

Britain we inherit, filtered through interpretations devised in the 1950s, relies on an attributed 'experience of war'. This turns out to be a complex of statements, shifting between social history and the history of psychology, which derives its authority from mutual appeals and cross-references. Each invents the apparent truth of the other.

Making sense of this history, significant as it is in the shaping of family policies, has particularly exercised feminist imaginations; but the inheritance of early 1970s radical psychology, mixed in with broader socialist assumptions about the machinations of the state, has not helped. Feminist writings, looking back, have often assumed that the return of women to their homes after the last war was intimately linked with, if not positively engineered by, Bowlby's psychology, whose anti-nursery tenets were in harmony with the government's desire to get shot of its wartime female labour force, and reassert its 'normal' male one. Not unreasonably, given all the orchestrated appearances, feminism tends to hold a vision of post-war collusion between the government and psychology to get working women back to their kitchens, and pin them down there under the weight of Bowlby's theory of maternal deprivation in an endless dream of maternity throughout the 1950s. But, as this book sets out to show, examining the details of the history undoes all this. The connections between government plans, the movements of women on and off the labour market, and the development of psychological beliefs were far more fragile than this version allows. There was, in fact, no concerted attack.

But making corrections to the narrative details is not enough, for the belief that psychology was acting in the service of the state to keep women at home is also the application of a way of thinking familiar in both socialism and certain radical psychologies – a form of functionalism, the notion of a fit between components, so that one works to secure the existence of the other (or others). This way of thinking can give rise to a good deal of confusion. Put to the test, its assumptions are disprovable. But such functionalism is, after all, a demand for explanation – a desire which will not easily calm down. The substitution of a more detailed history will not be of much use unless that history can satisfactorily explain what happened. The

11

now-despised conspiracy theories – that brand of functionalism which ascribes repression to deliberate state, class, or sex manoeuvrings – are bound to survive. This is not only because conspiracies can indeed sometimes be the truth, as well as the appearances. The desire to understand political transformations is both reasonable and determined; it will stick with functionalism, conspiracy theories and over-schematised notions like 'social control' unless there is something better to hand.

An awkward reliance on 'ideology' can leave socialist thought silent in those areas where functionalism clearly can't work. One instance of socialist embarrassment over coping with the ideological is afforded by the cases of sociobiology and ethology, which have enjoyed great success with their differing invocations of inevitable aggression, of the sexual imperative, of the 'selfish gene' – in short, the whole human jungle. This success has emerged in the large sales, newspaper and television presentations of writers like Robert Ardrey and Desmond Morris; while the work of E. O. Wilson and other sociobiologists has had a quieter but strong academic influence. An open and sensitive area has been well colonised – an area which socialist theory has largely vacated. Sociobiology (a reinterpretation of Darwinism which stresses genetic determinants of culture) and popular ethology (the study of the social behaviour of animals) have been caught up in reductive accounts of instinctive sexual aggression, to great effect.

To shake this alliance between science and common-sense naturalism – an alliance on which Bowlby's success also in part rests, as my fourth chapter describes – would demand a radical overhaul of ideas of nature, psychology, biology, history, and the social. Without this daunting amount of work, objections to sociobiology are at risk of sounding opinionated, sustained only by a childishly obstinate refusal to admit the real nature of the world and of 'man' in it – acknowledging instead only some ideologically acceptable but ethereal history and culture.

How can the shortcomings of 'ideology' as a tool to deal with these questions be avoided? The work of Michel Foucault has been enthusiastically received in this country as a lever for displacing the well-worn debates about ideology, especially in the wake of disenchantment with Althusserian formulations. Foucault was exercised, in his *Archaeology of Knowledge*, by the question of how *not* to bestow a life of its own on ideology, as if it had a course through history like the course of a mole across a lawn, surfacing and disappearing again. In that book he set out to free the history of ideas from its 'subjection to transcendence', to the problems of origin and subjectivity; and at one point he recommends doing this through the study of 'discourses in their specificity'. (A discourse can be approximately defined as an identifiable array of terms and statements which refer to a single object, in the widest sense of object: or, indeed, arguably constitute that object themselves; for example, the Judaeo-Christian discourse on marriage; the discourse of social hygiene.) The examination of discourses has been loosened from its anchorage and carried off by some as the means of revivifying political debates; it does avoid the old difficulties with the concept of ideology as distortion and misrepresentation, although new problems arise about where the edges of a discourse are, what guarantees its singularity, and how transformations between discourses occur.

In the *Archaeology of Knowledge* these difficulties are laid on one side. Foucault concentrates instead on characterising the dispersed life of psychiatry, which ran everywhere beyond its institutional confines. This phenomenon of discursive spreading is described again in his *History of Sexuality*, which argues that the nineteenth century was not a time of a straightforwardly repressive censoring of sex; and that the twentieth century is not a time of an enlightened speaking out about the unspoken. This book has been widely seized on as a source of fresh illumination; but I have reservations about its capacities to fulfil all the hopes invested in it. The drawbacks include, I think, a use of 'repression' which can suffer from inexactness and overapplication. Foucault's 'power' is atmospherically generalised; it describes the exercise of 'strategies' – the management of populations, for instance. But these strategies have no agency behind them, and power is everywhere, like air. How, then, can it be distinguished or resisted? Points of resistance, for Foucault, are themselves implicated, embroiled in power. A troubling difficulty is that the origins of power and strategies take on a theological

13

nature; although Foucault's intention is to erase the puzzles of functionalism, the result is as if a new and more religiously veiled functionalism were being hailed. Strategies which work, but work with causeless effects, their non-authorship the more remote and terrifying because their tracks are everywhere, are in that sense no convincing refutation of a Marxist functionalism which credits the state with diabolical intelligence in its inroads on personal life. To that Foucault objects, criticising the conviction that the state can efficiently tailor sexuality for its own needs. But, strangely, he then asserts bodies and pleasures as the points of resistance to what he calls 'the universal deployment of sexuality'. Why should 'bodies' remain as pure courts of appeal, especially after Foucault's insistence that sexuality is no natural given? And what would a 'non-deployed' sexuality be?

It's as if a half-secret anarchism were hanging around this work, a defiance of psychoanalysis which Foucault names as one of the confession-extorting strategies which serve to anchor sexuality to the family and to the law. There are many valuable aspects of the *History of Sexuality*, but it would be a pity if the wholesale adoption of its ideas also refused their particularity in favour of an unmodified assertion that, for example, 'sexuality is constructed at the level of the discursive' – is produced through, as well as described in, language. This could run a new risk of producing only a sociology of language for socialism – a linguistic reduction to oust those older forms of biological or sociological reduction in which the sexual was all nature, or all society. Is it much of an advantage to speak, for instance, of 'the language of populism' or of 'the rhetoric of domesticity' here, a measure often adopted now by historically minded socialists? For is it possible to isolate a single rhetoric, or 'language of', with much accuracy?

The last chapter of this book, discussing 'the language of pronatalism', illustrates the difficulties of finding a substitute for 'ideology' by this means. In the later 1940s, people were voicing many similar beliefs and sentiments, but in differing tones, through different organisations, political tendencies, and psychologies, each taking note of what the others were saying. 'Ideology' in that period became an orchestration of language, whose elements can be traced to their sources and disentangled. The prominence of the ideological here may be explained not by some greater secretion of ideology from a mysterious origin, but in the differing significance and weight of the political, the governmental and the psychological spheres. In this account ideology is not so much an independent spirit, or a series of representations only. Detecting ideology is more like taking the measure of the distances – or lack of distances – which obtained between politics, policies, and psychology as they paid attention to each other, as they drew on each other's formulations to produce an apparently seamless fabric of self-confirming references, an unbroken mass of language. Yet such a reliance on 'language', although placing the needed emphasis on all its powers, cannot finally close the account of the political.

CHAPTER 2

Developmental Psychology, Biology and the Social

'Psychology does not in the least possess the ''secret'' of human acts, simply because this secret is not of a psychological order.'
Politzer, *La Crise de la psychologie contemporaine*[1]

'Individuals producing in society – hence socially determined individual production – is of course, the point of departure [. . . .] The human being is in the most literal sense zoon politikon, *not merely a gregarious animal, but an animal which can individuate itself only in the midst of society [. . . .] Whenever we speak of production, then, what is meant is always production at a definite stage of social development – production by social individuals.'*
Marx, *Grundrisse*[2]

Discussion of the notions of 'biology' and 'society' employed in developmental psychology, and some socialist attempts to revise these terms as they occur both inside and outside psychology, at once encounters the difficulty of defining the nature of this pair, the 'biological' and the 'social'; how the two should be understood, and whether they can be united. This is the dilemma, whether or not voiced as such, of British developmental psychology – the science of child development.

It is not the aim of this book to review the whole range of competing theories about the biological versus the social in psychology, nor to answer the question of what a 'better' developmental psychology might look like. Rather it will dwell on how the broadest assumptions about how what goes to constitute 'biology' and what 'the social world' are overlaid, in developmental psychology, by more local versions of the innate/learned distinction, embodied in ideas about the growth and 'socialisation' of the infant and child. Any Marxist critique of these theories will be committed to trying to give some content to Marx's formulation, in the sixth of the *Theses on Feuerbach* – 'Feuerbach resolves the religious essence into the human essence. But the human essence is no abstraction inherent in each single individual. In its reality it is the ensemble of the social relations' – and to the idea, ventured by Marx in the *Grundrisse*[3], of individuation as something which takes place across history, through the means of production. Is Marx's 'social individual' – a phrase which, in its context, is at once seemingly pregnant with possibilities, and all too vague – of any help in clarifying what that uncertain goal of some socialists, a materialist psychology, might be? Or, on the other hand, if the concept of the social individual were pursued to its conclusion, would that point instead to the dissolution of the whole category of a psychology of the individual? Answering this will entail questioning some received Marxist and more broadly socialist assumptions about the nature of science, 'the dialectic', and whether indeed a consideration of biology leads ineluctably in the direction of reaction.

Some socialist onslaughts on psychology and biology have rightly seized on the thoughtless opposing of the individual to society, and the biological to the social. But if all which escapes the net of the social is swept out of sight as being a reactionary biologism, or abandoned to medical sociologists, then the original seesaw of social versus biological remains intact, with the weighting shifted to the social end. The result is an uneasy redistribution of balance, which leaves untouched the origins and references of the debates themselves, and merely tips the weight back and forward according to fashion between social and individual emphases.

British developmental psychology; humanism and theories of interactionism

How far do generally held notions – of what an individual is, what biology is, what society is – slip, uncriticised, into child psychology, and to what extent is this inescapable? The barest statement of the question often presented by British developmental psychology as being at the heart of its whole enterprise – how does a (biological) infant turn into a (social) being? – already assumes that it is a matter of starting off in the realm of biology, which is then gradually relinquished for a realm of society. Expressed thus, the question has received a multitude of attempted resolutions, including, for example, the assertions that there is 'a complex process of interactions' between biological and social factors in the individual, as in Schaffer's 1971 work[4] or that the infant is 'biologically structured', but adapted towards becoming human by means of the growth of 'communicative capacities', as in Trevarthen's 1975 paper.[5]

A less orthodox claim (made, for instance, by Ainsworth in 1974)[6] is that the infant is a social being from the start. This avoids shuffling biological and social 'factors' around by simply dropping 'the biological' altogether, in a way analogous to some socialist attempts to cope with the difficulties by bracketing everything together as 'social relations'. But this tactic provides no means for analysing how neurologically and physiologically differing newborn children do, indeed, develop differently.

And, in practice, the assertion that the infant is 'always – already' social – is never anything but social – has been voiced in a limiting manner, concentrating on 'communication' in an isolated mother-child dyad, a closed couple; and on the analyses of 'intersubjectivity' – interactions between the pair. In this way of considering the infant's development, the claim that it is born 'already social' is taken as the exact equivalent of 'already interpersonal' – and that within a severely restricted range of persons anyway. The emphasis on 'communication' solely inside this mother-child pair isn't an inevitable consequence of considering the infant 'already social'. The reason for this slippage between 'social' and 'interpersonal' has to do with the history of British developmental psychology.

The apparently neutral terminology of 'communication', in particular, grew up as a would-be humanising elaboration of earlier, 1950s 'attachment' theorising. This was itself an attempt to characterise the 'particularly human' attachments of the child, as distinct from the monkey. The notion of 'adaptedness to being human' as the key to infant development can be understood as a reaction against 'ethological', animal-based research; a liberal insistence that human infants do behave in human ways. But this 'adaptedness to being human' is invoked as if it accounted for some passage by the infant from a prehuman state into a full humanity. It acts as a solution to a problem already dubiously posed. Faced, for example, with experimental evidence like that of Friedlander in 1970[7] which indicates that an infant will from birth selectively respond to those sound frequencies which are the same as those of human speech, some psychologists have seized on the elements of an apparently helpful 'species-specificity' – the human infant usefully responsive to the sound of the maternal voice rather than to the sound of the creaking door. But it is hard to see why it should be thought legitimate to wring a theory of transition from presocial to social, from biology to society, out of the partiality of the infant for the frequencies of the human voice. For, in discovering that preferences for certain 'sensory stimuli' are detectable in infants a few days old, we may be saying something about neurology, but what else? Such preferences can hardly be taken as an index of 'humanity' in any more precise sense than that of the empty notion of 'species-specificity' – which says only that human infants do indeed grow up into human adults, and not into apes or primroses.

Nevertheless, one recent drift in British developmental psychology has tried to extract special mileage from fresh research findings about selective attention in newborn children. Using these findings to stress the sophisticated potential of the very young child for communicating, some, like Harré and Shotter, both in 1974, have described what they call a new humanist phenomenology.[8] In this kind of work the hunt for the sources of the quintessentially human has been couched in the vocabulary, common to that of some American psychotherapies, of 'transactional relationships' in the mother-child couple, and 'negotiation' between them: a kind of psychic business exchange. This is the diction used by some self-defined 'humanist psychology' when it looks at mother-child interactions in the quest to determine 'what it is to be human'. This

19

enterprise has also been inspired by Berger and Luckmann's socio-logical theory, which tends to take 'social' and 'intersubjective' as synonymous adjectives,[9] – as if the social was nothing more com-plex than a straightforward multiplication of what goes on between any two human beings.

Such moves in developmental psychology, comprehensible as flights from the limitations of a behaviourist approach, are like a longing for psychology to be able, once again, to speak about phenomena like 'consciousness of self', and so to recover its late-nineteenth-century kinship to philosophy. In practice, however, this humanism stops too short. It speaks only of the activities of a timeless, ahistorical, desert island mother-child couple, watched at its communicatings and interactings as in a bell jar; it is differen-tiated only – to use its terminology – by its degrees of 'sensitivity' and 'competence' at fostering the growth of such desired ends as social games, communicative skills, and conveying intentions. These activities are not modified by the exigencies of, say, housing or money – anything beyond the mere interaction of subjects in a vacuum is not entertained in this scheme of things. Development happens on a terrain of pure (inter) individuality.

The more progressive-looking versions of 'intersubjectivity' describe themselves as constituting a new humanist approach: they assert that it is the task of developmental psychology to ascertain the growth of 'the negotiation of shared meanings', or the start of 'autonomy' through self-definition. In Shotter's words, 'What is it then in the new psychology to be human? It is to be a growing system, which can, in interaction with other growing systems, increasingly localise within itself the power of responsible action.'[10] The moral duty of psychology is to study and facilitate the growth of this 'autonomy' in the individual: the relation that this apparently spiritual state has to questions of economics and power is left undis-cussed by its advocates.[11]

An unexplained notion of 'autonomy' as the hallmark of the healthy individual sits uncomfortably close to the 'autonomy' com-mended by some philosophies of the free subject as self-sufficient economic being. We can make more sense of why this humanist and intersubjectivist school of child psychology should have captured the 'radical' ground if we set it against the legacy of British Kleinianism – the work of Melanie Klein, and of others influenced by her, including Susan Isaacs, John Bowlby, D. W. Winnicott. This stresses the 'innate' – and grim – nature of the infant, and the isolated mother-child couple as the terrain on which the child's psychic development is fought out. Bowlby himself moved from a version of psychoanalysis into ethology – the study of animal social relations – and constantly made parallels in nature with human 'maternal behaviour' in his attempt to render psychoanalysis environmental, and, as he put it, consequently more scientific.

Developmental psychology and the problem of 'socialisation'

'Everyone has in his early life made the transition from a state of nature without memory or role to a state of self-conscious existence as a social being.'

Stuart Hampshire, *Thought and Action*[12]

This description encapsulates, in a fairly standard form, a dilemma about the relationship between 'development' and 'socialisation' which runs as follows. The child, or infant – the timespan of the phrase 'early life' is left conveniently inexact – is at some initial biographical point a tabula rasa – a blank slate. The process of socialisation 'then' occurs, over a similarly vague timespan, during which the child becomes a social being. Is there anything wrong with Hampshire's representative remark?

There is one ready objection to this kind of statement about the transition in the infant from (non-self-conscious) biology to (self-conscious) social being: how is this transition effected? To isolate the various conceptual positions which psychology has had recourse to here, it is worth briefly characterising the main work on infant development and socialisation, although there are difficulties in trying to reproduce 'typical' approaches without being hopelessly gestural.

British research work on the whole distinguishes between 'development' and 'socialisation'. 'Development' has been taken to cover the infant's acquisition of physical and mental skills and cognitive abilities; and developmental research is the business of making analytical and quantitive assessments of this process. The child's growth in 'linguistic competence' has been studied as a more or less distinct sub-specialism. 'Socialisation', on the other hand, has generally been defined with reference to the child's growing competence in social interactions – to employ this terminology unanalysed, for the moment. Earlier British, American, and European work on socialisation had examined the past lives of the children studied, who were often in vast orphanages – work, for example, like that of René Spitz, which blamed the institutional upbringing of infants for their adolescent delinquency or adult neuroses.

There is a more recent British tradition of work which invokes 'socialisation', and sets out to detect and analyse this as an observable set of occurrences. Much of its diction is inherited from ethological work of the 1950s: thus Schaffer, in *The Growth of Sociability*, sets out to explain the 'attachment' of the child to a preferred adult, usually the biological mother, like this: 'It represents a relatively clear-cut behaviour tendency occurring almost universally among animals as well as in man, the biological utility of which in a condition of infantile helplessness is obvious'. But, he adds, the human infant is distinguished by the fact that it has access to a larger behavioural repertoire than other animals, and that these responses are less rigidly arranged.[13] Despite these similarities of vocabulary with earlier animal work, Schaffer describes himself and likeminded developmental psychologists as pursuing a new study: that of how the infant learns to distinguish familiars from strangers by his repertoire of 'signalling abilities' used for specific individuals and situations, and 'above all, [how] he has formed his first love relationship; a relationship which many believe to be the prototype of all subsequent ones'. In brief, the crucial beginnings of the 'socialisation process'. These concerns are 'of very recent origin, for it is only of late that an empirical rather than a purely speculative approach has emerged in this field'.[14]

What are the salient features of this supposedly new empirical approach? A key is provided by Schaffer in his objections to Freudian concepts of infancy: the particular nature, he writes, of the experiencing child is left out of consideration, and 'variables' which modify the impact of particular events are ignored. The strong behaviourism of J. B. Watson comes in for a similar criticism, for in this, psychological growth was seen as determined solely by the infant's surroundings and by parental handling; the infant was shaped like inert matter, and 'the role of organismic determinants of behaviour was brushed aside'.[15] But Gesell's innate determinism (the stress on a self-unfolding maturation and the corresponding undervaluing of 'environmental influence') is seen by Schaffer as deficient for remaining 'every bit as much outside the skin of the infant as Watson had done'.[16] Stimulus-response theory, he thinks, is both naive and scientifically deficient because it treats its objects as invariant. But Piagetian cognitive development theories do possess virtue for Schaffer because of their interactionism; the infant constructs its environment actively, and through this process and the acting of the environment on it, develops more elaborate means of dealing with the world. But whereas under the Piagetian schema the dynamic infant, passing through operational stages, constructs its cognitive world, Schaffer would prefer to stress the growth of sociability. How does it come about, he asks, that infants are increasingly drawn to other people? 'What are the sources of attraction that impel the young to others of their kind?'[17]

This description of socialisation has affinities with earlier work on the topic. Animal-based ideas of the child's 'attachment' are retained, but it departs from that earlier work to try to delineate the effects of 'interpersonal contacts' in nonpathological development. Thus,

From birth, the infant is equipped with a species-specific cognitive structure which ensures that he is selectively attuned to certain types of environmental stimuli. Such stimuli tend to represent aspects of the infant's surroundings essential to survival and among these parental characteristics are particularly prominent. Thus from the beginning other individuals will exercise an attention-compelling influence on the young that is unrivalled by any other single feature of the environment. As, in addition, parents are similarly attracted to the infant, prolonged and frequent encounters are likely to take place and the stage is, therefore, set for an enmeshing of parent-infant interaction patterns. . . . Social responsiveness is therefore primarily derived on the one hand from the infant's sensitivity to certain kinds of sensory input and on the other hand from the fact that other people, considered as stimulus objects, are structured in such a way that they are best able to provide these inputs.[18]

This illustrates the fundamentals of this approach to socialisation; the schema of 'stimulus-response' is preserved, although the field of players has been extended from one subject, the child, to two mutually stimulating actors, the parent-child pair, and this extension itself ushers in the vocabulary of 'interaction'.

The types of study which have generated this approach have shown that the newborn infant has a far more extensive range of sensory abilities, and a greater capacity for selective perception of the 'human object', than had been imagined; the last fifteen years in particular have seen intensive research here. Schaffer comments, 'We need to know not only whether an infant is sensitive to stimulation but also how he organises and uses the information that is available to him. If every stimulus in the environment were directly to impinge on the infant, if every new event were to elicit yet another orienting response, then the infant's world would indeed be a booming, buzzing confusion'.[19] On the contrary, the 'selective perception' of infants has been demonstrated by Fantz among others.[20] Patterned rather than unpatterned visual stimuli are preferred by infants from the age of one week, as are complex rather than simple stimuli. Several studies from 1964–6 have shown – although some of their findings have now been qualified – that movement, brightness and solidity will be selectively attractive.[21] The 'social object' has a much higher impact than any inanimate part of the environment; infants of only two to six days old will pay special attention to a disc with human features painted on it in the correct order than to any jumbled-up approximation to a face. And auditory responses are similarly angled towards square-wave tones with low frequencies which possess a likeness to human speech sounds. Not only – this account runs – is the infant neurologically patterned 'in favour of' responses to stimuli which are human attributes, but crying and later smiling act as powerful signalling systems: and much investigation has tried to characterise adult responses to the child's signals and to the child's capacity to initiate encounters.

Experimental work here has taken two main drifts. The recognition that infants are 'active partners in even the earliest social encounters' has led to studies of 'reciprocal interaction' between child and adult, to trace the levels of 'stimulation' mutually provided by both mother and child at each stage.[22] Other work, starting from a similar position, has tried to describe exchanges; the timing, sequence and coordination of the child's and mother's gestures and interventions as 'communication'.[23] Characterising the growth of this 'social exchange' over the first year, Trevarthen, for instance, concludes 'that human intelligence develops from the start as an interpersonal process, and that the maturation of consciousness and the ability to act with voluntary control in the physical world is a product rather than an ingredient of this process'.[24] Research which uses such descriptions still tries to give some empirical content to the established concepts of socialisation and development. But these new analyses of the mother's and infant's responses and interventions in a 'behaviour sequence' have employed a new vocabulary of communication, of 'sensitivity' on the mother's part to 'cues'. The interest and empathy of the mother has become essential for the establishment of 'shared meanings': cognitive and social development here mesh with the idea of 'communicating'. The responsibility attributed to mothers has widened: they are seen as responsible not only for emotional development, as in the earlier 'attachment' work, but also for facilitating the child's 'communicative capacities' – its humanity.[25]

There is a modified approach which attempts, while placing emphasis on the 'human' social nature of the infant, to recapture the element of biology by characterising development as an 'interaction' of social and biological elements. This looks like an attractive compromise: the specific effects of, say, a particular neurophysiological state would not be written off, but nor would all infants be regarded as tabulae rasae waiting for the world to act on them. Yet how can this 'interaction' be described?

The uncertainties of psychology's approach to 'socialisation' rest on a failure to clarify a dense set of overlapping words and phrases, including socialisation, individuation and the acquiring of subjectivity. Before saying more about how the idea of socialisation causes such troubles, both in psychology and in socialist belief, some comment on the nature of widely held assumptions about it may be helpful.

Why is it that the child effectively becomes the exemplar, the touchstone for the detection of the truth about the interfaces of biology and society, presocial and the fully human? There is a strong presumption that the child as a unique knot of problems of origins does offer an especially valuable starting point for separating out the determinations of social from biological. And this looks impossible to do with blurred, 'fully socialised' adults, who don't permit the delineation of the biological under the encrustations of the social. The child appears to present a life caught at its start in an unmuddied form, a pure object for study. The child is in this sense the genesis of the adult, the 'father of the man'. It is a point of innocence before the effects of the world, a lookout from which the darkening accretions of the social can be seen approaching. Rather like Milton's Adam and Eve after their expulsion from the natural state of Paradise, – 'The world was all before them, where to choose their place of rest, and Providence their guide' – the child stands blank at the start of its life's journey away from its original simplicities, whereas adults become by contrast denser, harder, impenetrably complex and beyond any hope of separating out their components, their biology hopelessly riddled with the world's determinations.

This is an only slightly ironised account of a widely-diffused tacit supposition about the child as a privileged locus of a truth of origins. To think about the impacted nature of words like socialisation and individuation, we must recall the forcefulness of this culturally given sense of the child, and of ageing as a distancing away from the point of an original biology. (Ageing towards maturity only, that is: for the onset of old age represents a kind of return of the biological, a downhill slide to more invasions of the body.) But it is not enough to speak of merely cultural suppositions here, of some blend of the intuitively true, the common-sensical, and the 'ideological': there is a strong element of virtual necessity about this supposition too. It concerns the idea of biology's precedence over the 'social'.

It seems that there's a degree of circularity – which may well be inevitable, largely because of conceptions of *time* – in the use of the child as index of the adult both generally, and in the biology/society puzzle within psychology. There is a chicken and egg problem here. That analysis which sets out to tackle the inadequacy of a purely 'developmental', away-from-biology, concept of socialisation is itself nevertheless fixed in a background of thought which guarantees the child as the focal point of these problems. While the figure of the child remains an archetype of a biological-to-social knot, those theories which attempt to deal 'in a better way' with this knot may be concentrating on a symbolism which misleads. For although everything points towards the uniqueness of the child as the site for detecting the answers, this pointing may only indicate an illusion that the solution lies 'in' the nature of the child. But it's no naive illusion – it is very well founded.

How does developmental psychology cope with this? It is true that most work gets done without much worry about 'development' as an obscure concept in itself. Work proceeds in the conviction that empirical detection has the best chances of providing answers for the case of the young child: that it is easiest to work here in the clearest part of the wood, before the *selva oscura* of adulthood overgrows everything. Much research proceeds in a self-declared practical manner, which sets itself to meet objectives within an implicit framework of theory which itself is ignored, or else accepted for the sake of getting on with the business in hand. When anxieties do surface, they tend to be abbreviated expressions of larger underlying awkwardnesses, which stay unvoiced. Thus, for example, the question about whether what happens to the child at one stage has effects later – for instance, the short- or long-term influences of 'bad mothering', or the effects of drugs given to the mother in labour on newborn infants – is a manifestation of the whole question of what 'development' means, and how we can ever speak of 'stages' in it – and, indeed, about the extent to which studies in child development should imply ameliorative interventions. Although some research institutions – the Thomas Coram Foundation in London, for example – are concerned with interventionist policies, in that their work includes assessments of, say, preschool facilities for the care of 'normal' children,[26] developmental psychology on the whole is bracketed off as a self-sufficient specialisation alone.

27

Interactionism, Marxism, the dialectic

The use of 'interaction between social and biological factors' as a device to reconcile apparent opposites has been tried within developmental psychology. But this interaction has only been asserted, and its workings not explained in detail: unease about the gap between socialisation and development has tended to settle at the mere making of statements to the effect that 'a complex interaction' is at work, as if the problems were solved thereby. Biological and social 'factors' are invoked as if they formed a sum capable of giving a more realistically dense picture of what is going on 'inside' the individual. But how can the exact interaction at work be characterised so as to inform?

It looks as if there might be one quick way round this problem – to object to the construction of it: to say that the problem arises because different ontologies – categories of being, the social and biological – are jammed together. There is not really an equivalent status between the social and the biological – their relation isn't analogous to, for example, that of a knife and a fork, which can be included in the class of cutlery. This criticism – that the biological cannot intelligibly be said to interact with the social – was made in this way by the philosopher Lucien Sève in 1968:

The terminology individual-society comes to mean heredity versus milieu, innate versus acquired, nature and culture or nature versus nurture; in short, biological givens and social conditions. But if biological givens are really biological in an autonomous sense – nervous types in the Pavlovian sense – they haven't the least *unity* with social conditions, and are not even contraries in any dialectical sense. Rather they are the chance meetings of independent elements – they cannot have any reciprocal relations determined by a dialectical internal law of growth. Opposition cannot explain internal contradiction.[27]

It is questionable whether an interactionist model requires the sort of formal 'unity' which Sève describes as characterising the true dialectic. But his criticism *is* valid in respect of those blanket claims which, merely by virtue of employing the term 'dialectic', suppose that explanation is thereby guaranteed – claims put forward by a strong current of Marxist and socialist thought which has used the vocabulary of dialectics to cope with the problems of interactionism.

British work of a Marxist persuasion in the philosophy of science and particularly in biology took this approach in the 1930s and 1940s.[28] It marks a style of work which understood itself to be following Engels in his *Dialectics of Nature*, a style exemplified by the Russian scientist Zavodovsky, in the influential book of essays, *Science at the Crossroads*, edited by Bukharin in 1931.[29] Zavodovsky's chapter on 'The Physical and the Biological in the Process of Organic Evolution' is a good instance of that theorising of biology which rests on asserting interactionism. It criticises the 'metaphysical opposition' of this pair, the 'physical' and the 'biological'.[30]

Instead he suggests the relative independence of the biological, which advances not only through interaction with the physical conditions of its surroundings, 'but also as a result of the development of the internal contradictions latent in the biological sphere itself'.[31] The physical, by which he means the environmental in the the widest sense, is the necessary framework in which biological processes take place; but simultaneously it enters into the biological process as such. And Zavodovsky adds, 'the social-economic relation for man also acts' – but this is remarked by way of an afterthought.[32] The extreme complexity of interactions requires, for its analysis, a multidisciplinary approach, 'the consideration of all contiguous branches of science', to be done under the banner of dialectical materialism – the approved Soviet theory of knowledge, based on particular understandings of Marx and Engels.[33]

I have reproduced Zavodovsky's position since it presents itself as indubitably in the spirit of Engels. In this, it is representative of one Marxist tradition of 'the dialectics of interactionism' – a tradition which continues, with modifications. For in the face of the post-1960s leftist rejection of biology, or more accurately of reactionary uses made of it in the fields of intelligence testing, genetic determinism or evolutionary reductionism, some Marxists wanting to defend biology have had to find grounds to criticise these critics. Stephen and Hilary Rose, for example, in 1974 used 'autonomism' as a pejorative term for the rejection of neurological and biological referents in the description of human conduct; a refusal which they characterised as antiscientific and philistine. They attacked what they rightly saw as the writing-off of the natural sciences in favour of an untrammelled 'human subject'.

The newer versions of autonomism which, as with Laing, represent a rejection of biology that is but one aspect of the broader rejection of science advanced by Rosjak. It is easy to see how this rejection has emerged in its revulsion from the oppressive role of reductionism. Nonetheless, while one may sympathise with the attempt to counter the manipulation and objectification of the individual which reductionism imposes, and to replace the human subject as the centrepiece of events and actions, we must reject autonomism as inadequate; biology (and the natural sciences in general) cannot be disregarded.[34]

The Roses asserted a need for a transformed neurobiology, 'a nonideological and hence scientific and nonoppressive paradigm would be a version of interactionism – dialectical materialism; such a science cannot be fully realised except in a transformed society'.[35] Such confident hope occurs in both those Marxists who wish to continue an Engelsian understanding of science, and draw on Engels' *Dialectics of Nature* and *Anti-Dühring* in support of this, and those who want to save biology from relegation to reaction; but they tend to write as if the vocabulary of the dialectic adequately and sufficiently 'marxises' the problems.

But does it? To assert the dialectic like this not only raises severe problems in understanding Marxism, but is no advance on that interactionism which describes itself as studying 'mutually influencing factors'. (The invocation of the dialectic is by no means confined to a formal Marxism – see, for instance, Merleau-Ponty in 1964, or McMurray in 1961.)[36] It is not evident how any interactionism, whether calling itself dialectical and therefore Marxist or not, is capable of answering questions about the possibility of a transformed or radical psychology. For it leaves its own constituents unexamined, preserving the dualities at the heart of the interaction in their original and unsatisfactory shapes.

And where does interaction happen? It is usually postulated on three levels: one, *within the individual*, between 'internal' social and biological factors; two, *between individuals*, as with mother-child

interaction, (and one and two are often conflated in the same literature); and three, *between the individual and society*. And some or all
of these three approximate areas have been described as mutually
interacting, thereby producing a dense and borderless flux. The
introduction of an appeal to dialectics into this flux does not clarify
anything, for it is only to a particular form of interactionism – and
one which, misleadingly, claims to *guarantee* a truly socialist method.

Socialised biology, the 'social individual', and the process of 'socialisation'

If the appeal to the dialectic is abandoned as raising more anxieties
than it solves, there is another possible move: to try to undo the
opposition of the biological to the social. How could this be done?
Perhaps by saying that most of what is understood as biology is *lived
out* by the individual in a social form – though this is not to say that,
for example, one is aware of one's blood circulating – that, as with
questions of health and illness, of nutrition, of mental disturbance,
of fertility, sexuality, reproduction, what we might try calling *socialised biology* is as accessible to the same sort of analysis as any other
experiences.[37] And here there are links with European philosophical
work on physical being, that of Merleau-Ponty[38] in particular.

This might look attractive, because it permits thinking about
these considerations in the social and economic spheres, and does
not assume that giving attention to the biological is reactionary or
deterministic. However, many further questions need attention
before a concept of 'living out one's biology' can be other than
vaguely sociological. The first and hardest of these questions is the
nature of the individual's relation to society: Marx in his *Sixth Thesis
on Feuerbach* says that 'the human essence' is not a quality which
dwells in each private individual, but is something more like the set
of social relations. This formulation is one telegraphic attempt at
eroding the opposition of the individual to society. Can this be
expanded to have some meaning for psychology? What sense can be
given to the idea of the 'social individual' – beyond substituting
some group psychology for individual psychology, which would
hardly be an advance?

Althusser in 1969, discussing the *Sixth Thesis*, interprets it as a pointer towards political economy. 'To find the reality alluded to by seeking abstract man no longer but real man instead, it is necessary to turn to society and to undertake an analysis of the ensemble of the social relations'.[39] And social relations cannot simply be read off from an examination of the 'subject' of psychology, as if the individual formed the exact miniaturised centre of the set of social relations.[40] But the confused notion of 'socialisation' in developmental psychology does make just this assumption. 'Socialisation' in developmental psychology becomes a blanket term to describe the 'entry' of the child into social relations, and sometimes this gets a nakedly utilitarian definition. The psychologist Brim in 1966 wrote 'the function of socialisation is to transform the human raw material of society into good working members',[41] echoing the well-worn metaphor of the child as investment. More usually, socialisation is characterised as the passage from the presocial into society, located on a sliding scale at or soon after birth. Socialisation for Becker in 1972 meant 'the formation of human beings out of helpless, dependent animal matter . . . it explains the original formation of the social self'.[42] 'Entry' into society is seen as the gradual move away from the animal, the biological – whereas the truth is far more intricate; from (if not before) birth the human infant never inhabits a state of nature, unaffected by the world. The notion of socialisation here is dependent on the assumption that x biological factors + y social factors = a person: an additive, cumulative account, in which the process of socialisation has a clear start in time in and for the individual at various moments after birth, and that these can be practically determined. Much research has turned, for instance, on the extraordinary sophistication of the capacities of infants of a day or two old. But here a sliding over from a relatively neutral account of growth and development into a more normative account is inevitable. Examining the child's arrival at stages becomes the practice of developmental psychology: this means measuring the comparative achievement of 'milestones' across a lateral sweep of individuals, so that an account of a particular piece of language development, for example, might describe a temporal norm of attainment for some 'typical' individual infant, stripped of any cultural and economic background. This is what development comes to *mean* in practice: while there is still, in its theory, a free-floating area of how to understand the problem of 'the formation of the social self' – and it is this problem which gets taken over by the diction of humanistic psychology.

But this measuring of stages overlooks the general difficulty that socialisation as the acquisition of a social self cannot be a cumulative progress of hurdle-crossing, the familiar 'milestones' of development, because the individual is always already social, always there. You can never logically precede your own socialisation, or lag behind it: the individual is always the plenum of her or his own social experience and is necessarily saturated with it. 'Socialisation' is only a linear chronological process under a narrower definition to do with entering institutions, acquiring certain behaviour and so on – as distinct from the breadth of reference which socialisation theory does claim for itself. The idea that you get 'more and more social' as you age seems to have a strong subterranean connection with another assumption. It is not just that something is wrong with partitioning off development from socialisation and then sprinkling on a handful of 'social factors' for the liberally minded – but that, in a more profound way, the additive idea of socialisation connects with its implications of distance away from the biological. And this is a corollary of the assumed *priority of the biological*, mapped onto the start of the individual life's time. Socialisation theory claims to account, potentially, for the whole elaboration of the infant's 'becoming social'. Yet, because in practice it continually separates 'socialisation' from development, the illusion at its heart is the more marked: that of the child as the exemplar of pure nature, pure biology, capable of arriving at full humanity only through successive forays into a world it stands outside.

The priority of biology

The peculiarity of developmental psychology, that it must deal both with the appearance of 'progressive entry' into social institutions and the ageing of the subject in that process – a double history – does intensify the possibility of biology getting used here as a myth of origins. It is often stated that the infant is born in an animal-like state and over time acquires a social or a human nature. Being 'helpless' is equated with being 'animal-like', so that having to lose your animal nature is the precondition for achieving your humanity. All this is transparent enough to criticism on the grounds that such nature-to-culture transitions are implausibly voiced. What's harder to cope with is the wider supposition of biological primacy, the biological base. To transpose this into the terms of base and superstructure: socialisation or 'becoming human' is superstructural, while biology is what is eternal, underlying and primary – the base.

In child development, there appear to be very strong grounds for seeing 'socialisation' as a secondary process, which proceeds independently from the neurological starting point of life. At birth the child is the biological base; that moment, that start in time, seems to mark the 'state of nature' of the infant. This strengthens the assumption that not only is biology *in general* the base, but it is also the specific characteristic of the individual beginning in life, to which 'human powers' are gradually attached: the child is wild.

A secondary difficulty is the impacted language of 'socialisation' and 'individuation'. Developmental psychology's question about how the infant 'becomes a social being' refers not only to its becoming so *for others*, but also to how it 'becomes a social being for itself'.[43] The apparent travelling away from biology is also under a certain light a travelling to this acquisition of self-consciousness. So the infant is a subject which is not, yet, a subject to itself, in the sense of possessing reflective capacities. There are evident difficulties about this, including how much 'consciousness of self' is going to count as a guarantee of acquired subjectivity, let alone about what's meant by this 'consciousness of self'. Despite such anxieties, an approach which wants to speak of growing individuation in the infant must concern itself somehow with the problem of changes in 'consciousness' *over time*.

There is an incontestable truth about the entry of time into child development. Banally and obviously enough, first a child cannot speak or crawl, and then later on it can. When developmental psychology takes up the task of explaining the ageing of the child as its simultaneous travelling away from its biology and towards its society, biology becomes a pure point which stands, in a somewhat religious way, as a signpost at the start of (and at the end of) an individual life – a lay religion, though, in which the 'trailing clouds of glory' are no longer heavenly, but are the tracks of nature.

While there is clearly something wrong with the notion of a progressive entry into the world, nevertheless there are real problems of how the passage of time brings about changes. Age really does entail – in the vocabulary of psychology – both cognitive and social complexities. There *is* more as you go on; and as we get older things get harder – Wordsworth's 'Shades of the prisonhouse begin to close about the growing boy'. It is true that the child 'is always' immersed in social relations: but to say this leaves untouched the question of how to characterise change in and over time. We need to find a means for describing the ways in which the density of 'social relations' does indeed alter – but without accepting that the infant is inserted into the world and in this says a long farewell to its biology.

One way out of these difficulties is to reduce everything to the sphere of 'social relations'. But against such a reduction, I would argue that biology does indeed figure: but neither as a start, nor an end. And to discuss the persistence of ideas of biology as base and origin as merely 'ideological' would be cavalier and short-sighted. For the fact that the biological is so widely conceived as if it were a material equivalent to the Freudian unconscious – something which deeply underlies everything else – seems to have a great deal to do with the force of even concealed metaphor on our imaginations, and especially with the spatial metaphors lurking in words like 'base' and 'levels', as well as with temporal metaphors.

For the biological is seen as a literally *underlying* substance – in the way that if you put a sliver of brain under a microscope you will see cells of tissues and blood – and also as a base, something basic and primary, in the sense of possessing fundamentally determining powers. It's as if biology is in some quasi-literal way *closer to the bone* and therefore is also prior as an order of explanation: just because it is 'underlying', it is therefore fundamental as a means of explication.

This supposition also lurks in the depiction of 'civilised'

behaviour as a veneer over more 'basic' urges to aggression, territorial defence, blind sexual drives, and so on – the whole notion of the 'human animal'. This language of animality is a manifestation of the more subterranean, linguistically anchored faith in the underlying nature of the biological; and understanding the persistence of the latter assumption is a precondition for understanding the former. Modern versions of human animality may attract the label of being 'ideological', but that characterisation does nothing to explain their staying power or the reasons for their shortcomings. These reasons cannot be elaborated here: but one starting point from which to get a grip on them is an awareness of the complications in moving from biology to society.

Biology and psychology in some Marxist theories

I've mentioned those Marxist approaches to psychology and biology which have tried to deal with the problems of the social-to-biological relation by invoking the dialectic. This is only one possible route among many: the nature of psychology has been very differently conceived in past attempts at constructing, for example, an avowedly socialist psychology. Child psychology has received bare critical attention in Britain in recent years. It is psychoanalysis which has occupied the stage; and the history of attempts to 'integrate' Marxism and psychoanalysis is long, arduous, and continuing. This debate has been reanimated by examination of what psychoanalysis contributes to theories of sexual difference – this by feminism in particular.[44] In the 1970s and 1980s, concentration on the nature of psychoanalysis has largely examined only its theory: a tendency eased by the virtual absence of psychoanalytic practice from the British health services – unlike French clinics.[45] Psychology, however, has been criticised in Britain in the last decade chiefly on the grounds of what it actually does and not of its conceptual frameworks; and such criticisms have often emphasised the roles of psychologists themselves in inculcating banal or damaging notions of the 'normal' – producing, for example, conservative accounts of femininity or homosexuality.

To find a consideration of psychology and psychoanalysis which doesn't make a radical separation between these two, one has to look back to a point predating their postwar demarcations. The work which had most influence on socialist libertarian thought in this country, certainly over the last fifteen years, has been that of Wilhelm Reich.[46] Socialists have been attracted by the urgency of Reich's attempts to characterise, for example, the 'authoritarian family' as making its members susceptible to fascist ideologies.[47] What, for my purposes here, is most interesting and instructive is Reich's move from his determined early effort to insist – following the educationalist Siegfried Bernfeld – that psychoanalysis was no mere bourgeois fashion, but was potentially both 'materialist' and 'dialectical' and so congruent with the principles espoused by the German Communist Party.[48]

From this doomed polemic, Reich turned instead to an examination of how 'the economic basis works itself out in people's instinctual structure; how the social existence of men influences the fundamental biological instincts of hunger and sexuality, and how in the different classes the concrete living individual develops out of this, and not the abstract "human nature" the bourgeois talks about'.[49]

But ultimately the problem of deciphering those ways in which (as Erich Fromm put it) 'the instinctual apparatus . . . is only manifest in some *specific* form that has been modified through the social process',[50] gave way for Reich to a commitment to ideas of psychic healthiness. He abandoned his initial attempts at understanding the social formation of human needs, to emphasise instead the 'instinctive, biological' nature of these needs – a conception, however, he had never fundamentally queried. Other attempts, announced programmatically from 'within' socialist theory, to bypass Freud and to account for individuals as differently produced by material forces have concentrated on the 'social individual' as the bearer of needs, and on how individuality can be specified without recourse to empty quasi-psychological concepts like 'personality'.[51]

The socialist philosopher Lucien Sève, for example, in his book, *Marxism and Personality Theory*, written in 1968, sets out to criticise and improve existing attempts to develop Marxist psychology. He looks back to Georges Politzer, who held the dethroning of the psychological to be the precondition for any socialist theory of the individual: 'Psychology is held to possess the secret of human acts, but this secret is not of a psychological order'.

Sève, too, writes against Freudianism for its neglect of the effects on the individual's involvement in, or at the edge of, the labour force. Recalling Politzer, he settles on biography as a transformed social science, as the 'science of the real lives of individuals' based on the extent to which they are able to realise their capacities and needs, what opportunities they have for using any time of their own, what time is occupied by waged work, and so on. For Sève, biology drops out of the field in all this, never appearing in the world of lived social relations. Since he characterises biology only in its emergence as 'drives' or in deterministic accounts of 'personality' of the worst 1940s and 1950s American brand – he criticises, for example, the typologies of Sheldon with its 'endomorphs' and 'mesomorphs' – this is unsurprising. But he also leaves out of sight the question of how any biology is lived.

Sève continually criticises the conception of the individual who 'naturally' preexists society – especially this idea as it is carried over into the work of would-be Marxist psychologists. He argues, following the spirit of the *Sixth Thesis on Feuerbach*, that social relations are not to be thought of as 'external' factors to growth, but in themselves constitute the essence of personality. So this leads him to claim that to describe sexuality as 'always social', but to describe other 'biologically supported' needs, such as eating, as merely socially mediated, or as 'conditioned' by social factors, as untenable. He says that all need is social need. But I would argue here against Sève that to submerge biology into social relations is to ignore the highly specific forms of biology as lived – as with, for instance, illness, fertility control, even the provision of physical space in which to live. These are areas which *are* certainly intimately linked with the processes of production, but which cannot be lumped together as the mass of 'social relations' if their uniqueness is to be understood. In contrast to Sève, who deals with all biology by putting it down to social relations, the Italian philosopher, Sebastiano Timpanaro, though also writing from the standpoint of Marxism, insists in his *On Materialism* on the distinctiveness of the biological realm.

Timpanaro does agree with Sève in several areas, but insists on the importance of recognising, for any socialist concept of human need, human limits which cannot be reduced – or elevated – to the sphere of 'the social'. He claims, I believe rightly, that 'the most effective way to oppose apolitical or reactionary psychology is not to accept the dilemma, "sociopolitical science or biological science?" and opt for the former alternative against the latter'.[52] But he then goes on to identify biology with a realm of passivity and necessity, sickness and death, which he describes in a tone of aesthetic pessimism. The world, he says, is not only something to be worked on and be transformed by human efforts, including politics; it also blocks and resists. His 'materialism' includes evocations of the inescapability of death and decay – which 'we socialists' must also recognise.

But such an insistence on biology is dangerous when it takes this shape of ostensibly hard-headed, though in fact profoundly romantic, reminders of our unheroic mortality. If the reintroduction of biology to socialist thinking were to take this melancholic shape, then it would be rightly rejected for leaving the old gaps wide open: Timpanaro's suggestions, once again, keep the categories of 'biology' and 'the social' and their relationship separate and unexamined. Reminders that we will sicken and die do not help. Timpanaro limits his circumscribed recognition of biology to those conditions – ageing, decay, death – which aren't susceptible to alteration as occurrences – and then characterises this recognition as 'materialist'. But this position identifies materialism with the natural and the organic with terrible consequences. (What materialism actually is, what content – if any – can be given now to the term, is a crucial problem, and one to be faced by any attempts to incorporate biology with Marxist theory, given that materialism is a key term for many versions of the latter.[53]) Timpanaro falls into a curious and mournful aesthetic of resignation to our mortal frailty, a frailty proposed in such a way that it is beyond help. It is striking, too, that he misses out from his catalogue of biological inevitabilities the fact that the world is sexed, that there is gender. He remarks that old age arises and persists 'on the biological level'. But so does infancy, puberty, menstruation, the menopause, childbirth; all of these embody irreducible biological components. Despite the brutal intractability of illness, it can't be allowed a completely privileged grip on the category of 'biology'.

It seems to me to be right to argue that biology is never lived out in a pure form: to borrow a phrase from Merleau-Ponty, 'the body never quite falls back onto itself'.[54] But this does not then commit you to arguing that everything is merely vaguely 'social'. Certainly there are difficulties about what you do with the biological once you have insisted on its social nature but have also refused to drown in it in a pool of social-ness. But to speak as Timpanaro does of 'the persistence of certain biological data even in social man' is to remind us of what we already know daily and does not solve the problem.

It could be objected that appeals to a concept of social biology still leave biology unanalysed and out in the cold, and that socialised biology will only give a more dense account of 'social factors', and push back biology to a point of infinite regression. This may turn out to be true. But what is important here is that biology, as lived within particular lives, has for too long been neglected. The account of what is social as we have it is both too wide in its compass and too narrow in its definition; tacking on a 'biological' category, like illness, to the cluster of 'social factors' is inadequate: assimilation is not a critical process.

And to overlook the particular forms in which biology is lived out is to overlook the fact that this biology is simultaneously biography – and that lives differ in ways which general categories of the socio-economic do not capture. For women in particular it is evident that an extremely significant proportion of social experience *is* socialised biology – reproductive experience, for instance. Because it is so vulnerable to inroads – changes in abortion laws, for example – it has a clear *political* dimension. The question of the conditions for a real control of fertility are of obvious concern here. And this is why feminism in particular cannot avoid thinking through the problems about what meaning can be given to the biological and the social.

Just because it's not possible to give a content to the idea of pure biology without difficulties, that should not mean that 'the biological' should vanish undifferentiated into the mist of 'social relations' or indeed that the aims of developmental psychology should be abandoned. Full consideration of the question of how, say, development in different children takes on 'differently social' forms will involve rejecting the sort of strict environmentalism sometimes held in the belief that it is equivalent to materialism, and indeed the further belief that materialism is a self-evident and incontrovertibly socialist concept. Instead it will be necessary to understand social-ised biology as encompassing the ways in which disabilities, nutrition, reproductive control, conditions of work are lived out in aspects of the economy or at its margins.

There are indeed real problems in the history of attempts to estab-lish materialist psychologies, Marxist psychologies, and so forth. But when these problems are identified only with the applicability of 'the dialectic' and of materialism, and when weariness then forces an abandonment of these concepts, some socialist philosophies have instead swung in favour of a universal culturalism, putting all down to unbounded 'social relations'. But this rush away from the traditional intractable apparatus of certain socialist thought leaves the way wide open for a return of an unworked-through notion of the standard biology-society relation. This reappears, troublingly, either as a posited 'absence' in socialist thought which must then be filled (in the way Timpanaro tries to do it) by annexing an untrans-formed version of biology in the name of a truly full materialism. Or else it makes many reappearances as overinsistences on the natures of male, female, homosexual, heterosexual. These first put everything down to 'society', and then divide that society relentlessly and totally along the lines of gender and sexual being.

To remain continually aware that we are indeed embodied need entail neither a fetishism of 'the body', nor a dissolution into the clouds of the social. What, though, can be made of the contribution of psychology to all this is another history.

CHAPTER 3

Child Psychologies in Europe and America

> 'My mother groan'd! my father wept
> Into the dangerous world I leapt:
> Helpless, naked, piping loud:
> Like a fiend hid in a cloud.'
>
> William Blake, 'Infant Sorrow' from
> *Songs of Experience*

'. . . *greed, hate and persecutory anxieties in relation to the primal object, the mother's breast, have an innate basis.*'

Melanie Klein, *Envy and Gratitude*[1]

It may seem that 'the child' is a straightforward enough object for investigations, rather like the squirrel or the daisy in simply being there. But 'the child' is not transparent or trouble-free as something to be studied. I don't mean that, as is sometimes argued by historians of the family, 'the child' as a distinct category of humanity is the creation of the seventeenth century, or whenever: but, rather, that for the child to become an object of psychological investigation, it has to be transposed out of its background, usually the family; and there is nothing about the child which dictates the manner of such transposing. The history of child psychology shows that the ways in which the child takes a place in a science have, on the one hand, a great deal to do with 'extraneous' conceptions of the nature of child, mother, father, family, community even; and, on the other, with conceptions of what is to count as scientific procedure in itself. There is a weak sense in which this is true of any observation of any object – how you understand the squirrel depends on how you, as it were, detach it from the pine forest: that is, it depends on your understanding of ethology or of natural history. But there are, in the case of investigations of the child, particular difficulties, which can't be adequately detected by tracing the history of psychology alone.

The child in nineteenth-century psychology

The child – the infant in particular – did draw the interest of an embryonic psychology in the last decades of the nineteenth century. A crop of observational studies and reports appeared in rapid succession in Europe and America. Most of the authors had allegiances to physiology or to medicine; infant psychology was doubly embryonic where the investigators had previously worked on foetal behaviour in animals. Most influential was Wilhelm Preyer, Professor of Physiology at Leipzig; his *Die Seele des Kindes* appeared in English translation as *The Mind of a Child*. The most quoted English text was Charles Darwin's 'A Biographical Sketch of an Infant'; in the United States, Stanley Hall's 'The Content of Children's Minds' was well known. These celebrated texts were, however, not the first of their kind: both Preyer and Hall refer to earlier 'scientific' observers (as distinct from philosophers, like Locke and Rousseau who had been taken with child study). The scientific work on infants emanated almost exclusively from Germany. Tiedemann's 'Beobachtungen über die Entwicklung der Seelenfahrigkeiten bei Kindern' is one of the earliest declaratively scientific records of infant behaviour and development to be published and recognised; one of Tiedemann's subjects is, again, his own son.[2] H. Feldmann, a physician, published studies of the onset of speaking and walking in thirty-five infants in 1833, while the first known observations of newborn children, as distinct from older infants, were made by Kussmaul in 1859. He held that all the sense organs were capable of some degree of functioning at birth – not, at the time, an orthodox opinion.

While most mid-nineteenth-century work on infants was pursued by those with medical qualifications, some educators and pedagogues, like Pestalozzi, occupied themselves with child psychology as a distinctive subject. Towards the end of the century, both philosophy and a psychology unsure of where to differentiate itself from philosophy, seized on the questions of child development as offering the chance of clarifying speculation and surmise about the nature of mind by means of direct observation. Taine's 'Notes sur l'acquisition de langage chez les enfants et dans l'espèce humaine' – a series of anecdotal accounts of an infant girl's acquisition of speech – was soon translated in *Mind*, the British philosophical journal. That James Sully could write a popular presentation of the new but reputable field of psychological investigation in 1881 – 'Babies and Science' – suggests how far such work had become solidly established; while Sully's *Studies of Childhood* (1895, 1903) acknowledged a train of predecessors and contemporaries in Europe and America. Galton in 1875 had studied the psychological development of twins, introducing the nature/nurture terminology. He came down in favour of nature as decisive: 'There is no escape from the conclusion that nature prevails enormously over nurture when the differences of nurture do not exceed what is commonly to be found among persons of the same rank of society and in the same country.'

Charles Darwin's 'A Biographical Sketch of an Infant' was first published in *Mind*, 1877, although based on notes he made in 1840. It is preoccupied with elucidating that which is 'reflex or instinctive' as opposed to that which is 'acquired through experience'; and, less prominently, with the ontogeny-phylogeny axis, the theory of 'cultural recapitulation', according to which embryological development echoes the evolution of a species, and the development of the child repeats the development of adult human cultures, proceeding in stages from the primitive to the civilised. Darwin tried to observe the transition from 'spontaneous' to 'learned' behaviour, and so to classify what was and was not innate. Thus the infant's sucking is 'reflex or instinctive' since it occurs before 'experience and association with the touch of his mother's breast'; and 'winking of the eyes' is similarly inborn. As to 'early reflex grasping', Darwin argued that 'the perfection of these reflex movements shows that the extreme imperfection of the voluntary ones is not due to the state of the muscles or of the coordinating centres, but to that of the seat of the will'. The sources of emotion are described; smiling is noted at the age of forty-five days – a characteristically late dating by modern standards; while 'true smiles indicative of pleasure' are 'probably of mental origin', indicating 'inward pleasurable feelings'. The beginnings of anger and jealousy are detected – 'a tendency to throw objects is inherited by boys . . . I could never see a trace of such an aptitude in my infant daughters' – and tentative theories about coordination are advanced to explain the development involved in grasping an object. Inherited racial memories are posited:

The vague but very real fears of children, which are quite independent of experience, are the inherited effects of real dangers and abject superstitions during ancient savage times. It is quite conformable with what we know of the transmission of formerly well-developed characters, that they should appear at an early period of life and afterwards disappear.

Darwin notes analogous developments in language:

The interrogatory sound which my child gave to the word 'mum' when asking for food is especially curious; for if anyone will use a single word or a short sentence in this manner, he will find that the musical pitch of his voice rises considerably at the close. I did not see then that this fact bears on the view which I have elsewhere maintained, that before man used articulate language, he uttered notes in a true musical scale as does the anthropoid ape Hylobates.

Taine's notes, translated in *Mind*, 1877 as 'The Acquisition of Language by Children', share Darwin's interest in classifying particularly human sophistications. He writes, 'the delicacy of impression and delicacy of expressions are in fact the distinctive characteristic of man among animals and . . . in him are the sources of language and general ideas'. He emphasises the ability to make analogies as characteristic of the human developing intelligence: 'No dog or parrot would have done as much; in my opinion we come here upon the essence of language.' The theme of cultural recapitulation is again present:

The child presents in a passing state the mental characteristics that are found in a fixed state in primitive civilisations, very much as the human

45

embryo presents in a passing state the physical characteristics that are found in a fixed state in the classes of inferior animals.

The 'animistic' ideas which Taine reads in the child's speech provide him with the foundation for this conclusion. The spontaneous utterance of sounds fascinated him; it was 'a sympathetic articulation which she herself has found in harmony with all fixed and distinct intention. . . . a natural vocal gesture, not learned, and at the same time imperative and demonstrative'.

Again, in a similar fashion to Darwin's analysis, weight is laid on the infant's unique capacities to generate speech: 'originality and invention are so strong in a child that if it learns our language from us, we learn it from the child'. The infant, says Taine, 'learns a ready-made language as a true musician learns counterpoint or a true poet prosody; it is an original genius adapting itself to a form constructed bit by bit by a succession of original geniuses; if language were wanting, the child would recover it little by little, or would discover an equivalent'.[3]

In both Taine and Darwin, human-animal comparisons aim to elucidate the uniquely human properties of the human infant, and inventive capacities, particularly in the realm of language, are the point of demarcation. Here 'the infant' is set against 'the dog' and 'primitives'. Neither in Darwin's nor in Taine's papers is there much sense of the child in the family: an implicit nurse hovers in the background; Darwin refers in passing to brothers and sisters. Both Sully and Preyer, on the other hand, do draw attention to the fact that the new object of natural history was fixed in the nursery, and that this had consequences for its study. Sully's 'Babies and Science' is on the verge of whimsy; while it skates self-consciously around its own wit, it describes the nature of the new scientific interest in the infant to a general educated public. 'The evolutionist,' writes Sully, 'has found a meaning for this apparent defect [early helplessness] in the organisation of the human offspring.' A condition of dependence has a social evolutionary function – it calls forth 'impulses of tendance, protection &c, on the part of the parent; only on this condition could the family, the community or the race be preserved'. It follows for Sully that 'the period of infancy which produces . . . the germs of altruistic sentiments, affection and sympathy' is 'longer in the case of civilised man than in the savage'. Indeed, some comparative anthropology becomes necessary for the task of determining the origins of Mind; for 'the modern psychologist, sharing in the spirit of positive science, feels that he must begin at the beginning, study mind in its simplest forms'. Therefore

he carries his eye far afield to the phenomena of savage life, with its simple ideas, crude sentiments and naive habits. Again he devotes special attention to the mental life of the lower animals, seeking in its phenomena the dim foreshadowing of our own perceptions, emotions &c. Finally he directs his attention to the mental phenomena of infancy, as fitted to throw most light on the later developments of the human mind.

So the study of 'primitives', of natural history, and of the behaviour of the human infant might constitute well-ordered steps to the fuller knowledge of 'finished' mind.

A particular evolutionary interest – again that theory of cultural recapitulation – is invoked: 'the study of infant life may well be fitted to suggest by what steps of intellectual and moral progress our race has passed into its present state. The attentive eye may thus find in seemingly meaningless little infantile ways, hints of remote habits and customs of the human race'. But this theory is also treated with light irony by Sully: the father and scientific observer, who is also the author,

hints that the special interest taken by his child in reflections may be a survival reflecting the primitive feeling in respect of the second selves or ghosts of things, which anthropologists as Mr E. B. Tylor and Mr Herbert Spencer tell us, was first developed in connection with the phenomena of reflected images, shadows, etc. . . . he goes on to ask whether the fear called forth by the doll and the face of strangers at a certain stage in the child's development, is not clearly due to an instinct now fixed in the race by the countless experiences of peril in its earlier, presocial, Ishmaelitic condition.

But his own mildly parodic attitudes did not distract Sully, in his 'serious' scientific work, from staying within the same set of references. The late-nineteenth-century psychologist had simultaneously to keep an eye on underpinning evolutionary ethnography, note in infantile behaviour shadows of our forgotten ancestors, and observe the acquisition of Mind, memory, emotion, so providing conclusive escape from the dilemma of whether morality and intellectual capacities are 'acquired' or 'innate'. In this way, the psychologist might help to clarify a great philosophical debate.

The seriousness of psychology's undertaking is recognised by Sully, and treated too as an uncertain joke when it came down to practice: the absurdity of the scientific father in the officially female domain of the nursery is spun out to the point of tedium. At the same time, comments on the 'humanising', softening effect of the occupation of infant-watching for such men are half-seriously linked to the theory of the socially mollifying effects of childish helplessness – a perfectly respectable theory for Sully's contemporaries. Thus,

Science has become a champion of the neglected rights of infancy; it has taken a whole period of human life under its special protection. And in doing this it has constituted itself the avenger of a whole sex (women) . . . the first thing that babies needed was to have their existence justified and this service has been amply rendered them by the newer science of biology.

Science says 'to all male scoffers [that] the state of infantile frailty and imbecility is causally connected with all the blessings of social life. . . . Had there been no babies, there would have been no higher intellectual development, no sacred ties of kinship, friendship and copatriotism'.

The ironised presentation of the father as scientist, the scientist as father is linked (and linked uneasily, for at what point does the earnestness switch to parody?) to the notion of the elevating powers of infant frailty. Science

has become the ally of the natural admirers of babies in their endeavour to win over the reluctant interest of men. One may almost say that she has entered into a harmless conspiracy with mothers to lure the sluggish brain of man on to perceive something of the mysterious charm that surrounds the baby . . . she does so by awakening a scientific interest in the baby. . . . Science having thus declared the infant to be a valuable phenomenon for observation, there has of late grown up among the class of scientific fathers the habit of noting and recording the various proceedings of the infant. Men who previously never thought of meddling with the affairs of the nursery have been impelled to make periodic visits thither in the hope of eliciting important psychological facts . . . the tiny occupant of the cradle has had to bear the piercing glance of the scientific eye. The psychological papa has acquired a new proprietary right in his offspring; he has appropriated it as a biological specimen. This new zeal for scientific knowledge has taken possession of a number of my acquaintances. They are mostly young married men for whom the phenomenon of babyhood has all the charm of newness and who import a youthful enthusiasm into their scientific pursuits. . . . If you happen to call on one of them, expecting to find him free for a chat, you may, to your amazement, catch him occupied in the nursery trying to discover the preferences of the three-month's fledgeling in the matter of colours, or watching the impression which is first made on the infant mind by the image of its own face in the glass.[4]

With Sully's characterisation of 'the psychological papa' goes a predictable portrayal of the mother, whose way of regarding children

unfits her from entering very cordially into the scientific vein. She rather dislikes their being made the objects of cold intellectual scrutiny and unfeeling psychological analysis. . . . To suggest a series of experiments on the gustatory sensibility of a small creature aged from twelve to twenty-four hours is likely to prove a shock, even to the more strong-minded of mothers.

This characterisation is sewn up at all possible seams, for

if the mother gets herself in time infected with the scientific ardour of the father, she may prove rather more of an auxiliary than he desires. Her maternal instincts impel her to regard her particular child as phenomenal in an extra-scientific sense. She . . . is disposed to ascribe to her baby a preternatural degree of intelligence.

The mother who aspires to the (male) realm of scientific knowledge is an evident absurdity; she 'brings her supposed observations' to her husband who 'has trained himself in accurate observation . . . he is compelled to suspect the accuracy of these recitals'. The nurse is a second female obstacle; she resents the man's 'unhallowed prying' in the nursery.

Continuing with a thinly disguised description of his own son's

behaviour, Sully set this amid contemporary developments, referring to *Mind* and to Darwin:

An English journal which devotes itself to the interests of mental science has
recently published a number of notes made by industrious fathers on the
doings of their infants. A distinguished naturalist set the example by giving
a curiously methodical record of the development of one of his sons. And in
France and Germany we hear of similar results of this spirit of enquiry on
the part of scientific men who happen to be provided with the necessary
objects of observation.

He concluded on a note of mingled scepticism and self-parody:

I leave this transcript from the diary of a psychological observer to produce
its own proper effect on the minds of my readers . . . some of them, particularly among the mothers, who have had their own field of inspection, may
be disposed to regard certain of his observations as trite and commonplace.
Others, again of the cynical bachelor class, may think that they discover
now and again traces of weak paternal sentiment mingling with and
adulterating the pure one of scientific discovery. And finally, sober people
may find some of the social speculations put forward in the record far-
fetched if not absurd. . . . I feel I have done my task in letting them know
something of the nature of the new fashion in the domain of psychological
enquiry.

Sully – at the time Grote Professor of Psychology and Philosophy
at London University – continued his work on infants and published more than one standard book on child development. By 1895
the Preface to his *Studies of Childhood* could point to a solidly established body of work in Europe and America in 'the new fashion' for
psychology – which was fashionable enough for several magazine
accounts to have proliferated: Sully mentioned 'Baby Linguistics' in
the *English Illustrated Magazine* for 1884, and articles in the *Popular
Science Monthly* of New York and *Longman's Magazine*. Among his
predecessors and authorities, Sully praised Preyer as 'a pioneer',
acknowledged the help of Lt. Gen. Pitt-Rivers in 'studying the
drawings of savages', mentioned Galton's work as an exemplar of 'a
regular and methodical register of progress', referred to Baldwin's
Mental Development in the Child & the Race, and described Miss Shinn's

Notes on the Development of a Child as 'minute and painstaking . . . pointing to the ample opportunity of observation which comes more readily to women'.[5] He also stressed medical forerunners, particularly Sigismund, whose *The Child and the World* of 1856 was the work of one of the group of 'pioneers who struck out at this new line of experimental research [who] were medical men . . . doctors have a special access to the nursery'.[6]

Preyer's *Mental Development in the Child*, written as a popular exposition of his *Die Seele des Kindes* of 1881, treated the child observed in the family with a serious, even didactic purpose. Both Preyer and Sully recognised that the child's location in the family gave rise to 'problems' in studying it. But Preyer, not dismissing the class of mothers as creatures of incorrigibly unscientific temperament, wanted to enrol them as a special class of lay scientific observers:

The scientific observation of children by their parents has become more common in recent years. Much work remains to be done, and the persons who have the best opportunity to do it are the mothers. The object of this book is to initiate mothers into the science of child observation. The work requires great patience and skill.[7]

Referring to his earlier publications, Preyer added:

It is not too much to say that this new department of physiological psychology is now firmly established. Investigators in the most diverse special provinces of medicine, language, pedagogy, are turning more and more to the observation of their own children during those years in which speech is acquired, and we can foresee that at no distant date will appear special textbooks upon the physiology and psychology of the child from the first to the fifth year of life. Before that takes place, a great deal more work must be done. . . . But in order to initiate mothers into so complicated a science as that of psychogenesis, the results already attained in it must be presented to them in a form as easy of assimilation as possible.[8]

He proposed that 'teachers of both sexes, fathers and siblings' should be enrolled in this new field of enquiry. As a physiologist who had first worked extensively on embryology, animal and human, it was unsurprising that he had leanings towards what would now be called ethology.

The observation of untrained animals, especially young ones, and the comparison of the observations made upon them with those upon little children, have often been found by me very helpful toward an understanding of children; and I hope from the completion of a comparative psychology, together with the inauguration of psychogenetic observations, more results than from the prosecution of earlier psychologies of a more speculative sort.[9]

Preyer's extensive researches in embryology[10] had been concerned with the chronology of sensory perception. In the tradition of early experiments with foetuses, his physiological work with newborn children attempted to establish a calendar of the discriminations of touch and taste. This orientation towards physiological psychology did not preclude observations on the best handling of infants: he wrote with some passion of the effects of 'ignorance' of the child's needs:

For example, a child quietly sleeping is waked in order to be fed; or is allowed to cry uninterruptedly in the night without being once looked after in order to find out what is wrong with him; or he is swathed too tight. . . . Not only is the physical development disturbed considerably by such preposterous actions, but the character too, which unfolds itself very early, is spoiled. The waking of young children, in particular, I regard as extraordinarily harmful in both these directions.[11]

This movement from observation to advice-giving in one page underlines the almost ethical nature of psychology for Preyer; infant observation had direct implications for infant management. Both Preyer and Sully, despite their quite different interpretations of it, were well aware of the problem of how the father and mother were to stand in relation to the study of the child. Claims were made about the role of the new psychology as a special source of practical advice; Sully's general textbook, *Outlines of Psychology* of 1884, reached towards a definition of psychology which preserved its 'practicality'. While the aim of psychology was 'the scientific study of first, physical phenomena themselves and secondly, as subsidiary and complementary to this, of the connections between these with physical and particularly nervous operations', this entailed a concern with applied science too. Although psychology was 'a theoretic or speculative as distinguished from a practical science or art', this distinction itself, he said, could not be long maintained, 'for practical science though thus contrasted with the theoretic is really very closely connected with it'. In Sully's exposition, psychology was the basis of the practical sciences and of education, and entered into 'logic, aesthetics, politics and rhetoric' – with a special interest in 'the evolution of moral sentiment [which] follows a similar course in the case of the race and of the individual'.[12]

The 'new psychology' in the last decades of the nineteenth century was self-consciously located between the theoretical and the practical, and overlapped by other disciplines, notably natural history, anthropology, physiology and medicine. The elucidation of 'the physical bases of Mind' with the problems of method this posed was recognised as fundamental to both child psychology, and psychology in general. *Mind* in 1877 carried an extract from G. H. Lewes's 'The Physical Basis of Mind', which argued against a reduction to 'the material', and for 'historical and social conditions' as the other 'half of the psychologists' quest'. For 'the human mind, so far as it is accessible to scientific enquiry, had a twofold root, man being not only an animal organism but a unit in the social organism; and a complete theory of its functions and faculties must therefore be sought in this twofold direction'. Of the 'reductionist superstition of the nerve cell' which characterised certain contemporary drifts in psychology, Lewes wrote,

The conclusion has slowly forced itself upon me that on this subject there is a false persuasion of knowledge, very fatal in its influence, because unhesitatingly adopted as the ground of speculation both in Pathology and in Psychology. This persuasion is sustained because few are aware of how much of what passes for observation is in reality sheer hypothesis.[13]

The couplet 'nature/nurture', the invention of Galton, was quickly taken up, being pleasantly mnemonic. Sully's *Outlines of Psychology* (1884) stated approvingly: 'We may say that individual development is the action of what Mr Galton has happily called "nurture" upon "nature".'[14] Galton himself, in his *English Men of Science* (1874), subtitled 'Their Nature and Nurture', discussed his terminology thus:

The phrase 'nurture and nature' is a convenient jingle of words, for it separates under two distinct heads the innumerable elements of which personality is composed. Nature is all that a man brings with himself into the world; nurture is every influence from without that affects him after his birth. The distinction is clear; the one produces the infant such as it actually is, including its latent faculties of growth and mind; the other affords the environment amid which the growth takes place, by which natural tendencies may be strengthened or thwarted, or wholly new ones implanted. Neither of these terms implies any theory; natural gists may or may not be hereditary; nurture does not especially consist of food, clothing, education or tradition but includes all these and similar influences whether known or unknown. . . . The impress of class distinctions is superficial.[15]

Arguing from examples of twins, including twins in Shakespearean fictions, Galton concluded: 'In the competition between nature and nurture, when the differences in either case do not exceed those which distinguish individuals of the same race living in the same country under no very exceptional conditions, nature certainly proves the stronger of the two'.[16]

His *English Men of Science*, a supplement to *Hereditary Genius*, attempted to establish a body of statistical knowledge about mental heredity. It included interviews with 180 'men of science' with respect to their descent, parentage, distinction of family, education, individual qualities – head size, energy, truthfulness, innateness of strong taste for science, and so forth. Its aims were simultaneously pedagogic, moral, and political: for Galton hoped that a knowledge of intellectual heritability would join a eugenicist programme for social reform. The nation needed better scientists, and a scientific concept of how to produce such commodities:

Science has hitherto been at a disadvantage, compared with other competing pursuits, in enlisting the attention of the best intellects of the nation, for reasons that are partly inherited and partly artificial; this tendency to abandon the cold attractions of science for those of political and social life, must always be powerfully reinforced by the very general inclination of women to exert their influence in the latter direction.[17]

Galton's anxieties about population quality were directed, in his concluding remarks to *Hereditary Genius*, to a nightmare of the 'better classes' withering away and the worse inheriting the earth, as a consequence of leaving fertility control to individual sensibility and prudence.[18]

He believed the significance of his work to be its potential for lifting eugenics out of the realm of 'introspective' morality and into that of 'objective' science: it was 'one of the landmarks in the transition from introspective to objective methods in biological and psychological research'. Psychology, including child psychology, was aware of itself as both a technical and an ethical science. In the US, in fact, the establishment of a specialist psychology directed to 'practical' issues was marked by the appearance of the *Journal of Applied Psychology* in 1917. (A department at Harvard had been set up earlier under the direction of Professor Munsterberg from Germany.) The compass of this applied psychology is indicated by the article topics – 'The Psychology of a Prodigious Child', 'Stuttering', 'Industrialism', 'Psychology and the Businessman', and 'The Moral Issues Raised by Applied Psychology'. The latter article argues against the notion of the autonomy of means and ends.[19] A blend of pedagogy, performance testing, and the elementary tenets of Taylorism (the 'rationalisation' of labour processes) were included under the rubric of the 'applied'. However, the discipline was soon to act as a straightforward service to industrialism.

It was quite predictable that observational child psychology would be similarly transformed; it slid into new concepts of schooling. Typically enough, the American *Psychological Review*, whose first number appeared in 1894, carried a separate section for reviews of the new child psychology, where works on teaching, on children's performance in schools and the like appeared regularly. Pedagogic literature, though, was by definition not occupied with the very young child or the child placed within the family. How were these elements taken up as the 'new psychology' of the 1880s fragmented gradually into a series of discrete specialisms? By 1904, *Mind*'s reviewer of Kirkpatrick's *Fundamentals of Child Study*[20] could take a retrospective look at the literature in his field: 'Child study has in recent years occupied a prominent place in educational literature and at school conferences. Monographs dealing with individual children and groups of children are becoming common. . . . Infants and school children are being weighed, measured and observed by countless parents and teachers all over the world.' The President of the Child Study Association in 1903 wondered: 'How can the study [of children] be undertaken except by one who is a physiologist, by one who is also a pathologist, by one who is also a psychologist, by one who is also a practical educationist?'[21] Education was crucial: 'What a child is at any time depends upon what he was at the beginning and what he has acquired by his reactions'. An optimistic reading of nature versus nurture allowed for malleability in the child; and educational institutions were the places where intervention happened. The problem of the new science of child study was 'the outer and inner factors in human development and to determine how the inner factors are modified by the outer'.[22] This opened up an emphasis on the curative and elevating influence of 'the outer', and emphasised the original moral and practical tone which was so central to child psychology: although to say this much is not to minimise the effects of contemporary evolutionary theory – as well as anthropology and biology – on late-nineteenth-century psychology.

By the first decade of the twentieth century there was a strong move, in child-psychological writing, away from the home and towards the school: Kirkpatrick's *Fundamentals of Child Study* of 1903 was designed for 'investigators, students, teachers and parents' but in practice the family had dropped away.[23] The emphasis was on 'training and regulation', including self-regulation, of the child's 'instincts'; where the home appeared, it did so only as a training-ground. It became school-like, and the parts played by the mother and the father vanished. The vocabulary of 'training' was not a product of the start of the twentieth century alone, – but the differentiation of child psychology then taking place did bring about the development of a new pedagogical-psychological literature. Baldwin's *Mind of the Child* of 1895 advocated 'habits' and 'inviolable regularity'; it was the job of 'interested parents' to 'know your babies through and through. Especially the fathers! They are willing to study everything else. They know every corner of the house familiarly and what is done in it, except the nursery. . . . The best school in the humanities for every man is his own house.'[24]

Home *as* schooling was here a corollary of conceiving the infant as immediately social. Thus Baldwin: 'the child is bound up with others from the start by the very laws of his growth. His social action and feeling are natural to him . . . he is really social all the time.'[25] Child psychology in this account became a branch of moral philosophy; a 'psychogenetic' study investigated the social nature of the infant – 'the real self is the bipolar self, the social self, the socius'.[26] Baldwin described society as a psychological organisation, not a physiological one; and here his writings point to another branching out of child psychology, particularly evident in the United States – towards 'social' or, later, 'group' psychology.[27]

Stern's *Psychology of Early Childhood* (1914) rapidly became another contemporary classic. The Preface to the First Edition indicates its methodological tensions:

Child psychology itself, which for a long time consisted only of the collection of data and individual investigations, is badly in need *of clearly marked boundaries*, as to the extent, value and significance of its discoveries. Then, too, general psychology ought to enter into a closer relationship with child-lore. . . . Of late, too, historians have begun to take an interest in child-study, for they believe that the similarities between the early development of the individual and the intellectual growth of the race are extensive enough to open fresh paths for historical research. Then, too, educational interests are not without weight.[28]

Parents, teachers, physicians and teachers of defective children were held to need guidance from child psychology; and Stern referred them to courses in Training Colleges and University Extension work.

Along with the uncertainties about intellectual boundaries, the socially limited nature of extant studies came in for criticism – 'the want of scientifically unprejudiced and copious observations of the little child of the proletariat'.[29] The sole objects of detailed study Stern wrote, were

the children of the upper classes . . . it is of course probable that the main features of the child's psychic development share the same general character, but in details such as the relative time of development or the influence of certain conditions of environment, it is but reasonable to suppose that amongst the lower classes, variations will be found which so far are but little known and which offer a wide and important field for future enquiry.[30]

Stern's own method of infant investigation – in the nineteenth-century tradition – was to use his own children. He advocated 'direct observation of children by such persons who live with them in a constant relationship of confidence and familiarity'. This was the mother's part – 'she it is who seems destined above all others to do this service for child-psychology'. The old caveats appeared, nonetheless – 'few mothers' would be capable of combining objectivity with 'the necessary subjective mother-love and tenderness'.[31] Truly scientific work must remain the province of those with psychological training, although the right sort of mothers might supply extra raw material. Stern suggested that family observations should be supplemented by *in situ* studies of kindergarten pupils, including working-class infants. Referring to new developments in psychology, Stern included Gestalt, and 'personality' theory, and the new 'thought psychology' advanced by Bühler. To one side of these, he placed a class of 'offshoots', among them psychoanalysis. Here, 'once more medicine puts its hand to child psychology' with what Stern interpreted as unhappy results. He objected to sexuality being read in everywhere, and deprecated

the wish to see in the child nothing but the adult in miniature . . . the educational and therapeutic results are more especially dangerous for early childhood, since their tendency is to rob the child prematurely of his irreplaceable 'innocence', and this fact needs particular emphasis since, at the present time, at home and even more abroad, many enthusiastic followers of Freud are now recommending psychoanalysis of children as the general foundation of educational reforms.[32]

The work of the psychologist Adler, he thought, was safer, for 'this individual psychology in its method of interpretation aims at discovering in the child's psychic life not onesided sexual clues, but those of general application and logical in character'.[33]

Psychoanalytic psychology in America; Kleinian theory in Britain

In the first decade of the twentieth century, observational child psychology in Britain, as in America, disintegrated into several specialisms. Paediatrics and infant welfare, under the rubric of child health, constituted one leaning of enquiry, educational psychology and the testing of intelligence another. Work which called itself 'psychology' was oriented towards theories of infant 'management' and advice to parents; it was translated from European writing or imported from the United States – the work, for example, of Charlotte Bühler or Siegfried Bernfeld. The role which had been occupied in the late nineteenth century by 'the new science of the child psychology' had been taken over by psychoanalysis, and this was well entrenched in the 1930s.

In America, the earliest psychoanalytically oriented work on the family was later reinvigorated by the prewar immigration of European psychoanalysts and sociologists escaping from fascist Germany and Austria, among them many critical theorists of the Frankfurt School. The whole Frankfurt Institute from 1934 onwards emigrated to New York, including Marcuse, Horkheimer, Fromm, and eventually, Adorno.[34] About the Institute's main project, Horkheimer wrote, 'The central theme of the work is a relatively new concept – the rise of an "anthropological" species we call the authoritarian type of man.'[35] Despite important differences among the group,[36] there was a common commitment to understanding how sociology and psychology could develop a means for understanding the development of 'personality types', the authoritarian or fascistic 'character structure' in particular. Accounting for the rise of Nazism was morally and politically imperative for socialistic accounts of the 'authoritarian family'.

Positions taken by Frankfurt School theorists of the family are

59

instructive – those of Horkheimer especially – as instances of attempts to analyse the 'patriarchal' family. Horkheimer gave an ambiguous status to paternal authority. Would the dissolution of such authority predispose to a healthy critical rebelliousness, or instead to a conforming helplessness in the face of the advances of monopoly capitalism? This question depended on the notion of the 'internalisation' of authority taking place in the family. Horkheimer took it to be a fact that 'the family in crisis produces the attitudes which predispose men for blind submission,' despite his later references to it as a preserve of moral, humane resistance to a broader social dehumanisation. His 1936 *Studien über Autorität und Familie*, originally intended to include reports on the mentality of workers in the Weimar Republic, argued the conservative function of the bourgeois family.

The family, as one of the most important formative agencies, sees to it that the kind of human character emerges which social life requires, and gives this human being in great measure the indispensable adaptability for a specific authority-oriented conduct on which the existence of the bourgeois order depends . . . the bad conscience that is developed in the family absorbs more energies than can be counted, which might otherwise be directed against the social circumstances that play a role in the individual's failure. The outcome of such paternal education is men who without ado seek the fault in themselves.[37]

Like Reich, Horkheimer considered that the economic dependence of women in the family and monogamy caused the inhibition of 'important psychic energies'. The family, to Horkheimer in 1936, 'is becoming a simple problem of technological manipulation by government'; its function as a 'refuge' was less significant than its 'role in the authoritarian structure of capitalist society'.[38]

Despite the distance between work on the authoritarian personality and classical Marxism, the dominant late-1930s theories of the family shared a moral approach to the family, treating it as an integral unit. This is clear in the shifting analyses of the family as liable to produce conservative susceptibilities or radical tendencies, but anyway as a cornerstone of the state. Later writings were more diluted; the 1940s 'basic personality type' work reduced comparative studies of the family to cross-cultural work on child-rearing. The theme of the family as agent of sexual repressiveness, and hence political conservatism, resurfaced only with the second generation, 1960s, Frankfurt School's modified reworking of these theories, notably by Herbert Marcuse.

Certainly the work of the Institute understood the use of psychological categories within sociology to present severe problems. Horkheimer and Adorno in particular both refused to collapse sociology into psychology. Nonetheless, the Institute's preoccupation with how psychoanalysis and psychology could interpret social and political problems readily joined tendencies in American psychoanalytically influenced anthropology and sociology. Prominent among these was that framework of 'ego psychology' used by Hartmann and Fromm, although Adorno had strong theoretical objections to it. This understanding of 'ego psychology' sat well with the attempt to conceive of character in relation to culture – specific 'personality types' were produced by specific cultural norms.

The aim of this 'ego psychology' was to comprehend the formation of the 'healthy ego' in society: here considerations of the unconscious and of sexual differentiation tended to fall away. For although the diction of Freudian psychoanalysis was sometimes used, the theories which sustained 'ego psychology' were far from its Freudian sources. Whereas psychoanalytic psychology in Britain was captured by Kleinianism, in America a particular 'ego psychology' was decisive in the understanding of the child in the family: as a body of psychology it sat close to pedagogy. Its chief exponents were Kris and Hartmann, whose work is discussed below. Laplanche and Pontalis summarise the difficulties involved:

An entire school has set out to relate the acquisitions of psychoanalysis to those of other disciplines (psycho-physiology, learning theory, child psychology, social psychology) in an attempt to found a true general psychology of the ego. This enterprise has led to the introduction of such notions as that of a desexualised, neutralised energy which the ego can command and which has a so-called 'synthetic' function, and that of a conflict-free portion of the ego. The ego is looked upon above all as an apparatus of regulation and adaptation to reality, while an attempt is made to trace its origin and development through maturational and learning processes, starting from the sensory and motor equipment of the baby at the breast. Even supposing that any of these ideas could be shown to have some initial support in Freud's thought, it would still be hard to see how they could be said to represent the most consistent expression of the final Freudian theory of the psychical apparatus. Not that there is any question of setting out some 'true' Freudian theory of the ego to counter these tendencies of ego psychology: indeed, it is remarkably difficult to integrate the psychoanalytic contributions to the concept of the ego into a unified line of thought.[39]

Freud himself – despite the impression which the fame of 'Little Hans'[40] conveys – had said little about children as patients. He did not go in for analysing children, as distinct from tracing the aetiologies of adult emotions and neuroses in childhood sexuality. Child psychiatry was an established discipline which well predated Freud's formulations on the Oedipus complex as the childhood key to adult neuroses. In Britain, for example, Henry Maudsley's *Physiology and Pathology of the Mind* of 1867 included a chapter on 'Insanity of Early Life', and tried to differentiate between child and adult psychopathology. In Germany, Emminghaus's long textbook of child psychiatry, *Die psychischen Störungen des Kindesalters*, of 1887, emphasised taking individual case histories in order to isolate 'inherited' from 'acquired' causes of illness. The study of child hysteria relied on a belief in heritability: the hysterical mother transmitted a susceptibility to hysterical symptoms to her child. Child psychopathology became a province of both pedagogues and child psychologists: in Germany, the journal of character disorders in children, *Die Kinderfehler*, founded in 1896, furthered this study.[41] Charcot in France had, in 1872, underlined the importance of isolating the child from exciting environmental factors, chiefly its family, although he too stressed the significance of 'heredity' in hysteria.[42] European developments in child psychiatry followed a transition away from those accounts which relied on heredity; but they still retained some uneasy commitment to it. This newer work emphasised the psychopathology of childhood rather than the course of 'normal development' in children.

There was a different development in the United States – the early adoption of psychoanalysis. Freud had lectured in 1909 at Clark University on the significance of childhood experiences in the aetiology of mental illness,[43] and the main American early-twentieth-century absorption of Freudianism was in the sphere of preventive 'mental hygiene': sound childrearing practices might save trouble and expense later on. To a far more pronounced extent than in Britain, child psychology and psychoanalysis, as aspects of 'mental hygiene', became attractions for neuropsychiatry, philanthropy, child protection movements and public health theories. This tendency was furthered by the fact that American analyses were always carried out by doctors: there was no lay analysis. The 1921 Presidential Address to the American Psychiatric Association declared: 'The path of mental hygiene starts and ends in the community. Its course leads through the home, the school, the hospital, out again into the widening network of supervisory and helpful agencies in the community'.[44]

Psychoanalysis, as an adjunct to mental hygiene, continued its incarnation in America as social prophylaxis. At the same time, the study of the 'normal' child within psychology in the first decades of this century was coloured by the behaviourism advanced by J. B. Watson. Watson's own description, from his outlook in 1913, of the course of American psychology asserted the true scientificity of the break with 'an introspective psychology' addressed to problems of consciousness: he held that experimental behavioural psychology had generated the 'vigorous growths' of 'experimental pedagogy, the psychology of drugs, the psychology of advertising, legal psychology, the psychology of tests and psychopathology'.[45] Watson and Lashley together established the journal *Psychobiology* in 1918 from Johns Hopkins, as a vehicle for pure research in physiological psychology, and in experimental work on animal learning. Psychologies of the child were largely taken up with the business of mental measurement: broadscale studies, like Gesell's, set out, in the 1920s and 1930s, to establish 'norms' of attainment. (One experiment by Gesell in 1927, for example, under the auspices of the Yale Clinic of Child Development, set out to record 'the behaviour characteristics displayed in twenty-five different situations, instituted at fifteen age levels from four through fifty-six weeks' among 107 infants.)[46] Gesell saw his task as laying down those 'norms' which had clinical and diagnostic application: in paediatrics, he claimed, a revolutionary increase in medical and social control had already been achieved in principle, for behavioural measurements could act as yardsticks to detect physical handicaps, mental defects or endocrinal deficiencies. Gesell supported his work by a theory of 'maturation' which appealed to Piaget's early studies for intellectual confirmation: he believed that the infant's susceptibility to learning and conditioning would always be secondary to a preprogrammed 'maturation'; the individual child's growth would 'tend towards an optimum realization' of built-in limits. This teleological conception characterised the mainstream of American child developmental psychology in the 1930s. Drawing up clinical norms for diagnostic use was what child psychology consisted of, while mental hygiene and preventive management were adjuncts to the psychoanalysis of children.

The introduction, then, of 'ego psychology' in America in the 1930s and 1940s could address itself to a missing subject: the family. For the 'ego psychology' of Anna Freud, vigorously espoused and extended by American-based analysts like Ernst Kris and Heinz Hartmann, was 'triangular': it concerned itself with father, mother, child. The tendency of 'ego psychology' in America to take the family as its object sat well with a broad process of rendering psychology sociological which had established itself in social anthropology too. Writers and researchers as diverse as Mead, Róheim, Fromm, Erikson, Kluckhohn and Leighton were pursuing overlapping ends, including the cross-cultural study of the Oedipus complex; clinical work on child development which embraced the study of cross-cultural childrearing practices; and the struggle to establish some framework to harmonise research in anthropology, psychology, and sociology.[47]

These pursuits were joined by war-influenced studies of national 'character', which tried to extend work like Adorno's *The Authoritarian Personality* and Reich's *Mass Psychology of Fascism* in ego-psychoanalytic terms. Thus, volume 1 of Róheim's *Psychoanalysis and the Social Sciences* in 1947 carried an article by Spitzer which discussed 'Psychoanalytic approaches to the Japanese character' and Róheim's introduction to this volume claimed that 'modern anthropology has influenced dissident psychoanalysis, i.e. the Horney, Kardiner, and similar groups, to a considerable degree'.[48] Many articles produced in America under the banner of a psychoanalytic anthropology sought to analyse 'national character structure': representative titles include 'Psychological Aspects of Current Japanese and German Paradoxa', 'Oriental Character Structure', 'Trends in Twentieth-century Propaganda', 'Antisemitism and Negro Race Riots in Detroit', 'Japanese Character-Structure and Propaganda'.[49] This literature was extensive enough for Spitzer and Ruth Benedict to compile, in 1945, a *Bibliography of Articles and Books Relating to Japanese Character*, published by the Office of War Information.

All this work was based on hopes that a psychoanalytically oriented postwar education would modify the 'national character-structures' it detected in enemy nations, like Japan: Kris and Leites wrote 'if the appropriate education [psychoanalytically influenced] on a vast enough scale and at a rapid enough rate is not provided for, the distrust and privatization of the masses may become a fertile soil for totalitarian management.'[50] The study of national character types worked on an assumption of a group psychology that also claimed, in the case of Róheim anyway, some authority from the late writings of Freud in particular – such as his *Moses and Monotheism*, which in parts echoed the theory of cultural recapitulation: 'The archaic heritage of human beings comprises not only dispositions, but also subject-matter memory traces of the experiences of earlier generations. . . . If we assume the survival of these memory traces in the archaic heritage we have bridged the gulf between individual and group psychology: we can deal with peoples as we do with an individual neurotic'.[51] Róheim's wild project, given in *Psychoanalysis and Anthropology*, was to take whole cultures as incarnations of infantile psychic dramas, and, in order to reveal the truth about primitive societies, to enlarge on suppositions that the savage was tantamount to the infant.[52] More sober aspects of this widespread American welding together of anthropology, psychoanalysis and sociology were demonstrated in 'cross-cultural' work like that of, for example, Margaret Mead's *Sex and Temperament in Three Primitive*

Societies and Kardiner's *The Individual and His Society*.

This latter is the 'basic personality structure' work denounced by Sève.[53] Again it claims the authority of what it calls 'Freud's sociology': it takes Freud's *Totem and Taboo* as authorising the idea that the 'psychic life of the savage' represents a well-preserved early stage of our own development: taboo systems parallel the defensive strategy of an individual compulsive neurosis.[54] Primitive culture is the psyche writ large: the tenacity of the nineteenth-century theory of cultural recapitulation with its equation of child equals savage equals neurotic is witnessed by its reincarnation at least as late as the 1940s. But cultures were different: repressions, Kardiner wrote, 'do not always fall in the same place in all cultures' and so the generalisations made by Róheim were unsound.[55] Faced with the lack of homogeneity between cultures, Kardiner posited a 'basic personality structure' which underpinned cultural diversities through 'a delimitation of the human needs which all cultures must satisfy'.[56]

The postulate of a 'basic personality structure', then, acted as an opposition to functionalist accounts of the workings of society: the writings of Kardiner claimed for themselves a greater degree of humane-ness than the mechanics of functionalism. American 'basic personality structures' aimed to put a humanist impulse back into the study of society. For 'personalities' were socially produced, and their means of production were potentially open to inspection, and to intervention. Like the investigations of German and Japanese 'national character' psychology of wartime America, the 'basic personality' sociopsychology of Kardiner and Linton[57] lent itself to investigations of childrearing habits. If, as a wide spectrum of European and American social anthropological and social psychological work seemed to indicate, 'rigid' childrearing produced 'rigid' adults, then here was an indication for a more easy-going upbringing.

One main investigative focus of this American group marriage of psychoanalysis, psychology, sociology and anthropology in the late 1930s and 1940s was child psychology and child management. A distinct literature took it upon itself to elucidate cross-cultural childrearing practices. American Indians on reservations provided captive raw material for studying the primitive. Under the auspices of the Bureau of Indian Affairs, Kluckhohn and Leighton examined Navaho children: the former wrote 'Some Aspects of Navaho Infancy and Early Childhood' in 1947 and both produced *Children of the People* in the same year, although their investigations had begun in 1936. Erikson, too, studied children on a Sioux reservation and Yurok Indians on the Pacific Coast, publishing his findings between 1939 and 1945. The Kluckhohn and Leighton investigations were mainly descriptive, in an ethological vein: 'In essence, we studied these children in their families with the same simple natural historical kind of method that one would use in studying a colony of beavers.'[58] That this kind of anthropological work was done under the auspices of the US Bureau for Indian Affairs produced some unease on the part of its authors. It was 'explained [to the Navaho] (which was true) that tests were being given in the endeavour to help the Indian Service improve its methods of teaching Navaho. Otherwise the usual pretext was a desire to learn the Navaho language'.[59] The observations of Kluckhohn and Leighton were shot through with warnings that 'the very delicate adjustment' between tribe and environment could be upset by prohibitions on the part of 'certain physicians, missionaries, teachers, nurses and other well-intentioned whites'.[60] The Navaho, though afflicted in adulthood with 'morbid melancholia and endemic uneasiness', were at least also given to liberal practices of childrearing, which the authors thought more beneficial than the current white American childrearing customs. The free handling of infants, however, was a start only, and no guarantee of a good future: later on, strain would militate against the beneficial influences of such childrearing.[61]

Erikson's 'Childhood and Tradition in Two American-Indian Tribes' was published in the first volume of Anna Freud's *The Psychoanalytic Study of the Child* in 1945. His visits to a Sioux reservation and to some Yurok Indians on the Pacific Coast were intended 'to collect additional data concerning the rapidly disintegrating systems of child training in both tribes: and this, in order to throw further light on present-day difficulties of reeducation among the Sioux, and for the Yurok, to interpret some of the compulsive weirdness of their ancient tradition'.[62] Erikson, like Róheim, employed a collective psychology: 'the tribe as a whole behaves in a fashion analogous to an oral-dependent compensation neurotic: the victim of a one-time catastrophe has adjusted to "government rations" and refuses to feed himself'.[63] The 'educational difficulties' experienced by the US Indian Service in its attempt to 'reeducate' the Sioux, and their apparent obstinacy and demoralisation, were put down by Erikson to 'anachronistic' fears of extinction and fear of 'loss of group identity' on the part of both whites and Indians alike. Coercion by white officials would only serve to exaggerate Indian 'delinquency' in the form of 'a general and intangible passive resistance against any further and more fixed impact of the white standards on the Indian conscience'.[64]

Erikson's synthesis of psychoanalysis, collective psychology and pedagogy led him to conclude that tribal practices in childrearing directly produced adult culture: the Sioux handling of infants was 'an ingenious arrangement which would secure in the Sioux personality that combination of undiminished self-confidence, trust in the availability of a food supply and ready anger in the face of interference, the coexistence of which was necessary for the functioning of a hunter democracy'.[65] But Yurok infants, the children of 'capitalist fishermen', lived under a different regime – oral puritanism, early weaning, and strict mealtime system befitted an adulthood in which 'nobody speaks during meals so that everybody can keep his own thoughts on salmon and money'.[66] For Erikson,

Child training is not an isolated field governed or governable by attitudes of malice or love of children, insight or ignorance: it is a part of the totality of a culture's economic and ideational strivings. The systematic difference between 'primitive' and 'civilized' cultures almost forbids comparison of details.[67]

But details *were* compared, endlessly, transculturally: the American social anthropology of the 1930s and 1940s was constantly preoccupied with the 'primitives' on its own doorstep; it drew implications about white childrearing, while devising strategies to combat the 'degeneration' of the tribes. Erikson, in his amiable insistence that the severe stresses on the Sioux should be remembered in any investigation of their 'recalcitrance', made analogies with the psychoanalysis of the individual. The search for 'social factors' had to be included in individual psychology: 'the social function of psychoanalysis is not to free the patient from the ambiguity of his background . . . the patient, instead of blaming his parents, should learn to understand the social forces responsible for the deficiencies of his childhood.'[68]

'Ego psychology' was evidently an appropriate instrument for this task. Writers like Erikson saw conflicts of 'identity', whether tribal or individual, as the key to the nature of wartime and post-war America, with its disparate class and racial composition, its immigrants and its native primitives: to sustain 'ego ideals' was important in this world 'characterised by expanding identification and by great fears of losing hard-won identities'.[69] The American postwar 'national character' was tension-ridden – dependent, in the vocabulary of psychotherapies of the 1950s, on the maintenance of a 'strong ego'.[70]

Erikson himself was given to accounting for the surge of ego psychology and its search for 'social factors' as the outcome of rapid and vivid contradictions in an anxious America. At the level of individual psychology, too, he held that the ego was the 'central regulator, closest to the history of the day'.[71] The 'ego' of ego psychology had by now lost whatever location it once had in Freudian theory and come to mean little more than the conscious mind. In 1939, Hartmann's essay on 'Ego Psychology and the Problem of Adaptation' had emphasised the human capacity to act in the world through 'spheres of autonomy' of movement, dependent on 'conflict-free ego spheres'.[72]

A behaviourist interpretation of Freud in the late 1930s joined the 1940s blend of anthropology and psychology to emphasise the 'achievement' of a static adult character – that psychology of 'types' exemplified in the wartime pursuit of the Japanese 'personality type'. Margaret Mead, writing in Carmichael's *Manual of Child Psychology* for 1954, commented: 'The history of the uses to which psychology has put data about primitive children and data about primitive peoples when constructing theories of developmental psychology is a history of the changing relationship between anthropology and psychology.'[73] The mutations of the earlier debates

69

between Malinowski and Jones about the cultural specificity of the Oedipus complex[74] into a wide train of research on 'national character types' cannot, however be put down to this unstable anthropology-psychology link. The search which Margaret Mead described for the 'orders of congruence between sorts of character structure and politico-economic forms'[75] became nationally institutionalised. Her own introduction to *Childhood in Contemporary Cultures* carries a revealing list of acknowledgements: the book grew 'out of the Columbia University Research in Contemporary Cultures, inaugurated by Ruth Benedict in 1947' and included research done under the auspices of the American Museum of Natural History Studies in Contemporary Culture. Both foundations were

under grants from the Human Resources Division of the Office of Naval Research. According to the terms of the contract, all the articles stemming from these two projects may be reproduced in whole or in any part for any purpose of the US Government. We have also drawn on the materials of the American Museum of National History Studies in Soviet Culture, conducted under a contract with the Rand Corporation.[76]

Outside the institutions, the supposition that childrearing 'habits' were the key to healthy adulthood and to the formation of the effective 'ego' seeped well beyond the formal confines of psychology and social anthropology into manuals of child management, welfare, education and advice to parents. This prescriptive diffusion was one of the aspirations of ego psychology, as formulated, for example, by Hartmann. Its function was to 'bridge the gap' between developmental psychology and psychoanalysis; while 'prevention, which might well become more essential than therapy, is directly dependent upon the trends of research under discussion today'.[77]

The site of prevention, was, essentially, the family: and so psychology had to ally itself to social welfare and paediatrics. In this respect, the broad aims of wartime ego psychology consolidated prewar developments.[78] Kris and Hartmann in 1945, reviewing developments in the previous decades, considered that 'some of the dynamic propositions of psychoanalysis are finding respectful consideration in practices of social control, in welfare, and in the social services.'[79] The cultural wash of ego psychology in America far exceeded the impact of the British dilutions of psychoanalysis over the same period.

One of the main sources for ego psychology was the work of Anna Freud. Her lectures to the Vienna Institute of Psychoanalysis had emphasised her origins in an interwar Vienna concerned with therapy for adolescents and disturbed children. Her analyses of 'delinquents', had been carried out in cooperation with August Aichorn, whose book on delinquency, *Wayward Youth*, has a Foreword by Sigmund Freud. She referred to the work of Siegfried Bernfeld, too,[80] and his educational experiments, including the 'Kinderheim Baumgarten', a school for homeless children which formed part of American relief work in the period after 1918. In 1929, Anna Freud had been asked by Vienna's School Inspectorate to lecture on psychoanalysis and education: some indication of the scope of the extant social psychoanalytic experiments is given by her list:

The Vienna Psychoanalytic Society thus (besides training for the thera-peutic analysis of neurotic and delinquent children) sponsored one child guidance clinic for young children (directed by Edith Sterba), one child guidance clinic for adolescents (directed by August Aichorn), special dis-cussion groups for teachers of the City who dealt with problem children in their own classrooms. . . . To these ventures was added in 1937 an experi-mental Day Nursery for infants between one and two years of age.[81]

Postgraduate analytically influenced teacher training also took place in the city.

All this intense concentration of practical psychoanalytic work ended with the advent of fascism: by 1938, those working with Anna Freud were dispersed to Holland, England, America. 'Analytic' nurseries were set up by emigrés in Boston, Detroit, Los Angeles. In London, the Hampstead Nurseries and a Residential War Nursery were founded. The 'Viennese school' had lost its persuasive coherence in one city. Anna Freud in exile continued to hold out for the usefulness of child analysis as an adjunct to 'all modern educa-tion' which should enter deeply into education in schools, and not be restricted to treating established neurosis within the clinic – just as her 1927 lecture had claimed that the most important future application of psychoanalysis must be 'to pedagogics or the sciences of upbringing and education'.[82] For her work was moving towards an emphasis on normal development and preventive therapy, and away from attempts to formulate a psychoanalytic theory of the neuroses and psychoses.

The difficulties which Anna Freud presented in her lectures were those of the conduct and ethics of child analysis – such as the question of the delicacy of interference with parental sovereignty, where the home might be contributing to the child's neurosis. Given that complete removal of the child from a toxic environment wasn't acceptable, there might be the possibility of 'a school where psycho-analytic principles predominate and the work is attuned to cooperation with the analyst'.[83] Nevertheless, if parents became devalued in the eyes of the child, harm could result: 'its already extensively constructed superego is in danger of being lost or depreciated: so that it can reoppose no real inner volition to the instinctual impulses which press for satisfaction'.[84] Premature separation of child from parent could cause damage to the insufficiently established super-ego; and in 1946 Anna Freud, then based in London, cited the evacuation of children as evidence of this.[85]

Freud had formulated that particular topography of superego, ego, and id relatively late, in 1923.[86] In this admittedly uncertain arrangement, the superego is not a fixed point of conscious restraint in the interests of civilisation: but for Anna Freud and the American adherents of their version of 'ego psychoanalysis', commitment to a preventive analysis of children made it all too possible to take up the superego and render it fully, and only, sociological. The net effect of this was to identify the 'strong ego' as a kit for psychic survival, while the 'healthy' ego became a detached desirable possession. The teleology implicit in the whole project of child analysis – the advance to a psychically successful maturity – found its full expression in a new language of achieving a robust ego. This was the 'resolution', which rapidly dominated American thinking, of the difficulties of applying psychoanalysis to the study of children. But Kleinian psychoanalysis attempted its 'resolution' of the same problem quite differently.

Melanie Klein's theory took the child as inherently flawed: her decisive step was a special form of concentration on the child's psychic foundation as established in the first few months of life, when the psychic actors were two – the mother and the child. There is no theory of sexual differentiation in the child; and the father, in Kleinian theory, is present only in the infant's phantasy of the mother-with-a-phallus.[87]

The mother-child relationship in the early months was also the point when later psychoses were fixated. This timing Freud had also first entertained in 1897, and he was preoccupied by its connections with verbal formulations, the development of speech. While in Kleinian theory, the mother-child tie was crucial, this tie had more of the nature of a backdrop to a set of unfolding psychic processes: the infant was possessed of impulses which simply were there; and which exerted a vigorous and terrifying force, irrespective of the way the child was treated.

Although in an early paper to the Hungarian Psychoanalytic Society in 1919[88] Melanie Klein did see the psychotherapist as able to intervene between mother and child and so modify the closed nature of that dyad – if need be by eroding parental authority – her later work was more pessimistic. Her 1928 paper, 'Early Stages of the Oedipus Conflict', placed the Oedipus complex as an end point of a far earlier set of processes. She wrote, 'Oedipus tendencies are released in consequence of the frustration which the child experiences at weaning, and they make their appearance at the end of the first and the beginning of the second year of life'.[89] At this relatively early stage in the development of Kleinian ideas, there was a suggestion that childrearing practices did play some part in the psychic growth of the child: 'frustrations' at least had something to do with experiences imposed by others, although just what the link was remained ambiguous: 'Oral and anal frustrations, which are the prototypes of all later frustrations in life, at the same time signify *punishment* and give rise to anxiety'.[90] Punishment was *not* imaginary and solipsistic. Guilt and frustration in the child had their corollaries in the world: pre-Oedipal infancy, in the late 1920s Kleinian account, was marked by guilt and misery, but these emotions were, somehow, connected with what was done to the child.

Considerations of the effects of childrearing were prominent in the work of Melanie Klein's mentor, Karl Abraham. His 1925 paper, 'The Influence of Oral Erotism on Character Formation', referred closely to the mores of his contemporaries, and their possible influences on psychic shifts in infancy. He used the vocabulary of sadism to describe the actions of infants, but linked this to the child-handling practices of the European middle classes in the 1920s. Abraham's work stood behind Klein's: but Abraham had not detached his descriptions of the psyche of the pre-Oedipal child from that child's location in a particular family. The bestowing of innate psychic attributes on the infant was a Kleinian tendency. Aggression was *in* the infant from the start: the possibly aggressive behaviour of its parents paled before the original sin of aggression which came with the infant. Like the child of Blake's poem from *Songs of Experience*, the Kleinian infant was indeed 'a fiend hid in a cloud'. In 1933, Melanie Klein wrote, 'The repeated attempts that have been made to improve humanity – in particular to make it more peaceable – have failed because nobody has understood the full depth and vigour of the instincts of aggression innate in each individual'.[91]

It was not only that such postulated instincts were inborn, it was that they were essentially incapable of being modified (except that, to a limited degree, associated behaviour might respond to psychoanalysis). The infant of three to four months suffered, in Kleinian theory, persecutory anxieties, the 'paranoid-schizoid' position: the mother was the focus of this innate anxious hostility. The infant's 'early expressions of pleasure in biting the breast' were indicative of a 'primary ambivalence' between greed and anxiety. Feeding, in the Kleinian account, was crucial for the emotional state of the infant; and 'greed' became a shorthand for an inborn deficiency: greedy infants of a few months of age who did not like being left on their own were credited with 'unstable and transitory object-relations which could be described as promiscuous'.[92] Greed was as fundamental to the infant as persecutory anxieties and a 'schizoid' understanding of the world in terms of 'part-objects'.

This idea of Melanie Klein's develops a line of Karl Abraham's thought. She meant by part-object the bit of the maternal body (usually the breast) which in the infant's phantasy is credited with benevolent or malevolent powers – as in 'the good breast', 'the bad breast'. The gratifying breast is loved, the bad breast is the target of infantile aggression; these emotions are projected by the infant, with the early emphasis on destructiveness. As a defence against resulting anxiety, the infantile phantasy splits the object into 'good' and 'bad'. The Kleinian infant traverses two successive stages of psychotic anxieties in relation to this splitting mechanism: firstly, the paranoid (the first four months of life) and secondly, the depressive stage – the rest of the first year, during which the part-objects are gradually resigned in favour of an approach to the whole object, the mother.

All these imaginative struggles of the young infant were directed towards objects of 'phantasy' and were not, in general, connected with actual people or events external to its own terrifying imagination.[93] Only rarely – and then rather inconsistently, as in her 1952 paper, 'On Observing the Behaviour of Young Infants' – did Melanie Klein return to her earliest reference to the treatment of the child: here she commented, 'the unconscious is strongly influenced by his actual experiences at the hands of the mother'.[94]

For on the whole the infantile unconscious pursued its inexorable path in loneliness, directed by emotions of frustration and persecution that had little to do with the external life of the child. Differences between infants arose from their 'inherent capacities' rather than their histories: a stronger ego, a more depressive ego, were propensities which were not acquired, but which arrived with the child. The mother in Kleinian theory remained curiously invisible and almost irrelevant: a cloud behind the 'good' or 'bad' breast. Since the infant would endure hell whatever she did or did not do, it followed that there was a sense in which she was hardly responsible for its wellbeing at all. This corollary, however, was not adopted either by Klein herself, or most markedly, by sociologised Kleinianism.

Envy and Gratitude, for instance, in which Melanie Klein looked back in 1957 over the course of her earlier work, vacillated between ascribing some significance to maternal handling, and then swiftly moving back to an assertion of the natural inflexibility of the infant's psyche: 'In passing I would say that the very favourable changes in feeding children which have come about in recent years, in contrast to the rather rigid way of feeding according to timetable, cannot altogether prevent the infant's difficulties, because the mother cannot eliminate his destructive impulses and persecuting anxiety.' She concluded, 'greed, hate, and persecutory anxieties in relation to the primal object, the mother's breast, have an innate basis . . . envy is also constitutional'.[95] There were, though, recommendations about how parents should respond to expressions of emotion: here a morality of 'suffering is good for you' intervened. Children should be allowed to cry without being comforted, since this would make for 'enrichment' of the future personality: 'conflict and the need to overcome it is a fundamental element in creativeness'.[96] But ultimately Melanie Klein's occasional concessions to the effects of the child's treatment were laid aside:

My accumulated observations, however, have convinced me that the impact of these external experiences is in proportion to the constitutional strength of the innate destructive impulses and the ensuing paranoid anxieties. Many infants have not had very unfavourable experiences . . . and we can see in them every sign of great anxiety for which external circumstances do not account sufficiently.[97]

In her summary of her analytic history she reiterated the inborn nature of character: 'I have had many opportunities in my analytic work to trace the origin of character formation to variations in innate factors'.[98]

If original constitution decided character, there was little guidance in Kleinian theory as to what might make this process successful, given the virtual autonomy of terrible impulses unfolding in the infant. In *Envy and Gratitude* she wrote that, through a successful mother-child attachment, 'the basis for a satisfactory development is laid. Innate factors contribute to this bond'.[99] But given that the innate had been so strongly empowered, the *nature* of this space left over as the terrain for failure or success is hard to ascertain. It was the emphasis on what might be termed a version of infantile 'original sin', built into the deepest foundations of

76

Kleinian theory, which was unique: misery was incorrigible.

The Kleinian infant had no equivalent in Freudian psychoanalysis, and as things fell out, it was Kleinian psychoanalysis which became known as the 'British School' and Kleinian theory which swept the board of the British Psychoanalytic Society. This body, which had a false start before the First World War, was reestablished by Ernest Jones in 1919. Jones, an enthusiast for the work of Karl Abraham,[100] extended this admiration to Abraham's follower: in 1925 he invited Melanie Klein to give a series of lectures to the British Psychoanalytic Society in London.[101] Kleinian analysis had little initial impact in most of Europe, or, indeed, America. But the decisive developments in London did not escape the alarmed attention of orthodox Freudians. A prolonged but unproductive skirmish developed between Freudians, neo-Freudians, and the new 'British School'. Anna Freud herself commented, with some acerbity, in her introduction to her *The Psycho-Analytic Treatment of Children*, that her lectures had not been published earlier, because psychoanalytic circles had been

concentrating their interest on Mrs Melanie Klein's new theory and technique of the analysis of children. The British Psychoanalytic Society devoted a 'Symposion on Child-analysis' to a severe criticism of the author's efforts which ran counter to Mrs Klein's outlook. The *Introduction to the Technique of the Analysis of Children* was rejected when offered to the International Psychoanalytic library for publication, and the matter lapsed, so far as England was concerned.[102]

It was indeed American and not British money which funded Anna Freud's Hampstead Nurseries – the Foster Parent's Plan for War Children, Inc., of New York.

The struggle of tendencies continued in the annual *Psychoanalytic Study of the Child*, the first volume of which appeared in 1945, published by Imago in London with an Anglo-American editorial board: its managing editors were Anna Freud, Heinz Hartmann and Ernst Kris. Its first number carried a critique and history of Kleinian analysis, a retrospective by Ernest Glover over fifteen years of antagonism. He objected, speaking for Anglo-American neo-Freudians, to the Kleinian neglect of the Oedipus complex, and to the theory of part-objects, naming Otto Rank as one who had also been enticed to push back formative experiences earlier and earlier. Rank was the main proponent of theories of birth trauma:

Readers who followed the history of Rank's deviation from psychoanalysis will not fail to note that by this time the Klein group had also committed itself to a monistic theory of neurosogenesis [i.e. the origin of neuroses]. The validity of Klein's view was also accepted without reservation in papers given to the British Society by Winnicott, Rickman, Scott, Isaacs, and Rosenfeld.[103]

The main criticism which Glover made – recognising, in 1945, that a rearguard action was being hopelessly fought – was to the Kleinian projection

of moral values . . . a bio-religious system which depends on faith rather than science. . . . Instead of Rank's birth trauma we have offered to us a 'love trauma' of the third month which is as fateful for subsequent development as Rank thought the birth trauma to be. . . . In my opinion, the concept of a three month's old love trauma due to the infant's imagined greedy destruction of a real loving mother . . . is a variant of the doctrine of Original Sin.[104]

Glover objected to the neglect of 'environmental factors',[105] a consequence of the Kleinian examination of the child in isolation: 'the parent's self-valuation is accepted at face value' as if mothers always 'really' acted benevolently.[106] Ernst Kris made the same point in 1950: 'the drama between breast and mouth, visceral tract and muscular apparatus is enacted with little regard for external trappings'; and he claimed that not Kleinian but 'ego psychology' would bridge the gap between psychoanalysis and a developmental psychology of the child.[107] For instead of taking the lonely child as a bundle of inbred phantasms, he preferred the work of ego psychologists, developing in the United States, as being 'environmentalist'. But this environmentalism consisted of seeing the mother-and-child as a unified system, a joint object for preventive treatment: 'Prevention, which might well become more essential than therapy, is directly dependent upon the trends of research under discussion today,' wrote Hartmann, in the same volume in 1950.[108]

This gradual shift of emphasis in America could easily abandon the unconscious since this was redundant to the objects of the newer 'ego psychology'. The Kleinian hegemony over British psychoanalysis also in effect broke with Freud: the field of players were reduced from the Oedipal triangle to the pair of mother and child, and the critical Freudian elements of sexual differentiation fell away from the regard of Kleinian psychoanalysis.

But there was a paradox at the heart of Kleinian theory: for while the infant was possessed of dangerous and melancholic impulses, nonetheless the fact that not all infants emerged into fully blown adult psychotics meant that either degrees of this innateness, or some influence of experience, had to be added to the Kleinian account. The irony of the relative indifference of Melanie Klein's theories to the impact of childrearing and education lies in the extensive spread of a Kleinian following, which was deeply concerned with such practices.

CHAPTER 4

The 'Popularisation' of Psychoanalysis and Psychology in Britain

'Those analysts who are optimistic about the popular propagation of psycho-analytical ideas are making a mistake. It is precisely this popularisation which is a symptom of the decline of psychoanalysis.'
        Wilhelm Reich, *Dialectical Materialism and Psychoanalysis*[1]

'Nor, as yet, did Freud seem to ask the question: why is the father always assigned the role of withholder of knowledge, rather than the mother?'
        John Forrester, *Language and the Origins of Psychoanalysis*[2]

'It seems to me likely that studies of motivation in young children, especially the study of the way in which the mother and infant develop their highly charged relationship, will gain greatly in precision and clarity from the application of concepts and research methods derived from the European School of animal behaviour studies, headed by Lorenz and Tinbergen, and often known as ethology.'

        John Bowlby, 'Psychoanalysis and Child Care',
        Psychoanalysis and Contemporary Thought[3]

Winnicott's revision of Klein

D. W. Winnicott, the child analyst and paediatrician, saw the entrenching of Kleinian theories in Britain as an accident of time: the lesser influence of Anna Freud's work he put down to the 'very great development that took place in London in the twenty years after the end of World War I, before Miss Freud came over with her father, refugees from Nazi persecution'.[4] In this span of years, theories of chronology itself in psychoanalysis had altered. 'In the 1920s everything had the Oedipus complex at its core,' wrote Winnicott, and he described how, as a practising analyst, he had found the Oedipus complex could not account for disturbances in the children he had treated; for these

showed differences in their emotional development in infancy, even as babies. Paranoid hypersensitive children could even have started to be in that pattern in the first weeks or even days of life. Something was wrong somewhere. When I came to treat children by psychoanalysis, I was able to confirm the origin of psychoneurosis in the Oedipus complex and yet I knew that troubles started earlier.[5]

But if these troubles 'started earlier', where was this starting point? In the Freudian account, the age of three was critical, but this appeared to be too late. Winnicott had written in 1936, in a paper on 'Appetite and Emotional Disorder', 'the theory of psychiatric illness must be modified to allow for the fact that in many cases the history of the abnormality reaches back to the first months or even the first weeks'.[6] The Kleinian concept of greed, hostility and anxiety in infants, at the time going strong in British psychoanalytic circles, provided one description of early childhood pain; Winnicott said that he had studied and learned from Melanie Klein; and had found most analytically useful her ideas of the progression from guilt to restitution and reparation as necessary to psychic health, and her theory of 'reactive depression'. As dubious elements of the Kleinian apparatus, Winnicott mentioned her stress on heredity and inborn envy as the sources of infantile 'destructiveness'.[7]

Most important, though, was his reservation about the Kleinian equation of 'most significant' with 'earlier'. He observed lucidly: 'I think it is here that she has made mistakes, because deeper in psychology does not always mean earlier'.[8] His paper, 'On the Contribution of Direct Child Observation to Psychoanalysis', continued to insist that what was most 'deep' in the psychoanalytic sense could not necessarily be identified with what, in the chronology of infant development, was most 'early'. Such an identification he saw, rightly, as endemic to the Kleinian approach: 'On looking into the matter, we see that 'deep' is a matter of variable usage and 'early' is a matter of fact, which makes a comparison of the two difficult and of temporary significance. It is deeper to refer to infant-mother relationships than to triangular relationships, to refer to internal persecutory anxiety than to refer to the sense of external persecution.'[9] Against such suppositions, Winnicott argued, 'In two words: a human infant must travel some distance from early in order to have the maturity to be deep'.[10] Under the category of 'deep', however, Winnicott listed elements of buried emotional complexity, including 'internal anxiety', 'splitting mechanisms, disintegration, an incapacity to make contact'. This apparatus of terms is the Kleinian catalogue of miseries all over again. The revision of Klein which Winnicott proposed differed from the original, not by any radical conceptual rewriting, but by a shift in timing. Dangerous emotions of 'splitting' were not, for Winnicott, implanted at birth: while they still held sway in infancy, they had a different genesis in a form of 'environmentalism' – the relation with the mother.

In Winnicott's account it was the quality of the mother-child relation which was decisive. As he noted, Melanie Klein 'paid lip service to environmental provision, [she] would never fully acknowledge that . . . the dependence of early infancy is truly a period in which it is not possible to describe an infant, without describing the mother, from whom the infant had not yet become able to separate itself.'[11] For Winnicott, 'the infant and the maternal care together form a unit'.[12] This mother-child unitary system, which included a concept of the mother's 'adequacy', introduced what Winnicott held to be a necessary 'environmentalism' into child analysis:

Melanie Klein . . . has always admitted that childcare is important, but has not made a special study of it. On the other hand, there have been those who developed an interest in the childcare and infant-care techniques. Those who did this always ran the risk of being considered traitors to the cause of the internal processes. The work of Miss Freud and Mrs Burlingham in the Hampstead War Nursery led to a development of the study of external conditions and their effect. It is clear that this dichotomy between those who almost confine their researches to a study of the internal processes and those who are interested in infant care is a temporary dichotomy in psychoanalytic discussion, one which will eventually disappear by natural processes.[13]

This optimism on Winnicott's part proved unfulfilled: the problems of reconciling 'internal' and 'external' accounts were not subject to dissolution through time; or through the efforts of Kris and Hartmann, whom Winnicott named as likely bridgers of this gap. Elsewhere he argued the need for cooperation between direct observers of infants and psychoanalysts in order 'to correlate what is deep in analysis and what is early in infant development'.[14]

Such a correlation was rendered harder by Winnicott's retention of the Kleinian categories of infant destructiveness. The presence and behaviour of the mother, on the analytic revision proposed and practised by Winnicott, fed into consideration of the child, but the Kleinian repertoire of infantile emotions was kept virtually unchanged. While emotions were no longer 'innate', no alternative explication of their nature was offered: they were now fixed *in* the mother-child couple, but their generation there was not explained. For instance, Winnicott's paper 'Psychoanalysis and the Sense of Guilt' dealt with a significant part of Kleinian theoretical equipment: the infant's experience of a sense of guilt which sprang from its attacks on the mother. With Winnicott's measure of rendering guilt 'environmental', the continual presence of the mother in the life of the young child became necessary for the child to 'make reparation and restitution'.[15] Guilt became a virtue in so far as it was the first step on the road to reparation: guilt and punishment are both necessary for the child's psychic health; and both require the uninterrupted presence of the mother. To give one example of the analysis which ensued – children steal to mitigate an unrelieved sense of guilt, to induce that punishment which was not inflicted by the absent mother of early childhood.

There are two striking features about all this. Firstly, the acceptance of the inborn presence of 'guilt and aggression' in the infant, deriving from Klein, fed into the active and critical consideration of the role of the mother in the psychic health of the child: rather than Kleinianism being 'replaced' by environmentalism, Kleinianism was itself being rendered environmental. Secondly, this account of stealing in children as evidence of a thwarted need to 'make restitution' by inviting punishment so as to satisfy an independent sense of guilt lay behind Bowlby's idea of 'maternal deprivation' as likely to lead to 'delinquency'. But this account missed out its own Kleinian genesis, innate aggression and guilt causing the 'need to make reparation': it became, instead, a piece of common-sense sociopsychology which lacked any memory of its own origins. A critical middle term was blurred into invisibility. That 'environmentalism' which Winnicott tried to introduce as a progressive move in psychoanalysis became a banal piece of social theorising – absent mothers *just did* breed delinquents, potentially; and these psychoanalytic theories which had originally supported this were forgotten – much as America, forgetting the particularities of Freud, had transposed him into sociological personality theories.

'Popularisation'

Winnicott's rewriting of Klein, then, was hardly fundamental: it tacked a more active consideration of 'the mother' onto the given framework. That this was so is, I believe, well illustrated through Winnicott's own popularisations. But what is this 'popularisation' – is it truly a process of dispersion which proceeds more or less independently from the theory which it purports to represent?

Juliet Mitchell, who must suppose that it is, given her project of restoring Freudian theory to a serious feminist regard, wrote,

By the end of the fifties, sociology had established itself as a major academic discipline and there was an efflorescence of sociological studies on various aspects of family life and society – family interaction. Within psychology, the stress was all on mother-care; from the child psychologist Bowlby, whose work was popularised on radio and in women's magazines, we learnt that a person sucked his emotional stability literally with his mother's milk. . . . Evacuee children were 'maternally deprived' – bombs and poverty and absent fathers didn't come into it. Psychoanalysis, persecuted out of existence on the continent, emigrated to America or resurrected itself in England. The debates of the thirties bequeathed, instead of an interest in the psychology of femininity, a heritage of a mother-child obsession. It does not amount to an estimation of the intrinsic merits or otherwise of the work if one points out that the developments of child psychoanalysis contributed very neatly to the political demands of the epoch.[16]

But 'popularisation' is less straightforward than this suggests; nor can the relations between psychoanalysis and the 'political demands of the epoch' be left as one of a neat contribution.

'Popularisation' is an opaque notion. It is employed as if it offered an informative account of a process; but it actually explains nothing, and only acts as an ostensible redescription, without much content to it. For 'popularisation' doesn't tell us anything about *why* a particular theory should at a particular moment lend itself to dilution, or to being broadcast to a wider audience: it assumes the essential purity of a theory which then, through no fault of its own, suffers a process of coarsening once the world gets hold of it. And it says nothing about the 'responsibility' of theories for their own popularisations.

Many of the analysts and psychologists who were most influential in Britain in the late 1930s, the 1940s and the 1950s were the authors of their own 'popularisations'. They turned not only to the clinical practices of psychoanalytic treatment but to the business of giving advice to parents, broadcasting on national radio programmes, writing articles in newspapers and women's magazines, and generally hurling themselves with apparent enthusiasm into the dissemination of their theories. This fact alone does not, it is true, bear on 'an estimation of the intrinsic merits or otherwise of the work', as Juliet Mitchell puts it: but it does make it hard to decide what is 'intrinsic' to the work or, indeed, *is* the work itself. It is not possible, especially in respect of this particular period in the history of British sociopsychology and psychoanalysis, to hold 'popularisation' at a safe arm's length from 'theory'. An unexamined notion of popularisation tends to assume, too, that it is more or less equivalent to 'vulgarisation'. But what does this really mean: have many 'popular' renderings of psychoanalytic theory been vulgarisations? Are Freud's *Introductory Lectures*, for example, safe from this generalisation?

Kleinianism and child management

The contributors to the 1936 volume, *On the Bringing Up of Children*, included Susan Isaacs and Melanie Klein: this book was the outcome of a public lecture course entitled 'Can Upbringing be Planned?' Melanie Klein's chapter on 'Weaning' reiterates her ideas of the ubiquity of infantile phantasy and the inevitability of guilt stemming from primary emotional conflicts. At the same time, it gives a set of sparse recommendations of a broadly libertarian persuasion about the handling of infants, though it stresses the virtues of emotional 'self-control' on the mother's part. Susan Isaacs' contribution was a tolerant and liberal extension of these principles. Merell Middlemore's chapter on 'The Uses of Sensuality', influenced by Charlotte Bühler's work, recommended mildly progressive precepts, while cautioning mothers that 'stimulation' was unpleasant for the infant of less than three months. The book as a whole set out a liberalism in childrearing which distanced itself from prohibitive practices, like forbidding thumb-sucking. It was sustained by a weakened Kleinian emotional armoury. A deeply pessimistic philosophy of the nature of the infant was similarly accompanied by recommendations for benevolent handling in many books of advice to parents – as with one of Susan Isaacs' popular books in this vein, *The Nursery Years* (1929). (Susan Isaacs' own school, The Maltings, in Cambridge, which furnished her with material for her books,[17] was run on lines so libertarian that its memory remains a source of scandalised anecdotes in the town about its pupils' wildness.)

Not all Kleinian-inspired diffusions were restricted to the sphere of 'free' education. The Kleinian stress on the significance of breast-feeding and 'orality' as a seat of painful emotions inspired Merell Middlemore's *The Nursing Couple* of 1941, where the 'couple' is not marital, but is the mother and child. Margaret Ribble's *The Rights of Infants*, which first appeared in America in 1943, was very close in vein to British work, with a strong weighting on the figure of the mother as both the emotional and the biological source of all. A regime of maternal tolerance with the husband as 'the supporting power', was appropriate to 'the woman's greatest creative venture', childrearing: any maternal absence was deprecated accordingly. Thus,

perhaps with new psychological insight into the dynamics of a child's mental growth, the meaning of motherhood and fatherhood may assume its rightful dignity, interest and joy and the temporary withdrawal from a career for a woman in order to create and nurture a new life may not be regarded as demeaning or as an unwanted interruption or sacrifice. Association with womanly women who have enjoyed the experience of childbirth and infant rearing will often help a young expectant mother to relinquish any artificial attitudes and to get the unique mental stimulus which comes from contact with the first principles of life.[18]

This widely read book was an old compendium: a humanitarian reaction against earlier and harsher infant-feeding regimes; a libertarian philosophy which nevertheless stressed the ills of infant autoeroticism and insisted on the need for the correct 'guidance' of mothers, a conviction of the necessity of 'separate spheres' for the male and female parent. 'Two parents who have achieved maturity and happiness in their respective biological roles are the native right of every child.'[19] These qualities alone, though, were not enough; the best of contemporary science must inform the parents. The book concludes with the firm recommendation that 'they will have to cultivate a new form of fastidiousness founded on knowledge of biological and psychological reality. There is no other way to guide the baby towards mental health'.[20]

This blend of ideas, curious though it seems now in its swaying between naturalism and scientism, was common enough as a legacy of Kleinian thought in Britain. A style of childrearing was proposed which was to be 'cool' but not prohibitive. Most striking is the relegation of the parents, in this literature, to 'separate spheres': that male should remain firmly distinct from female is, it's claimed, essential for the psychic health of the developing infant. The man remains a shadowy presence providing financial and moral support to the mother, who is stage-centre in her 'unique' task, spotlit by an increasingly intense focus on her and her child. Paternal authority in the home had decayed for psychology as well as for sociology:

Kleinianism in this sense bore out the observations of Reich and Horkheimer.

Winnicott's advice to mothers as 'popularisation'

Winnicott himself was a prime mover in all this: his series of wartime broadcasts on maternal advice done in 1944 for the BBC were republished in the January 1945 issues of the magazine *The New Era*, a publication which dealt with broadly educational developments.

In his broadcast 'What About Father?' Winnicott, following Kleinian principles, depicts the male parent as a remote bearer of the authority of the outside world: he is 'the human being who stands for the law and order which mother plants in the life of the child'. He is a useful psychic sponge for the inevitable aggression of the infant: 'One parent can be felt to remain loving while the other is being hated, and this in itself has a stabilising influence. . . . Every now and again the child is going to hate someone and if father is not there to tell him where to get off, he will hate his mother and this will make him confused, because it is his mother that he most fundamentally loves.'[21] The baby, said Winnicott in another broadcast, 'has raging lions and tigers inside him. And he is almost certainly scared by his own feelings. If no-one has explained all this to you you may become scared too. . . . He needs you to help him manage the awful transitions from sleeping or waking contentment to all-out greedy attack'.[22]

While such perilous psychic negotiations between child and mother were being pursued, the wartime father could unfold the nature of life outside the jungle of the home: 'they [the children get a new world opened up to them when father gradually discloses the nature of the work to which he goes in the morning and from which he returns at night, or when he shows the gun that he takes with him into battle'.[23] The father is dropped out of the picture altogether to return only as a weapon-demonstrating visitor; this theoretical vanishing of the father from most current psychoanalytic speech coincided with the social stress – which was indifferent to the actual numbers of absent men – on the vanishing of the father to the war.

Winnicott's broadcasts of advice to mothers, intended to instruct and reassure, in fact contain an alarming menagerie of wild beasts of the mind: the child *is* the tiger in the nursery; or his emotions are 'rather like what being put in a den of lions would be for us'; he fears that 'wild beasts will eat him', while at the same time he will greedily attack the mother. The infant is at once a dangerous animal, and assailed by animal dangers. In his BBC talk on 'Why Do Babies Cry?' Winnicott sketched the 'value' of crying for the infant, as the therapeutic expression of rage, or else as self-consolation: he added, optimistically, 'some people think that sad crying is one of the main roots of the more valuable kind of music'.[24] Crying was, on the whole, good for babies, except, he said, for the 'hopelessness and despair' of institutionalised infants: 'it is in the institutions that we hear the crying of helplessness and disintegration, where there is no means of providing one mother for each baby'.[25]

The mother, the wartime broadcasts emphasised, was all-important: 'She is a specialist in this matter of her own children and if she is not overawed by the voice of authority she can be found to know well what is good and what is bad in the matter of management'.[26] The aim of the broadcasts, said Winnicott, was to underline for their hearers this self-sufficiency of the confident mother to tell people why they know what they know: 'To support ordinary people and to give them the real and right reasons for their good instinctual feelings'. Winnicott's comfortable commentary strayed outside the confines of this strange brief: in his 1944 talk, 'Their Standards and Yours', he reiterated the desirability of full-time motherhood: 'Talk about women coming back from the Forces not wanting to be housewives seems to me to be just nonsense, because nowhere else but in her own home is a woman in such command'.[27] The same tendency to slip into expressions of conservative asides had marked Winnicott's earlier writings at the start of the war. *The New Era* published his discussion on 'The Deprived Mother' in March 1940: the mother of evacuated children, he wrote, ought to be recognised to be in a bad way, whatever appearances were. 'The opinion has been expressed that mothers are having such a good time, being free to flirt, to get up late, to go to the cinema, or to go to work and earn good money, that they will certainly not want to have their children with them again'.[28] But, on the contrary, the mother may 'even be to some extent aware that she may value being continuously bothered by her children's crying needs, and this holds good even if she openly complains of her family ties as a plaguey nuisance'.[29] Several of Winnicott's comments on the minds of wartime mothers have undergone a mild bowdlerising for the susceptibilities of present-day readers. In the 1964 Pelican compilation by which he is now best known, *The Child, the Family, and the Outside World*, the sharper remarks have been smoothed out.

The sentiments of Winnicott's broadcasts and magazine articles are not unique in so far as they mirror a broad Kleinianism: other writers in *The New Era* repeat the need for enlightened but firm routine control of the inevitably raging infant, and the value of frustrations for its maturing.[30] But Winnicott commanded the wider audience of the BBC and the freedom to elaborate or simplify his theories for a larger audience. Like Susan Isaacs, and like John Bowlby later, he took these opportunities to retell some of his own ideas for popular consumption. Juliet Mitchell detects a difficulty here: 'Winnicott's very sensitive work nevertheless had an effect somewhat like Bowlby's in its earliest popularisation. Paeans to the family obscured its more interesting content. . . . Susan Isaacs' theses, again exploited for ideological purposes, contributed to creating a stultifying status quo.'[31] But to speak of 'exploitation for ideological purposes' only preserves an impossible disjunction between the innocence of a theory and the corruption of its deployment.

Psychology, psychoanalysis, social welfare: problems

What was the responsibility of variants of psychoanalysis and sociopsychology, in Britain in the 1940s, for their effects in other discourses; and are words like responsibility and effects right here anyway? How contingent is the relation of psychology and psychoanalysis to their political location? Clearly there are, and have been and will be, 'leftist' uses and interpretations of analytic work, as with a whole vein of post-First World War libertarian educational experiments which understood themselves to be also socialist (like those of A. S. Neill; or of Wilhelm Reich, or Siegfried Bernfeld or

August Aichorn in Vienna; or indeed Vera Schmidt's Kindergarten in Moscow). The British psychoanalytic developments did not proclaim for themselves any particular political location, although, especially by the end of the war in 1945, a widespread pronatalist appeal agreed well enough with them.

On this point, Juliet Mitchell writes,

The political reconstruction of the family in postwar and cold war Britain was buttressed by social welfare, which was family oriented, and by sociology, psychology, and psychoanalytic theories, massively popularised. In a way, it was a logical turn of the screw when the family, having been made – by conservatives – to bear the brunt of personality reconstruction was suddenly – by radicals – made responsible for personality destruction. Either way, trapped at the centre of it, were the mother and child.[32]

This is elegant, but, I think, mistaken. As an account, it seems a consequence of allowing a free-floating nature to sociopsychology. It portrays a 'leap' in psychological and psychoanalytic history which was not so sudden as all that. Certainly it's true that for both 'conservative' and 'radical' theorists (and one can include Bowlby among the former and Laing among the latter) the mother-child dyad was at the centre. But the time sequence she describes is not right, nor is the swing from conservative to radical thought as put here: no such neat opposition occurred. There was not such a capricious movement first to praise, then to blame the family. Bowlby and Laing started out from the same analytical nursery – the Tavistock Clinic; and Bowlby himself was, in 1940, writing analytic papers about the destructive role of certain kinds of mothers in the 'family constellation' as apt to produce neurotics.[33]

It's not that I'm trying to blur Laing and Bowlby together into an undifferentiated heap of Kleinian reaction: that would be a heavily exaggerated response to the commoner tendency to set the two at opposite points of radicalism and conservatism. But there is a broad, common and powerful source of their work in Kleinian theory. This, committed to an innate wretchedness on the part of the infant but at the same time to a weighting on the mother-child couple, does indeed, as Juliet Mitchell suggests, lend itself well to conservative uses. But to say just this only returns us to that separation of 'theory' from 'use made of theory' which is so implausible to sustain.

Bowlby's work, its development and theories

John Bowlby, as the architect of the theory of 'maternal depriva-tion' and associated ideas, has drawn upon himself a copious litera-ture of praise, analysis and hostility.[34] Feminist interpretations of 'Bowlbyism' have taken it as no coincidence that, after the Second World War, childcare facilities for the children of working mothers were withdrawn and Bowlby's ideas widely promulgated.[35] Yet while it looks as though there is excellent evidence to back up this view, on closer examination it falls away – in that form, at least.

Bowlby, born in 1907, began his working life as a clinical assistant at the Maudsley psychiatric hospital in 1933, after first qualifying as a medical student and beginning an analytic training. He then moved to the London Child Guidance Centre, where he stayed until the war began: during the war he was an army psychiatrist, and after 1945 was Deputy Director of the Tavistock Clinic, later Centre, and Head of its Child Guidance Department which was later renamed Department for Children and Parents.

His first book chapter, 'Personal Aggressiveness and War', in *War and Democracy*, was written with Evan Durbin. It tried, from their viewpoint in 1938, 'to examine the bearing of some recent biological and psychological work upon theories of the cause of war'.[36] Like American writings, it used studies in comparative anthropology; it also drew heavily on notions of innate human aggression, which it justified by drawing analogies with the behavi-our of apes. The authors dissociated themselves from what they termed 'economistic' accounts of the origins of war, and emphasised instead their belief that 'fighting is a form of behaviour funda-mentally natural'.[37] The 'reduction of repression' in the upbringing of children was no panacea, they wrote, for this natural bellicosity: 'internal conflict' was inescapable, although a more liberal regime of discipline was preferable.

The authorities which Bowlby and Durbin quote for these observations are Zuckermann's *Social Life of Monkeys and Apes* and

Susan Isaacs' *Social Development of Children*, written in 1932 and 1933 respectively. Bowlby and Durbin wrote,

Children, like baboons, are not natural pacifists . . . the theory which we wish to put forward is that man, having so much of the baboon in his nature, has the greatest difficulty in living in peaceable and cooperative relations with his fellows in a group, and that he is enabled to do so far more easily when he diverts his antisocial impulses against other groups.[38]

Bowlby and his co-author move swiftly from ape to man, from ape to child, from individual to group: 'all men' are equivalent, and the 'psychological forces' conducive to waging war are as weighty as economic causes. 'All men' have a 'latent need' for a scapegoat: a need 'to which such movements as anti-Semitism or anti-Fascism appeal'.[39]

This fits with the later turns of Bowlby's work – its flattening of specificities into generalisations, its appeals to animal analogies, its depiction of the child as the repository of intense, innate, unexplained emotional impulses. Bowlby's earliest uses of psychoanalysis were shot through with ideas of the instinctual; from the start of his career, animal references and human-animal analogies abound.

In 1940, Bowlby wrote his first book, *Personality and Mental Illness*, an account of sixty-five patients he had seen during his work as a clinical assistant at the Maudsley Hospital. He classified types of 'personality', rather than symptoms – the 'Shameless Anti-Social', for instance – and considered that while 'a tendency to mental illness is inherited and . . . the major functional psychoses breed true', nonetheless to the genetic components in mental disturbance the influences of 'early surroundings' must be added. These influences include the effects of separations of the child from the mother,[40] the impact of parental disturbances, and the experience of being fostered. Here again environmentalist and hereditary theories sit in that uneasy balance which characterises many theories of development from the nineteenth century on.

Bowlby's 1940 paper, 'The Influence of Early Environment in the Development of Neurosis and Neurotic Character', published in the *International Journal of Psycho-Analysis*, laments 'the very meagre attention given to the role of environment in analytic literature'. He recommends that psychoanalysts should station themselves in child guidance clinics and mental hospitals as observers: 'Psychoanalysts like the nurseryman should study intensively and at first hand (1) the nature of the organism (2) the properties of the soil and (3) the inter-action of the two'.[41] By 'environment' he means an environment of one person only: the mother and her behaviour constitute the child's 'environment'. Thus, 'in place of the term "broken home", I prefer to use the more accurate and comprehensive term "broken mother-child relation" '.[42] Interviewing the mothers of disturbed children is therefore a sensible course to take:

It seems probable that most mothers are reasonably good but that the mothers of neurotic children are frequently bad, in the sense that they have very strong feelings of hatred and condemnation towards their children, or else make inordinate demands from them for affection . . . it would be senti-mental to shut our eyes to their existence or to think that they do not have a damaging effect upon their children.[43]

This recalls R. D. Laing and Aaron Esterson's work on forms of mental illnesses as only comprehensible in the light of the 'family constellation' and the schizophrenia-inducing mother in particu-lar.[44] There is not, at this stage of Bowlby's work, any insistence that it is only 'the broken home' which produces neurosis in its chil-dren: children in 'stable homes' can also, because of 'unconscious emotional attitudes of mother to child', develop 'great anxiety and guilt'.[45] Mothers should not be assumed by the analyst to be irrele-vant to the psychic state of the child: they ought not to be relegated to the sphere of the patient's 'fantasies' about the past only. As far as the need for the mother's continuing presence went, Bowlby remarks: 'Provided breaks are not too long, and continuity is pre-served, there seems no evidence to suppose that the child who is always with his mother is any better off than the child who only sees her for a few hours a day, and not at all for odd holiday weeks'.[46]

Bowlby's work and the war

On the evidence of this 1940 paper then, Bowlby's opinions were not at all identical with the 'Bowlbyism' of the 1950s – the persuasion that mothers ought never to leave their children, on pain of inflicting serious psychic damage if they did. Nevertheless, while Bowlby's clinical paper casts a critical eye over the assumption that mothers were always beneficial presences, his more sociological articles in *The New Era* restore the figure of 'the mother' to an altogether unqualified prominence. In March 1940 this journal ran a special issue on 'Emotional Problems of the Evacuation', to which Winnicott and Susan Isaacs contributed articles. Bowlby's 'The Problem of the Young Child' expresses the anxiety that 'it would be tragic if more damage were to be caused by our precautions than by the weapons they were designed to protect us against'.[47] Younger children would suffer seriously if evacuated without their mothers from danger areas: yet billets would produce strain – 'with the best will in the world, few women can share their house with another'.[48] A policy which enabled mothers and infants to remain together had to be formulated as a matter of great urgency, for 'air raids may begin at any moment'. Meanwhile, after the so-called 'phoney war' of 1939,

plans for the evacuation of children in large groups and day nurseries have mercifully been abandoned although a large number of children are still being cared for in this way. . . . *Very serious attention* should be given to see that the children remain in the care of one woman who should always bear the official title of foster-mother.[49]

British psychoanalysts in this period hailed the phenomenon of evacuation as offering golden material for research. John Rickman, for instance, wrote in his foreword to this special issue of *The New Era*:

If we can withdraw ourselves to a distance as scientists are wont to do and yet observe minutely the effects of the disruption of family life, we may learn much from this event. But we must behave with true detachment, having no axe to grind, no special opinion to propagate nor political or social doctrine to substantiate. . . . We believe for instance that the things we most value are due to our living in families and that they are derived ultimately from our early experience of parental love, but we do not fully realise what the family means to us until it is disorganised.[50]

95

The New Era's articles, Rickman hoped, might 'help in seeing the foundations and structure of that nursery of our social life – the normal family . . . [they] throw new light on the meaning of "home" '.[51] Such a blend of previously established conviction and claims to a 'scientifically' neutral scrutiny marked the approach of several of the Tavistock group.

Bowlby's chapter, again published in 1940 in the *Evacuation Survey*, repeats the gist of his *New Era* remarks. Any wartime policies on the care of evacuated children which included group care for under-fives would, he considered, be dangerous: such children ought to be in the charge of their mothers, or else with a 'stable substitute'. 'Research into the origins of persistent delinquency in childhood has recently thrown this question into high relief,' wrote Bowlby, introducing the thesis which permeated his subsequent work.[52] The 'chronic and persistent delinquent', the adolescent thief and truant, was possessed of a

bad character which can be traced unequivocally to prolonged separation from his mother (or mother substitute) in early childhood. Some have been in hospital for long periods, others in a succession of foster homes, in others again mother has been ill and the baby has been in a hostel. The one common factor, however, is separation from the people who are known and being looked after by complete strangers in strange surroundings for long periods – six months or more. . . . The conclusion [i.e. from Bowlby's research at the London Child Guidance Centre] is that the prolonged separation of small children from their homes is one of the outstanding causes of the development of a criminal character. No scheme for the evacuation of young children which ignores this fact should be considered.[53]

By 1940 Bowlby had developed the preoccupations which were to sustain his work thereafter. These were not formed through observations of the ill effects of evacuation; they claim for their experimental authority the piece of research, described below, done at the Tavistock by Bowlby just before the war. So from its start, Bowlby's emphasis was already on the mother or mother substitute: before the war he had committed himself to the belief that 'separation' in itself was the agency of lasting psychic damage to the young child.[54]

Bowlby and postwar 'separation'

The research mentioned in Bowlby's comments on evacuation was not published until 1946, when it appeared as *Forty-Four Juvenile Thieves: Their Characters and Home-Life*. It was, though, a product of the late 1930s; based on work done between 1936 and 1939 at the London Child Guidance Centre, it first appeared as a paper in a 1944 volume of the *International Journal of Psycho-Analysis*.[55] In it, Bowlby set out to produce 'empirical testing for pyschoanalytical hypotheses', an attempt which pervaded his subsequent work. 'Separation' in itself was not, in orthodox psychoanalytic theory, an accepted source of anxiety: Bowlby's aim was to prove, by clinical demonstration, his conviction that 'separation' of the young child from its mother or mother substitute was inherently traumatic. The biographies of the 'forty-four juvenile thieves' revealed, he claimed, a significantly high number of such separations: whereas a control group of forty-four 'problem children' – but whose problems did not include stealing – had not suffered so many separations.

That Bowlby's own evidence did not fully warrant the conclusions he drew is a point made in detail by psychologists like Rutter in his *Maternal Deprivation Reassessed*; what I want to point out here are Bowlby's recommendations in his report on his research. His Preface is more reserved and hesitant than is his text:

That prolonged separation in the early years is sometimes the principal cause of the development of delinquent character can in fact hardly be doubted. What proportion of children who have this experience remains, however, unknown. Nor do we know the precise factors which determine whether a child will weather such an experience or will succumb. A follow-up of the large numbers of children who were in residential nurseries during the war would, of course, supply the answer to these questions. It is to be hoped that this opportunity will not be lost.[56]

No such study did in fact take place. Bowlby made a practical commendation: 'Since it is possible to diagnose an Affectionless Character at the age of three years and possibly earlier, a strong plea is made for early diagnosis and treatment. Above all, attention should be given to prevention: many prolonged separations could be avoided'.[57]

The forty-four juvenile thieves, thus dissected, proved deeply influential: Bowlby, partly on the strength of this research, was invited by the World Health Organisation to produce the report published in 1952 as *Maternal Care and Mental Health*. This was planned in 1948: at the third session of the Social Commission of the United Nations, it was decided to make a study of the needs of homeless children, to which the World Health Organisation would contribute a study of 'the mental health aspects of the problem'.[58] Bowlby's report included a summary of the copious literature from several European countries, Scandinavia and the United States, which throughout the 1930s and 1940s had surveyed the retarding effects of institutional unbringing for infants.[59] He emphasised that there had been 'a very high degree of agreement existing both in regard to the principles underlying the mental health of children and the practices by which it may be safeguarded' in his discussions with international childcare workers,[60] and he saw himself as a synthesiser and continuer of this earlier body of work; whereas the impression conveyed by much of Bowlby's more popular writing is that of a lone theoriser arrived from nowhere, lacking a history.

Many subsequent critiques of Bowlby have assumed this to be really the case, so rendering the whole phenomenon of 'Bowlby-ism' much more *ad hominem* than it actually is. The World Health Organisation report, however, cited the papers and books of Bakwin, Ribble in the United States, Spitz and Wolf, Goldfarb, Simonsen, Rondinesco and Appel, Burlingham and Freud, and Edelston, who used data from hospitals, nurseries and other institutions, like orphanages, for the care of children. Bowlby's summaries of these were advanced by him in a pioneering spirit, 'calling attention to matters of grave medical and social significance'. On the long-term effects of 'institutionalisation' on children, he quoted psychologists including Levy, Lowrey, Bender, Goldfarb, Powdermaker, and studies of war refugees on the Continent, concluding that 'the prolonged deprivation of the young child of maternal care may have grave and far-reaching effects on his character and so on the whole of his future life'.[61] The analogy he drew was between maternal deprivation and the stortage of vitamin D in infancy: as the latter would result in rickets, so the former would result in delinquency, 'affectionless' behaviour. Embryological analogies are drawn – not for the first time in the history of psychology, which had used it in the theory of cultural recapitulation:[62] the 'psychic tissue' of the young child could be scarred by separation from its mother, as could foetal tissue through exposure to German measles. 'This is a discovery comparable in magnitude to that of the role of vitamins in physical health, and of far-reaching significance for pro-grammes of preventive mental hygiene'.[63] The dangers of maternal deprivation ought to be accepted as fully established, wrote Bowlby: research should turn to 'matters of immediate practical significance on which information is needed', like the 'safety margin' which could be allowed for inevitable deprivation. He suggested the use of 'animals as experimental subjects': work on dogs might 'perhaps gain insights which could then be tested with human beings'.[65] Research in future, he proposed, should be carried out by a team of 'the experimental psychologist, the statistician, the psychoanalyst, the psychometrist and those with other trainings': the task of establishing what he terms the 'embryology of the personality' required interdisciplinary work[66] by a veritable committee of experts.

Much of this 1951 report is concerned with preventing 'mental ill-health' through the reform of institutions, encouraging fostering, treating children in residential homes in small groups, liberalising regimes in paediatric wards, and so forth. In this, its recommen-dations were not dissimilar to those of the Curtis Report on children in care, which was published by HMSO in 1948. There were other features of Bowlby's philosophy which were being widely voiced in postwar Britain: the emphasis on the virtues of family life; the plea for the education of schoolgirls and women for 'mothercraft'; and the anxiety about the 'problem family' and the discouraging of 'delinquency'. He recommends, despite his own insistence on the paramount virtue of the mother, that unmarried mothers should be encouraged to submit their children for adoption in the interests of securing a 'stable' family for them. However, as long as the mother is married, 'children thrive better in bad homes than in good institutions'[67] and the removal of apparently ill-treated children from their parents is not to be undertaken where it can be avoided. 'It must never be forgotten that even the bad parent who neglects her child is nonetheless providing much for him'.[68] 'Problem families, however, embody the 'cycle of deprivation' – that conviction popular throughout the 1950s, and still periodically invoked according to which disadvantages are transmitted down the generations, – and 'this vicious circle is the most serious aspect of the problem.'[69]

Bowlby did, though, recognise that there were some children with a mother or mother substitute 'whose attitude towards him is unfavourable': in such cases, 'parent treatment is an essential part of child guidance'.[70] Help for the home, however deficient this was, ought to come first: such 'preventive mental hygiene' called for the widespread professional training of social workers.

The period in which Bowlby's work was being disseminated had already absorbed a large literature of the 'problem family', a category well established before the war. Bowlby's WHO report fell on fertile ground: a simplified Penguin version of it was published in 1953, as *Child Care and the Growth of Love*: this ran into many editions and reprints, and is the book above all responsible for defining the 'Bowlbyism' of 'keeping mothers in the home'.

It is true that in *Child Care and the Growth of Love* Bowlby does not say that the mother *can never* leave the young child without causing irretrievable damage. This, though, cannot fairly be used, as some writers[71] have tried to do, to dissociate Bowlby completely from the charge of instilling guilt and suffocation in a generation of mothers. What Bowlby said was the corollary – that the young child 'needs her as an ever-present companion: this usually continues until about his third birthday'.[72] But this would be an academic quibble – especially given the tremendous emphasis which the need of the young child for 'continuous' mothering received. 'Bowlbyism' as tantamount to the assertion that children must *always* be in the company of their mother is indicated by the title of pamphlet written by Bowlby himself: this is, 'Can I Leave My Baby?'. It is now little known and rarely alluded to: it was first published in 1958, as one of a series of leaflets offering advice to parents, by the organisation then entitled the National

Association for Mental Health, which continues as Mind.

The question – and one wonders who is asking – of 'Can I Leave My Baby?' receives the *literal* answer of Yes – the child *can* be left briefly with its father, granny or a neighbour for emergencies, or for a trip out for the mother. But the real answer implied is No. Such expeditions are potentially dangerous, needing careful preparations: brief diversions, or brief necessary work is permissible for the mother, but it is a risky undertaking. 'This exacting job [of motherhood] is scamped at one's peril.' The mother is the child's security: she 'is going to be his anchor – whether she likes it or not – and separations from her are going to give rise to problems'. Like Klein and Winnicott, Bowlby continues the assignation of the father to a remote and instrumental sphere: he provides morale and money for the mother: yet 'remove Father permanently from the scene – by death or divorce or any other reason – and the whole picture changes tragically for the worse'. This leaflet is curiously unspecific about where it derives its authority, and who it answers.

The compensation it holds out entails a frequent metaphor of the mother as worker, albeit unpaid: 'A mother's job is inevitably exacting, especially when her children are small. It is a craftsman's job and perhaps the most skilled in the world. But what worthwhile job is not exacting?' Its reward for mothers is, Bowlby writes, the feeling 'that they *really* matter, that no-one else will do'.

Bowlby: instincts, ethology, 'science'

Why should Bowlby have been drawn to ethology – the study of the behaviour of animals and their reaction to their environment – above all? What did he mean by wanting psychoanalysis to become 'scientific'? The particular attraction of ethology seemed to lie, for Bowlby, in its observational nature and what he took to be its consequent straightforwardness. Concrete, systematic observation and experiment guaranteed, he believed, a rigour which psychoanalysis needed before it could claim 'scientific' status. Ethological theory rested on postulates of instincts: this was true of the work of Lorenz and Tinbergen especially in their studies of young birds and animals. In Bowlby's view, the problem for psychoanalysis lay in this area of instincts. Ethology, for him, had the great merit of simplicity of conception, and it had things to say about instinctive behaviour. Psychoanalysis, Bowlby believed, was already committed to a theory of instincts as central to its own axioms. But while the word 'instinct' is indeed used to translate both the terms 'Instinkt' and 'Trieb' in Freud's work, these terms in German carry different connotations. Freud's 'Trieb' was used to describe a psychic pressure which need not carry a stable, invariant aim or object, in contrast to 'Instinkt' in the classical zoological sense.[73] But Bowlby – like others – obscured any concept of the indeterminate nature of instincts. Wishing to get the zoological, ethological version of instincts into psychoanalysis, Bowlby hoped to be able to ground his theories of the gravity of disturbances in the 'instinctual' mother-child tie. His contribution made in 1953 to the World Health Organisation Study Group on the Psychobiological Development of the Child proposed that 'instinct is the central case of psycho-analysis', and quoted Freud's 1915 'Instincts and their Vicissitudes' to justify the search in biology for an adequate theory of instinct.[74]

In a recent interview[75] Bowlby has described his aims: 'What I've been trying to do, really, is to rewrite psychoanalysis in the light of ethological principles. . . . I've always felt that traditional psychoanalytical metapsychology was out of date, grabbed from nineteenth-century physics. My main concern right back from the thirties has been to get psychoanalysis onto a decent scientific basis. I want it to progress, not go round in circles or break up into cliques' – an ambition which repeats the nineteenth-century wish to secure the founding moment of psychoanalysis somewhere else; to anchor it in anthropology, or biology. The investigation, he said, of mother-child separation appeared to him 'one of the few islands of dry ground in a rather swampy scientific field, and that one had here a definable experience which demonstrably could sometimes produce a particular type of personality outcome. I have stuck very rigidly to it, with two or three purposes in mind'.[76]

These purposes were to establish the centrality of the mother-child tie to mental health, and to plan for concrete preventive action and interdisciplinary research. Bowlby had discovered Lorenz and Tinbergen on 'imprinting' and 'following' responses in young birds and animals, and seized on theories of 'imprinting' in childhood as possible keys to the development of adult neuroses: if an 'instinctual' progress was disturbed at a critical early stage, subsequent disaster might ensue. 'One possible explanation may lie in the extraordinary fact (which may well prove a key for psychoanalysis) that a response can be imprinted long before it becomes operative. It may well be that human sexual responses are imprinted in earlier childhood and not later'.[77] The study of mother-child separations might be advanced, Bowlby believed, by the study of the 'following response' in birds: ornithology could provide paradigms for psychoanalysis. And the possession of conscience itself, he considered, 'has an instinctive root': this he illustrated with reference to Lorenz's studies of wolves, whose attacking impulse against their own kind was self-checked.

While Bowlby's observations on the psychic urgency for continuous mothering were absorbed by social work theories of the 1950s, his search for a respectable 'scientific' underpinning continued to draw him to the growing literature of ethology. His convictions were unfolded at length in 1958 in 'The Nature of the Child's Tie to His Mother', published in the *International Journal of Psycho-Analysis*. This drew an unsurprisingly hostile response from psychoanalysts. It posed a 'primary social bond': the 'instinctual attachment' of infant to mother which could be observed as 'inbuilt responses, . . . the function of which is to promote social interaction between members of species'.[78] Freud's remark in 'Instincts and their Vicissitudes', to the effect that it would be desirable if assumptions concerning the theory of instincts could be taken from some other branch of knowledge and carried over to psychology,[79] was mentioned by Bowlby as further justification here.

As an elaboration Bowlby offered an analogy: the workings of the instincts appeared to him to parallel the workings of the unconscious: 'Once activated, the animal of which they form a part seems to be acting with all the blind impulsion with which, as analysts, we are familiar'.[80] Later in this same 1958 paper, the analogy became a virtual identification: 'When the response is not free to reach termination . . . we experience tension, unease, and anxiety. As observers when these responses are activated in another, we commonly think and speak of the individual as the subject of conscious and unconscious wishes and feelings.'[81] Moreover, wrote Bowlby, responses like the attachment of infant to mother had an evolutionary value for the species as well as a survival value for the individual. The vocabulary of 'species-specificity' permeated Bowlby's descriptions: he was insistent that this was apposite and necessary for the furthering of psychoanalysis, and reconcilable with existing work on infants: 'concepts derived from ethology may link with those in regard to infantile phantasy which have been elaborated by Melanie Klein and her colleagues'.[82]

Phylogeny repeated ontogeny for Bowlby too: a study of man's instinctual responses, he held, would demonstrate an equation of 'more primitive' with 'more instinctual': 'as we trace man back to his ontogenetic beginnings we shall find them responsible for an increasing proportion of his behaviour'.[83] The responses dominant in early infancy suggest the early history of Man-as-animal: 'There will be found active beneath the symbolic transformations and other trappings of humanity primeval dynamic structures which we share in common with lower species'.[84] The observational study of infancy, for Bowlby as for the European nineteenth-century psychologists, would furnish evidence of the origins of the species: 'The theory of Component Instinctual Responses, it is claimed, is rooted firmly in biological theory and requires no dynamic which is not plainly explicable in terms of the survival of the species', he concluded.[85]

Although Bowlby's appeal to ethology and the study of instinctual behaviour did not need recourse to the concepts of the unconscious for its underpinning, nevertheless Bowlby, himself a Tavistock clinician, located his ideas firmly within psychoanalysis. Where American revisions of psychoanalysis had looked to anthropology and the practices of 'tribes', Bowlby looked to zoology and ornithology, comparing human maternal behaviour and 'man's nearest relatives, the anthropoid apes'. Yet these analogies are pursued with a curious lack of specificity. Bowlby writes, quoting the 1954 research by Robert Hinde,[86] 'like the cock chaffinch referred to earlier, he [the human infant] is often restless and vocal when alone, content and quiet when in the presence of a mother figure'.[87] But the cock chaffinch described in the original ornithological study is a male courting an adult female. 'The couple' described by Bowlby is an 'attached' mother-child pair: the comparisons he makes are not only cross-species, but cross-generation and cross-gender too. Nevertheless, some constants remain: he claims that 'throughout the length and breadth of the animal kingdom', the mother remains the supreme object of the infantile 'attachment'.

The lack of reserve with which Bowlby drew psychoanalysis towards ethology was maintained in his subsequent work. A 1958 collection (published, ironically, in honour of Freud's birth centenary) entitled *Psychoanalysis and Contemporary Thought* carried a piece by Bowlby on 'Psychoanalysis and Child Care'. This argued that Lorenz and Tinbergen's ornithology and zoology proved the innateness of human aggression, for 'all recent research in psychology and biology has demonstrated unmistakably that behaviour, whether in the lower organisms or in man himself, is the resultant of an almost continuous conflict of interacting impulses'.[88] Under this rubric, Bowlby observed, Melanie Klein's theories of innate aggression and guilt might be vindicated. Bowlby understood his own innovations to be in the spirit of recent British psychoanalytic work – although he kept his distance from Melanie Klein's effective pessimism, and held out hopes for the 'germ of innate morality' which was advanced, he considered, in Winnicott's work. The 'guilt' and 'ambivalence' of Kleinianism could, he held, be demonstrated by observed animals, so confirming the 'universality' of such emotions.

The rapidity of Bowlby's juxtapositions is exemplified in this essay of 1958.

Inevitably the presence of mother or father evokes primitive and turbulent feelings not evoked by other people. This is true even in the bird world. Young finches quite capable of feeding themselves will at once start begging for food in an infantile way if they catch sight of their parents. . . . Parents, then, especially mothers, are much maligned people: maligned, I fear, particularly by professional workers, medical and non-medical alike.[89]

This leapfrogging from a 'psychoanalytic' approach to zoology to recommendations about childcare drew much criticism from other psychoanalysts. Yet the theories of Kleinian psychoanalysis, couched in terms of the innateness of aggression, were wide open to being 'borne out' by behavioural observations. The course adopted by Bowlby was neither unpredictable nor surprising in its directions.

Bowlby: criticisms

Ethology continued to inspire Bowlby's subsequent work: papers on 'separation anxiety' and on 'affectional bonds' continued, throughout the 1960s, under its influence. A particular interest in grief and mourning produced several papers,[90] and *Attachment and Loss*, published in three volumes between 1969 and 1980. It has not, however, been the 'ethologising' of psychoanalysis which has drawn attention to Bowlby's work. Instead, several objectors have taken it to be a fair instance of psychoanalysis, and have imagined Freud and Bowlby to constitute a two-headed hydra.

This has had odd results: one book devoted to criticising Bowlbyism, Patricia Morgan's *Child Care: Sense and Fable*, carried a foreword by the behavioural psychologist Hans Eysenck which, like the body of the book, denounces 'psychoanalysis' as 'unscientific'. It assumes that Bowlby's is a Freudian psychoanalysis, which must fall before the stern eye of the exact science of psychology. A similarly unqualified identification of Bowlby's work with 'psychoanalysis' was made in 1959 by Barbara Wootton, the sociologist.[91] Her opposition rested on research from the late 1950s, and on statistical doubts: she also attacked Bowlby for arriving at 'platitudes' and 'homely truths'. The number of 1950s critiques she mentions[92] make it evident that 'Bowlbyism' did not hold sway over every sociopsychologist and sociologist in postwar Britain, as a reading back through the 1960s might suggest it did. But Barbara Wootton, too, identifies Bowlby with 'psychoanalytic' determinism; she argues that infant experience should be regarded as less traumatic than psychoanalysis indicated, and that the effects of heredity on the child should be considered. The opprobrium which attached itself to Bowlbyism also fed into a later feminist opposition to psychoanalysis, which saw the latter as an instrument for the confining and diminishing of women, especially women as mothers.[93] That Bowlby's theories were to some extent the legacy of Kleinian theory, and that British Kleinianism was distinguishable from Freud's psychoanalysis, were not points which sprang to the attention of these critics. History was disregarded: if Bowlby was deficient, this was yet another nail in the coffin of psychoanalysis.

Bowlby, however, regarded his own work as a radical extension of psychoanalysis in Britain, a humane and liberalising departure from the narrow insistence on 'orality' which he attributed to his fellow analysts. In 1968 he summed up his work in a BBC broadcast on 'Security and Anxiety', as making a benign break in

intellectual circles. I emphasise 'intellectual circles', because it may well be that plenty of ordinary people thought otherwise – and perhaps thought more wisely. But in psychological and psychiatric circles it had been rather blandly assumed that the reason children become interested in mother is that she feeds them, and the reason they are upset when separated from her is that they are afraid that their unsatisfied desire for food will become unbearably painful. . . . I never thought this fitted the facts. . . . Nevertheless a great deal of thinking in academic and clinical circles has been fixated on feeding. It was studies of animals that first called this notion in question.[94]

Bowlby believed his postulate of an 'attachment instinct' in humans to combine evolutionary soundness – 'animals who do not develop attachment behaviour are unlikely to leave any offspring, while those who do develop it live to breed' – with a comforting obviousness. The attachment of children to mothers, as 'instinctual' did not need further explanation. 'In fact it is as natural for a child to maintain an attachment to a mother figure as it is for a young man to maintain an attachment to a young woman,' he remarked in his 1968 broadcast, pursuing that parallel of adult heterosexuality with the mother-infant pair which was itself such a remarkable forgetting of psychoanalysis.

There is no doubt that Bowlby was well aware of the implications of his ideas.

Studies of this sort raise practical questions about mothers going out to work, the age when a child should start nursery school, how children should be cared for when ill. As time goes on, the best solutions will become clearer. Meanwhile, we are wise to be wary. Any move that separates young children from their mothers needs scrutiny, for *we are dealing here with a deep and ancient part of human nature.* (my emphasis)

This passage is from Bowlby's 1968 broadcast, yet it represents many of his comments from 1940 onwards. He knew that a theory which claimed that to separate children from their mothers might do violence to 'human nature' also embodied a powerful sentiment.

How far can Bowlby be credited with responsibility for the extension of this powerful sentiment into the conviction that mothers must at all times remain with their children and, by inference, must not work even part-time, or make use of crêches or nurseries at all? Establishing answers to this question is not made easier by the tendency to consider Bowlby as an isolated and monolithic phenomenon, inflicted upon an otherwise innocent English culture out of nowhere; whereas his work is part of a wider grouping of ideas. For British psychology tends to behave as if it had no history, and could constitute its discoveries on previously unturned ground; a characteristic encouraged by the absence of full accounts of British psychoanalytic ideas and institutions.

CHAPTER 5

Policies on War Nurseries:
the Labour Market for Women

'Destructive impulses let loose in war may serve to fan the flame of aggression natural to the nursery age.'

Leader, *British Medical Journal*, 1944[1]

'The relative importance of industrial productivity can of course only be assessed by national governments; but the committee is convinced that in many cases such a decision, which should depend on weighing in the balance the needs of children and the demands of industrial productivity has been taken in complete ignorance of the price to be paid in permanent damage to the emotional development of a future generation.'

World Health Expert Committee on Mental Health, 1951[2]

War in the Nursery: policies and politics

The course of Bowlby's work cannot, in itself, be held fully account-able for the phenomenon of 'Bowlbyism' – that is, the intense con-centration on the married mother permanently in the home with the child as the unique and adequate guarantee of the child's psychic health, the defence against delinquency, and family and therefore 'social' breakdown. What, then, laid the ground for Bowlbyism? What was there about a diluted Kleinianism which proved amenable to its virtual national adoption? It is sometimes suggested that the way to understand the congruence of wartime and postwar child psychologies with the figure of the mother-at-home is to under-stand psychology as acting in accord with social philosophies. But what is the nature of this 'accord'? For the mosaic of ideas about the family and the child are not confined to some untainted realm of 'theory' alone deliberated by psychologists, only to become 'practice' and 'politics' once they come under the gaze of policy makers. How, though, is the connection between psychology and policies to be conceived? Has a social policy called in a psychology to do its work for it – to produce convictions tailor-made to its needs?

As an example of this means of explanation, we can trace two widely held beliefs about postwar Britain's policies for the care of children and for women's employment. One of these attributes to Bowlby's work the blame for the vanishing of those nurseries established for the children of working mothers during the war. The second makes a broader claim about the service of psychology, throughout the late 1940s and the 1950s, to a government given to promoting an 'ideology of domesticity' for its own ends. These beliefs – whose origins are by no means 'irrational' – claim the allegiance of much socialist and feminist reflection: but they do much to obfuscate the history of the period, and reinforce misapprehension of the broader theoretical relations.

The history of the war nurseries is an especially entangled example of the interactions of policies and psychologies: it is often presumed – especially by a postwar generation – that the belief that a young child must at all times be at home with its mother, and vice versa, was generated by a popularised psychoanalysis and led to the withdrawal of state provisions for childcare after 1945. But, in brief, such a belief was *not* instrumental in the demise of the war nurseries. Nor was it invoked in immediately postwar governmental plans for postwar nursery education – beyond an occasional mention in respect of the under-twos. How, then, did it become so dominant later on, so that for years it has held sway in debates about nursery provision?

The ordinary wartime day nurseries were indeed criticised on the grounds of the health of children – but here the health was physical, not emotional. The most sustained opposition to the war nurseries issued from medicine and paediatrics, rather than psychology: it came largely from the Committee of the Medical Women's Federation who conducted two surveys from 1944–5 on nursery

110

children. They concluded that 'the outstanding fact is the constant and considerable increase of respiratory tract infection'.[3] Against this, both survey papers agreed that children over two in day nurseries showed a better general physique and weight gain than children who stayed at home. One writer makes the point that children who had nursery meals didn't thereby lose their ration books. (This advantage was widely mentioned as being an incentive to women to work, thus giving the lie to the straightforward ascription of 'patriotism' to women: 'Many mothers were believed to have taken up war work or kept on with it because they themselves could eat at canteens and their children could eat at nurseries, all without any surrender of rations'.)[4]

Rather than dwelling on the admitted resulting gains in the children's growth and weight, the Medical Women's Federation reports emphasise the high incidence of minor infections. But not all medical criticism based itself solely on this criterion, although it was certainly the dominant objection to nurseries. *The Lancet* published a report from the Medical Officer of Health for Leyton in 1946 which suggested that poor weight gain in children under two might be due to 'emotional disturbances'.[5] And *The Lancet* in 1943 had carried a report from a speaker at a conference of the Medical Women's Federation denouncing the war nurseries as places of 'a high incidence of infections and a low incidence of happiness'.[6] There was some objection to the prospect of very young babies in nurseries, on the grounds that breastfeeding would decline. But Medical Officers of Health also emphasised the useful contribution of nurseries to maternal and infant welfare, though the shortage of 'trained personnel' and provisions was widely lamented. Medical Officers of Health who were enthusiasts for nurseries argued their advantages: children might usefully be taught 'regular habits' and be well fed; and those infections which might be missed at home could be identified promptly and properly treated. The rate and significance of infections in the home versus the nursery remained a debated matter; the findings of the Medical Women's Federation were not universally accepted. And in a sense the objections of the latter had to remain academic, since the Government had committed itself firmly to its wartime nursery scheme, and was hardly likely to reverse its operations in mid-war. What is of more interest is the nature and the sources of those anti-nursery arguments which survived the war, and were used subsequently to stress the 'need' for mothers to remain in uninterrupted contact with their young children. And here considerations of 'infection' were secondary.

What developed into the main arguments, those on 'psychological' grounds, were subdued throughout the war, and barely heard in relation to day nurseries. Certainly descriptions of the psychic dangers of institutional care were well established mainly in the American, French and Scandinavian psychological literature – but this was well before the war. Although René Spitz did first publish his results in full in *The Psychoanalytic Study of the Child* for 1945 and 1946 (in a methodologically dubious paper) this work on the psychiatric consequences of 'hospitalism' in institutionalised infants had begun in 1936, and was by no means unique.[7] Studies on the dangers of impersonal care of infants in hospitals and founding homes were spasmodically in progress throughout the thirties, not specifically occasioned by the war. But later use was made of such work as if it had originated and had been verified through the 'experiences of war'.

A 1942 *British Medical Journal* leader quotes another American study, by Bakwin, on children in hospital, and slides into a denunciation of English war nurseries;

while plans are being rapidly advanced for the accommodation of a quarter of a million little children in war nurseries it may be as well to take note of the observation that in infancy the loneliness involved in separation from the home may be not undesirable but lethal . . . it is obviously difficult to establish the perfect nursery in wartime when the ideal staff is more than ever hard to find and the demand is enormously greater . . . the elderly hospital nurse who is too often in charge with fifteen to eighteen-year-old assistants as the bulk of her staff, is apt to look on the emotional needs of the small child as luxuries . . . a mother too tired by long hours of war work to be loving and patient if the daily change from one environment to another makes him hard to handle . . . if, as seems established, the biological unity of mother and little child cannot be disregarded with impunity, it is well to hesitate before supporting a policy that separates so many young children from their homes. It might even be better for the national effort to direct into the factories most of the large army of labour required to equip and maintain war nurseries and to leave the mothers to do the mothering of the 'under-fives'.[8]

On similar grounds, a paper given to the 1942 National Conference on Maternity and Child Welfare by Dr Marguerite Hughes, atypical only in the scope of its proposals, suggested that nursery workers themselves should be released for work in munitions factories; that they should be replaced by minders and nursery classes; and that mothers should be paid ten shillings a week to stay at home.[9]

Embryonic maternal-deprivation theorising, blended with popularised Kleinian ideas, produced in a 1944 *British Medical Journal* leader a prophecy of doom. Entitled 'War in the Nursery', it describes how 'in the years from two to five the battle between love and primitive impulse is at its height. . . . Winnicott, Bühler, Isaacs, Bowlby and others all note the turbulent characteristics of the age. . . . Destructive impulses let loose in war may serve to fan the flame of aggression natural to the nursery age'. If 'the nerves of staff strained to breaking point' cannot hold out, delinquency may ensue; 'the Age of Resistance may thus be prolonged to adolescence or adult life in the form of bitterness, irresponsibility, or delinquency'.[10] The War in the Nursery was the infantile psychic parallel to the War in Europe. By implication, state-provided childcare under wartime conditions would reinforce the existing psychic war.

It's true that Anna Freud was in London at this time, and her work might have been expected to counteract this Kleinian tendency to stress inevitable innate aggression so exhaustively; her Hampstead Nurseries – residential homes for children who in various senses were war victims – formed the basis for her and Dorothy Burlingham's 1943 study, *Infants without Families*. But by 1945 Anna Freud had turned to theories of 'ego psychology' for work that led ultimately, as outlined in Chapter 3 above, to a comparative anthropology of childrearing: close work on the construction of sexual identity was replaced by 'personality' typology.

Thus, on all fronts, either by intention or default, the emphasis was firmly on the mother per se as psychic agent. Nevertheless, calls to 'prove' the psychological and psychoanalytic theories by using the golden opportunity of the war as raw material for studies went unanswered. While analysts as different from each other as John Bowlby and Anna Freud expressed the wish that systematic comparisons be made of home versus nursery conditions, little such work was actually carried out. The comparative comment that exists is either anecdotal or very brief. There is more on the different question of evacuation itself – the 1940 Evacuation Survey Report to the Fabian Society,[11] the Hampstead Nursery Reports in the *British Journal of Educational Psychology* between 1941 and 1943, Susan Isaacs' own reports on evacuees and her *Cambridge Evacuation Survey*. Unlike nursery provision, evacuation was an unambiguously sanctioned policy, possessed of an incontestably temporary nature, to which London mothers had been urged to respond for the good of their children.

The stress on the wartime absence and return of the father and the need for family unity as a precondition for psychic development are not only originally located in psychoanalytic and paediatric work but are part of a more generalised speech, though they may refer back, inaccurately, to such specialised sources for authority. References to the 'evidence' of wartime nurseries thus construct a false history.

The comment of one history of welfare services, written in the 1960s, is a bundle of representative cross-attributions here. Bruce in *The Coming of the Welfare State*, writes,

Psychologists, studying the social phenomena of war, gave scientific warrant to the need for family life in development, which mankind had always instinctively known, and the Ministry of Health, surveying the working of evacuation, acknowledged from its experience the impossibility of finding a substitute. . . . [Restoring the family] was the policy that underlay the Children Act of 1948.[12]

What was the genesis of these confusions? In part it lay in the history of the residential nurseries. These, like day nurseries, shot up in number during the war years; and they, as opposed to the day nurseries, give a clearer indication of shifts within social welfare and psychological theories. Financed by varied resources, like American and other voluntary funds, they tried to meet a huge need not created by the war, but rather exaggerated or revealed by it.

Children whose fathers were killed in the war or away in the services, or whose mothers had to work in such a way that no semblance of a family could be maintained, swelled the numbers of those whose parents were single, or destitute, or dead. Although the main work was done on a voluntary basis, the Treasury took over in 1941. The rationale of the new residential nurseries was to cater only for young children from the evacuation areas in need of care; but then they slowly changed from being an adjunct to civil defence during air raids to being a social service for war 'victims' in the most general sense. It was these residential nurseries which became the focus of arguments already established before the war (and which were to extend long after it) about the harmful effects of institutional care, and the necessity of conventional family life to produce the balanced member of civil society.

Anna Freud and Dorothy Burlingham's *Infants Without Families* is an isolated attempt to evaluate the effects of residential care on emotional development; its conclusions are oddly unrelated to its text, and the changing tone of its Forewords is a good index to the strengthening of anti-nursery feeling; a later edition in 1965 pins a vehement denunciation of nurseries to the same text.[13] But there is little evidence that either the medical criticism of day nurseries or the psychological criticisms of residential nurseries cut any governmental ice during the war. Nor was much official notice taken of expert opinion solicited from psychological or paediatric bodies during the time of confusion in the early part of the war; as Dorothy Burlingham and Anna Freud wrote, 'The continuance or discontinuance of residential nurseries after the war will probably be decided by social and economic needs and not on the basis of psychological requirements.'[14] That nursery policy was determined by expediency alone was on the whole true. Fearing this, the World Health Organisation's Expert Committee on Mental Health concluded in 1951:

the social and fiscal policy of many nations appears to be designed to press the mothers of preschool children to undertake productive work outside the home. The provisions of crêches and day nurseries is often one of the instruments of Government policy in encouraging such a tendency. The

115

relative importance of industrial productivity can of course only be assessed by national governments; but the committee is convinced that in many instances such a decision, which should depend on weighing in the balance the needs of children and the demands of industrial productivity, has been taken in complete ignorance of the price to be paid in permanent damage to the emotional development of a future generation.[15]

This committee's report, based on Bowlby's presentation of the largely interwar European and American literature on institutional deficiencies, was indeed influential, and this at an international level: its findings can, though, in no way be predated to represent British governmental policies in 1945. Certainly, the general spirit of Bowlbyism in Britain in the mid-1950s would have made the question of the provision of child care for working mothers almost unaskable – but this is a quite different proposition from putting the events of 1945 down to psychology and psychoanalysis. Yet if the psychology of the sanctity of the mother and child in the home did not occasion the closing of war nurseries, what did? To say that psychology and government were not in an unholy alliance to return women to the home is not to exonerate either, but to launch into a more mundane story – of misrepresentations, imaginative failures, evasions and indifference: less highly coloured, but no less deadly in its effects.

A full account of all this assigns to psychology only a marginal role in closing the nurseries – and must refer also to the needs of a particular war economy to speed up the temporary flow of female labour, and to internal governmental politics – like the ways in which the division of labour in the governmental machinery itself, and interdepartmental conflicts between the Ministry of Health and Labour entered forcefully into the setting up of nurseries. The requirements of industrialists, the position of the unions, the role of local authorities were all significant, as were the public presentation of nurseries, the ascertaining of women's 'needs' and the role of the professional nursery movement supporters. To speak of the 'state' in these areas as if it were a vast and united agency is actually counterproductive: the assignations of nurseries to 'welfare' or 'Labour adjuncts' and to local or central government were critical in the formation and the muddled results of policy.[16]

For, at the level of central government, tracing the many tensions between the Ministries of Health and Labour demonstrates their administrative dilemma of how the nurseries should be portrayed: as a 'Welfare service', or as a reaction to the immediate demands of war and the labour supply. The Ministry of Labour, feeling itself under some pressure from 'big industrialists', added that pressure to the confused urgency of the Ministry of Health's plans; concerned with speeding up the flow of female labour without regard to the finesse of nursery and childcare politics, it favoured paid child-minders, to be registered and overseen. This plan, though, was labelled as unsuccessful by November 1941. Nevertheless, the Ministry of Health remained enthusiastic about voluntary child-minding; a draft for a Ministry of Health circular suggested that those women who weren't already out at work 'will be in the position of explaining why they do not volunteer for the care of children' although 'the appeal will, however, be a positive one for service and not one of peevish menace'. This appeal was to be launched in areas which served the key factories: the slogan was; 'if you can't go to the factory, help the woman who can'.[17]

This notion of pulling together in an emergency characterised the presentation to the public of childminding plans. The Ministry of Health's propaganda called on the principle of 'neighbourhood mutual aid', for 'self help is often the best help'. To this end the status of minding was to be raised: 'caring for the children must be made as important as working in the factories'. The designation itself of the volunteers was a sensitive matter needing ministerial thought. For 'volunteer foster parent' smacked of illegitimacy, while 'daily child guardian' was reminiscent 'either of newspapers or of the poor law'. And while the local authority Maternity and Child Welfare Centres would dislike plans for large-scale voluntary and therefore unsupervised minding, it would have to be made clear to them that this should be pragmatically accepted. After all, it was not politic to countenance criticism of women minding their neigh-bours' children, when those who had taken in evacuees 'were told they were performing a public service'.

This capitalising on self-help extended to an official Ministry of

117

Health admiration for local traditions of childminding, especially among the Lancashire cotton workers. Pointing out such sterling examples of sturdy self-reliance, it hoped that 'most' women might rely on older established arrangements. A Blackburn councillor was quoted approvingly by a Regional Officer of the Ministry of Health as explaining that he had been 'put out' by his mother – and that if he had a child now, he would 'put it out' rather than send it to a day nursery.[18]

The principle of retaining parental responsibility – or, in effect, maternal responsibility – despite massive state intervention emerges most clearly in these proposals for childminding. Nonetheless, the government recognised that here was politically dangerous ground. The organised labour movement was demanding official governmental provision of nurseries and not the arbitrariness of private minding. The Ministry of Health itself observed in 1940: 'There is a political point in this. The TUC and our Factory and Welfare Board put these arrangements well ahead of any others in their programme, and are extremely reluctant to give any blessing to anything in the nature of "childminding".'[19]

And the notion of a national childminding network was also poorly received by various women's organisations: resolutions of criticism came from the Women's Co-operative Guild and Labour Women's Advisory Councils. As well as these expressions of disquiet, the stand taken by the Trades Union Council against 'makeshift' childcare is striking.

Once the scheme for state-financed local-authority nurseries, resembling that desired by the TUC, was eventually established, it drew on a wide pool of users: it had been originally designed for the use of munitions factory workers, where the demand for women's labour was most pressing. But it had proved impractical to restrict admission; the nurseries opened to workers 'on government contracts' and then to others who could be classed as essential war workers – like bus conductresses; while some showed a high proportion of mothers employed in service industries and shop work.

When the war nurseries closed down they did so at speed, and in a manner which reflected the inter-Ministerial tensions: while the responsibility for educational policy was the Board of Education's, the actual shutting down was the responsibility of the Ministry of Health. That this action did not live in the realms of pure pragmatism was obvious to all.

Although there was an official governmental commitment to providing nurseries after the war, the existing ones were not to be allowed to act as any foundation or to raise hopes for postwar policy: indeed, it is highly questionable whether this commitment was more than gestural. For the nurseries were, the government had repeatedly emphasised, intended as aids to war production and not social services in themselves, and their limited status as factory adjuncts had to be maintained in their public presentation. The Ministry of Health had commented, 'It is important in any reference in the national papers to make it clear that the urgency and extensive scale of this work is localised and not in the country as a whole'.[20] One civil servant, exasperated by delegates of professional nursery enthusiasts, hoped that temporariness could be made clear by a special name for childcare facilities – nursery 'centres': 'The very fact that a Nursery Centre is neither a nursery school nor a day nursery would stamp them as a purely temporary expedient to deal with war conditions and would make it easier to get rid of them after the war'.[21] But the involvement of a Ministry of Health militated against these ends. The Ministry had been obliged to sell nurseries as both educationally and physically good for young children – in its correspondence with concerned paediatricians, or against the opposition of the Medical Women's Federation.[22] And when it came to justifying the shutting down of the war nurseries, the Ministry of Health was unable to argue that children had been harmed by them. Although it had made an irresolute attempt at suggesting that under-two-year-olds needed to be at home with their mothers, this was never the main ground for defending the closures. Instead it set great store by what it presented as working mothers' apathy: no 'real demand' existed – just as no 'real demand' had existed at the start of the war. It overlooked the circularity of its own arguments; those nurseries which were closely associated with particular industries were emptying as those industries vanished. On this, the *Times Educational Supplement* pointed out in March 1945 that the Ministry 'was unable to promise that vacancies could be filled by children whose mothers are not technically "working". This is a vital point.' The *Daily Worker* commented in the same month; 'there are strong grounds for believing that the nurseries are merely being tolerated preparatory to their closing down'.[23]

The rapidity with which the war nurseries were dwindling in 1945 drew critical attention to the good faith of the Ministry of Health, which had to fend off several questions about the closings from pro-nursery Members of Parliament. To the question of whether the Minister was aware that his decision had caused 'deep disappoint-ment to many working-class mothers' and had drawn protests from a number of local authorities, the reply was that nurseries had been set up 'as a war service under emergency powers, and these powers cannot be used to provide a normal welfare service'. In similar spirit, Florence Horsbrugh, then Parliamentary Under-Secretary, claimed for the Ministry of Health that nurseries were underused, and that evidence of demand was dubious – petitions purporting to be from concerned mothers were not all signed by genuine nursery users. While the Labour member for Aberavon described 'a keen and lively demand' from miners' wives that the nurseries there should stay, Miss Horsbrugh stated that 'no local authority which had asked to keep a nursery open has been turned down'.[24] Agitation from many others, including nursery workers and educationalists, went by the board.

The grounds on which the closings were opposed by those profes-sionally concerned with nurseries are clear from the 1945 Deputa-tion to the Ministry of Health and Education on Nursery Provisions: The sudden expansion of state childcare at the start of the war had proved a source of anxiety to the old guard of nursery enthusiasts. They feared that hasty provision would discredit their aims, and that what was being developed was in no way educational, thorough or progressive. But by 1945, the prospect of the removal of the wartime nurseries suggested a serious attack on the foundations for any future or better institutions and training. This deputation was large. It included representatives from the National Council of Maternity and Child Welfare, the National Society of Children's Nurseries, Froebel teachers, nursery nurse training colleges, Barnardo's and services' children's homes. They were anxious for the war nurseries to stay on until properly qualified teachers could be trained, and that training itself should be transformed, and move away from the narrow hospital orientation towards the new category of 'child welfare'. Places should be found, the deputation said, for women who'd worked in the war nurseries and who wished to carry on. The wartime nurseries 'are accepted and they function', and should stay until better things superseded them. New courses for girl school-leavers must be developed; although this was introduced with the obligatory remark that 'the course would have value for them as potential mothers', there was much serious talk of new forms of entry into childcare professions.

The many other efforts to have nurseries kept and extended also got nowhere: for example, the London Women's Parliament National Nursery Campaign,[25] and the comments of the *Co-operative Review*, the Socialist Medical Association, the Women Citizen's Association, and local public health committees like Coventry's. The authenticity of 'demand' could always be queried by a Ministry committed in advance to ignoring it.

As the Ministry of Health's behaviour in 1945 ran counter to the broader governmental stance on nursery education, this further confused the issue, especially since it was also widely known that women workers would be wanted after the war; so that the Ministry's actions were seen as being idiosyncratically at odds with national need, as well as with stated governmental policy. This again raised questions at a parliamentary level: as Edith Summerskill asked in the Commons in 1945, 'in view of the fact that the Ministry of Labour had indicated that as many women as possible would be needed after the war', how could there not be nursery provision, in the end? This expectation of a coherent and inescapable plan for the care of children of wage-earning mothers weakened the force of protest against the war nurseries' demise. It looked as if what was at stake was only the exact form of the new nurseries inscribed in the Labour government's social service plans.

After 1945, the exchequer's grant to local authorities was halved; requisitioned buildings were returned to their peacetime uses; and the responsibility for running the nurseries now settled on local authorities. This was a very significant change, for the shift from the central governmental control to local control threw the whole matter open to the idiosyncracies and histories of the regions. Some medical officers of health, for instance, were opposed to nurseries on principle, whereas others were actively sympathetic; some authorities had no prewar local traditions of women's employment. The halving of the Treasury grant meant that nursery costs would now have to be met out of the rates, and compete with the local block grant for other health and welfare services. By the end of 1947 there were 879 day nurseries being maintained by local authorities – a drop of almost 700 compared with the wartime peak.[26] The Ministry of Health, as the internal memoranda of its civil servants make clear, was perfectly aware of the likely outcome of the transfer of responsibility from central to local government. The 1944 Education Act's wording did not, as the Ministry noted, make the provision of nurseries unambiguously statutory.[27] The Ministry had correctly anticipated that nurseries, once earmarked as 'welfare' and charged to the rates, would get little sympathy from many local authorities. And given the bottom-of-the-barrel nature of the employment of mothers, there was no sustained and enduring pressure on subsequent governments to enact nursery policies. How did the history of the war nurseries enter – if at all – into later government childcare policies? Did women's engagement in war work have any emancipating effects? To answer this, it will be necessary to turn to the whole question of the nature of women's war work and its particularly heavily gendered nature. I will concentrate on women industrial workers; a large group of which included those in traditionally 'male' employment, for whom the bite of gender might have been expected to be less deep.

The work of married women in industry during the war

On a rough estimate, at least three-quarters of a million women in industry during the war had children under fourteen. It is not possible to arrive directly at a more exact figure, since the Ministry of Labour did not collect statistics for the whole of the female work force by marital status and number of children (although the 1941

122

registrations of women under the Registration for Employment Order are analysed by marital condition).[28] The usual source of information about numbers and ages of children, the censuses of population and certain other household surveys, do not exist for the war years; there was no 1941 census. So it's only possible to make approximations by calculating from the information we have from limited sources. It seems safe to suppose that a very good third of the $2\frac{1}{2}$ million women in industry had children at school or under school age.[29]

Women with children under fourteen were never conscripted, or subjected to the effective civilian conscription of the 1941 Registration for Employment Order and the 1942 Control of Engagement Order. Mothers who did work, then, had the ambiguous status of volunteers. The proportion of all married women with children engaged in war work is masked, too, by the amount of unpaid voluntary work done by organisations like the WVS (Women's Voluntary Service). It is also hard to work out what proportion of mothers in the wartime industrial labour force were new workers; but proportions here varied so much on a regional basis and by the kind of employment that any overall figures would not be informative. Women's prewar labour histories affected their reception of details like new nursery plans, as well as colouring their attitudes to what they found themselves doing in the war. The enforced mobility which carried younger, single women in great swathes around the country at the behest of the Ministry of Labour did not affect women with children directly, nor did it affect soldiers' wives. As a character in Elizabeth Bowen's novel of wartime London observed, 'a Mobile Woman dared not look sideways these days – you might find yourself in Wolverhampton (a friend of hers had) or at the bottom of a mine, or in the ATS with some bitch blowing a bugle at you till you got up in the morning. It was well, she remarked, for Louie being a soldier's wife, though if she had half a head on her shoulders she should have started a kid also!'[30] But married women were indirectly touched by all this shifting labour. Some factories could change their function and to some extent keep their original work force, including their married women; soap-wrappers might become tool-makers, for instance.

123

At the start of the war, women from the Luton hat industry, for example, and from Lancashire cotton, Leicester shoe and hosiery factories became munitions workers: any one work force could be composed of women with very different histories of employment. A manager in 1941 noted amongst his new conscripted labour:

Scotch servant girls, from Dundee jute mills, from breweries in Sunderland, Irish girls of various types. Some were good, some bad, some indifferent. Scotch servant girls we found good hard workers. A Yorkshire girl was a hopeless case and had to be sent back home – pregnant. . . . Two Irish girls came on night shift, smoked, idled and swore at the foreman, refusing to work. . . . A hotel chambermaid; a sensible girl who'd made up her mind to do her job to the best of her ability and put up with the rough side of it. Note she's the domestic service type. This type is used to hard work and undefined hours of work at that.[31]

Married women, interspersed with such managerial heart-sinkers, were hailed as thoroughly reliable. The married woman as steady worker emerges through journalistic and managerial comment as an icon of decency and stability, sharply distinct from younger, single women. But remarks like, 'they seem to carry over their household pride into their job', 'these married women seem really keen to do the job somehow, and to keep at it', flattened the facts of the widely disparate work experiences of the married women in industry.

Again, it's only possible to get a sense of the latter on a piecemeal basis; the variety of regional differences makes national figures for the previously employed rather academic information, and obscures sharp variations between one work force and another.

Mass-Observation's *People in Production*, for instance, compares two extremes of 'morale' in two war factories. One factory was making life-saving devices and although it employed many new workers, it had 'a tradition of continuity of employment'. There was an active works council and: 'morning and afternoon rest pauses, an excellent canteen, radio in the factory, an average wage of about £3 and upwards, lowish time rate . . . an excellent sick bay and a firm's doctor and dentist scheme.' The work force of 1,000, almost all women, was credited with a strikingly cheerful enthusiasm for work by the Mass-Observation watchers. A Northern factory, by contrast, did similar production, but

has expanded with extreme rapidity after being plonked down in a small country village. . . . Most of the labour force consists of women who only two years ago were country girls doing domestic service, farm jobs, and like work. . . . The workers feel that the district has been invaded by the factory, which now dominates the area, but which will (they think) go away immediately after the war. Earnings for girls are up to £4 a week, and most of them have never seen so much money before in this village. . . . There is very little union organisation. A particular difficulty here is that every worker has to sign an oath of secrecy, is not allowed to say anything about the work being done, under fear of prosecution. Secrecy must be observed even with one's family in the village. . . . The management uses in conversation to describe the attitude of its workers the word 'cottonwooliness'.[32]

Whatever one makes of 'morale', it is clear that even factories turning out similar equipment were marked by regional histories and expectations.

The proportion of women in engineering and allied industries had risen from eighteen per cent in June 1939 to thirty-nine per cent by December 1943, but unskilled or semiskilled labour predominated, with a very small proportion of workers reaching the ranks of the highly skilled. The mass production of small aircraft parts, for example, might involve only half an hour's training to run machines used for stamping and drilling holes in aluminium pieces. Each drilling might take less than ten seconds to complete. Shell-filling in munitions factories was notoriously monotonous. Government training centres for teaching skills did exist, but the largest employers of married women on work new to them were munitions and engineering industries, where most of the work was simple and repetitious (and sometimes heavy, noisy, and dirty as well). Its temporary nature was underlined by the slight training and low pay, and by the practices of dilution already established prewar but intensified during the war. Under the 1940 Extended Employment of Women agreement between the Amalgamated Engineering Union (AEU) and employers, for instance, women, defined as 'temporarily employed', could only get the men's basic rate after thirty-two weeks of doing the job without assistance. Only those qualified for the work went straight onto the men's wage. Those who needed supervision received seventy-five per cent of the male rate for the job.[33] This agreement, which proved troublesome to operate, did guarantee women parity in the uncommon event of their being qualified to take up a 'male' job straight off. From the point of view of the engineering unions, it safeguarded the skilled male rate by underlining the temporary extent and terms of women's employment: it was this atmosphere of 'for the duration' which hung over women's work in general and over the employment of married women with children in industry in particular. The spirit of the nursery provisions accorded with this too.

The under-use of potential skill gave rise to much grumbling which intensified as women who had been in effect drafted entered factories. Married women, especially those with a history of factory work, were on the other hand often represented as docile employees unbothered by repetitive tasks, the details of factory organisation, or the best use of their labour. These women were held to accept, and accept willingly, the traditional position of economic and prestige inferiority. Their employment was given a personal meaning: making technology to get through the war quickly, to safeguard the lives of sons and husbands – if you could see a point in your work, you could put up with it. Mass-Observation quotes a conversation in a British restaurant queue:

F40B How do you like it?
F30B Well, it's monotonous, but you think *what it's for*, you know.
F40B That's right; it makes all the difference, doesn't it, if you think what it's for?[34]

Most complaints about the under-use of women's abilities are concerned with efficiency from a managerial point of view: women, undertrained, were not able to replace men, to the detriment of the war effort. The Ministry of Labour itself found it necessary as late as 1943 to issue a pamphlet, 'Women in Shipbuilding', aimed at employers. This was intended to stretch their imagination: even, wrote the Ministry, in the fourth year of the war when all labour power was needed, women were too often underemployed as

unskilled assistants and yard cleaners, when with a little encouragement and training they might replace skilled craftsmen. Former
housewives ought not to be underrated, although 'apt to underrate'
their own capacity themselves.

It is no exaggeration to say that the average woman takes to welding as
readily as she takes to knitting, once she has overcome any initial nervous-
ness due to the sparks. Indeed, the two occupations have much in common,
since they both require a small, fairly complex manipulative movement
which is repeated many times, combined with a kind of subconscious
concentration at which women excel. . . . Electrical work generally, and
wiring in particular, has a special appeal for women and their natural
conscientiousness combined with their love of making a neat job makes
them ideal 'wiremen'. Few women who have had a home of their own can
have resisted the temptation to use a paint pot and a brush and they take
with enthusiasm to paint work in the shipyard. . . . A healthy, and not too
heavy, sensible woman who has to run a home is marvellously adaptable,
and will turn her hand to anything with good will, once she has made up her
mind to do it. She has more balance than the young ones. . . .[35]

This text is interestingly stuck between a kind of naturalism and an
undercutting of that naturalism; it vacillates between asserting the
natural aptitude and neatness of women and stretching away into a
'try them and be surprised at what they can do' tone. Thus, it
continues, if women are trained with the closer cooperation of the
industry, there is no reason why they should not do skilled work on
the ships and in the workshops.

   One photograph of two women is nicely captioned, 'Working on a
Warship, they are Welding the Superstructure'. Another photograph of a driller and his woman helper adds: 'This is the right type
of woman for work aboard ship. She gives her mind to the job and
vanity does not prevent her wearing sensible boots'. Women paint-
ing 'seemed indifferent to such trifles as getting paint in their hair'.
Labour relations between the sexes, the pamphlet advises, could be
eased by the appointment of women supervisors in large yards to
supplement the foreman: '. . . they are admirable channels for
settling the grievances and misfits that the men in charge find so
difficult to cope with. . . . Such difficulties as do arise do so chiefly

because men are not used to dealing with women, so it is suggested that the first prerequisite is the appointment of an experienced woman labour officer or welfare superintendent.' What is striking about this Ministry of Labour offering, apart from all the raw material it provides for arguments about whether this language is sexist or not – and my sense of it is that analysis based on 'sexism' here would be wrong, because it would collapse far too much together – is the late date of its appearance. Debates about skill, training, and factory and ministerial inefficiencies in the best use of female labour flourished right through the war, even at the 1943 high point of women's employment. (And alongside the copious literature of congratulations and tributes to the resourcefulness and daring of somewhat glamourised Land Army girls, firewomen, and the like.)

The length of the working day caused some commentators to wonder whether the findings of industrial psychology on the counterproductive effect of long hours were unknown to management.[36] A munitions factory, for instance, might work between a sixty-five and an eighty-hour week; ten- or twelve-hour working days were not uncommon, with an hour off for lunch and then often no break after that until six in the evening. Arbitrariness, confusions, no dovetailing of factory shifts and nursery hours, no shopping provisions, and transport difficulties marked the lives of women workers. All this, despite the fact that the large-scale employment of married women had been anticipated from 1939 on. 'She starts on the washing-up, but even with me helping it is not nearly half done before she has to rush back to the factory. She says, "It's no good, I can't keep up with it. I thought I'd like to do a bit and bring in some more money, but I can't keep up with it. If I could just have a couple of days to get straight, then it would be alright, you could keep it under, but I can't manage like this!" '[37] This is from a Mass-Observation report on an unskilled fifty-year-old. The women interviewed by Thomas in 1943 all said that what was hardest was not the tedium of work, but the strain of 'managing' at home. Many women did take time off to 'get straight'; the figures for female absenteeism were consistently higher than those for men; two to two-and-a-half times as high overall. But again this hides great factory-to-factory differences, and a lack of uniformity in the assessing of absences: one indication of the 'worst' is the Ministry of Supply Filling Factory which had nearly a quarter of its women workers off at any one point.

There is a huge literature on female absenteeism which suggests adaptations at least to render physically possible the lives of women workers, who might well be faced with two- to three-hour journeys off to munitions works on top of getting older children to school.[38] A ten- or twelve-hour working day could mean leaving the house at five or six before daybreak in the winter, and coming back at ten or eleven at night, with the housework still to do. This rush for time was institutionalised enough to make good advertising copy: thus in *Picture Post* there appeared a woman at her sink with a Rinso packet: 'Me boil clothes? Not likely! I've got to be at the factory by two!' Under pressure of absenteeism, managements fitted work shifts with nursery hours; gave half an hour off a week for shopping; used priority shopping passes; organised women to collect lists from other workers and do the shopping for them; or let their workers off at midday Saturday. Two factories visited by Mass-Observation took literally cosmetic measures to cut down their absentee rates; they 'issued a weekly ration of cigarettes and cosmetics to every female member of the staff, and did it on a Saturday, their worst absentee day normally'. The success of this is not recorded.[39]

Part-time work, although constantly recommended by investigators, factory welfare officers, medical officers of health, industrial psychologists, was rare. It was as if management, whether Ministry of Supply or private industrialists, had been taken by surprise by an outlandish new work force with incomprehensible needs. For despite governmental flourishes about the importance of workers' welfare, and innovations like the 1940 and 1943 Canteens Orders, the provision of British Restaurants, and the gradual introduction of women factory welfare officers, the absolutely predictable problems for women in trying to combine long hours with responsibility for children and homes had not been predicted and were not met. The results further emphasised the implausibility of women with children as real workers. An apparently intractable labour force (allowing for that 'greater steadiness' of older married women) was working at a low-skill level 'for the duration' only. It had the status

129

of a temporary nuisance requiring piecemeal 'adaptations' as a response.

There were, though, some advances: the unionisation of women in industry shot up during the war, while some unions like the AEU and the Electrical Trades Union (ETU) admitted women for the first time in the course of it. The peak point of unionisation and female employment in 1943 saw some twenty-three per cent of employed women unionised.[40] This was an advance on the position at the start of the war, when only about five or six per cent of women in industry belonged to any union. Women's low level of unionisation was popularly attributed to an essentially feminine lack of interest in union concerns:

'Women in general are much less critical; they demand industrial change less than men. They take a much lower degree of interest in subjects like nationalisation, cooperation and supply organisation.'[41] On the other hand, women, particularly unskilled women, were taken to be especially concerned with 'personal' or 'local' issues: local labour arrangements, unsuitable jobs, tyranny by supervisors. My point here is not the objective truth or untruth of these attributed characteristics, – but to indicate a further instance of the designation of the women worker *as* female, as difficult to unionise for reasons to do with gender understood as innate temperament, as *essential* difference. And the most strikingly different women workers were the mothers.

Given the poor working conditions and the extreme difficulties of combining paid with domestic work, how important was the money as an incentive? At July 1941, the Ministry of Labour census of earnings of wage earners gave average wages as 99s 3d for men, 40s 7d for youths and boys, for adult women, 44s 4d, for girls, 25s 2d. In a war factory, women working long hours might earn an average of 66s in 1941.[42] Thus, while the strong wage differential between men and women was in general maintained, women's earnings weren't bad, on the face of it. But these earnings were largely based on increased overtime. The rise in the cost of living, plus transport costs and nursery fees, could mean that industrial work did not bring in much. Nonetheless, the money was important for servicemen's wives in particular. Their allowances stood at about unemployment benefit rates of the 1930s; 17s 0d from the state, 7s 0d from the husband, with 5s 0d for the first child and less for any others. The earliest mention of any women's economic discomfort due to war which *Picture Post* printed, in fact, was a report in 1941 on the Women's War Emergency Committee: a deputation, including Sylvia Pankhurst, lobbied for better allowances for dependants. In 1944, *Picture Post* published a letter 'from a Wartime Mother':

As a soldier's wife I find it virtually impossible to live on my allowance; as soon as the baby is old enough to be left in the nursery (if I can find one) I shall go back to work to supplement the family income . . . one of my best friends told me I had deteriorated mentally since I became a mother . . . nearly all the men are abroad and out of touch with home affairs and all the women are busy looking after babies (yes, in spite of the falling birth rate) in factories, or in the services.[43]

The acknowledged hardship of service wives, widows with children, and unmarried mothers, who could only pull up their earnings by long hours, led to frequent assertions that the apparently good industrial wage rates were illusory. The Labour Research Department in early 1942, for instance, commented that, 'Employers want to keep women's labour cheap, so that it will act as a brake on the men's wage standards after the war.' Most women were entering war industry at the low 'women's rate' and women continued to get on average half or less than half of the male wage.[44] The significance of the higher rate of the women's industrial wage as opposed to the average women's rate depended on whether or not it had to be used to support dependants; a woman who needed to work to keep her family could manage to do so by entering munitions works, but only at the cost of long hours.

The postwar production drive for women's labour

The process of women's withdrawal from the labour force was gradual, though it was established well before the formal end of the war. Married women had been placed in a priority class for release. By 1945, engineering and munitions work had dropped many women as the needs of war industries for intensive labour fell away.

Nonetheless, while labour controls were being lifted for the majority of women, urgent appeals were made to them to remain in or enter employment. Sir Stafford Cripps, speaking in 1943 as Minister for Aircraft Production to the National Conference of Women called by the Government, voiced the hope that once again women workers would be willing to shift jobs; war work was folding, but, he said, there would be 'a vast expansion in civilian production which will absorb large quantities of women workers'.[45] And, addressing the British Federation of Professional and Business Women in 1943, he reiterated the expectation that women workers would be increasingly needed after the war. His speech is a model text of the progressive invocation of the sexless 'citizen':

I have already stated that there are still problems to be solved with regard to our own country, especially on the economic side and I think that the key to the solutions of these problems is that people of both sexes should be regarded as citizens rather than as male or female citizens. The incidents of life will always make a difference between the sexes, but this relates primarily to the young mother and should not persist throughout adult life and certainly should not lead to any general discrimination. The experience of war has once again enabled us to see and experience the true quality between men and women, and the comradeship which has been demonstrated both in our factories and in our services should eliminate that suspicion of economic rivalry between the sexes which made the results of the last war so disappointing. . . . The theoretical problem of sex equality has gone, we now face the practical problem, and its only solution is to avoid intersex economic competition by making the field wide enough for all to enjoy.[46]

The 1947 production drive, however, had no such pretensions to undifferentiated sexual democracy. The Ministry of Labour had in mind a limited campaign, aimed at increasing British exports, which would require women's labour mostly in textile factories, but also in agriculture. Its *Gazette* in June 1947 specified where women were most wanted: in the cotton, wool and worsted, and clothing industries, in hospital domestic services and laundries, in the Land Army, iron and steel, boots and shoes, and transport. An address to women workers by Bevan emphasised that women were not being asked to do men's jobs, that the labour shortage was temporary, that part-time work would be made available, that 'he [Bevan] was not appealing to women with very young children although for those who wanted to volunteer and who had children a little older, there were in many places day nurseries and crêches'. Film trailers, cinema slides, shop window displays and special recruiting centres were introduced in sixty-nine designated districts of female labour shortage. There were 300,000 outstanding vacancies in the summer of 1947 for women workers; and the Ministry of Labour envisaged the potential employment of three times that number, while the pressure on production lasted.[47] Geoffrey Thomas's second survey for the Ministry of Labour (conducted in 1947, published in 1948) calculated that if nurseries and enough part-time work were offered, some 900,000 women might be persuaded to return to or enter industry.[48] Towards the end of 1947, the Ministry of Labour estimated that an extra 22,000 women had responded to the appeal and that the true figure might turn out to be 'considerably higher': by January 1948 they had calculated that the working population of women was some 70,000 larger. 'The number of women (in November 1947) was seventy per cent greater than before the war. The proportion of women in civilian employment thus increased from twenty-seven per cent in 1939 to thirty per cent in November 1947: it was thirty-eight per cent in mid-1945.'[49]

It was in areas of traditional employment that, from the outlook of 1945, conditions were unenticing. In factories set up before the war, pay was low and the comparatively good standards of canteen and childcare provisions were vanishing. Consumer and export industries had lost many workers to the war factories, and when the latter closed, as G. D. H. Cole wrote:

there was nationally a widespread reluctance to return to the old conditions of low pay and lack of amenities in squalid and obsolete factories. . . . It soon became evident that, if the required redistribution of labour was to be brought about without a great deal of friction, it would be necessary to make large improvements in both pay and conditions in the industries which had previously relied on the abundance of workers to get their labour on the cheap, and not to have to bother themselves too much about the conditions of work.[50]

The Lancashire cotton industry, for example, which had relied heavily on women workers before the war, found itself in trouble. Its lowpaid women had been swept into munitions works during the war, and

Experience of these factories made many people reluctant to return, or to send their children, to the textile mills. This attitude was reinforced by the bad repute into which employment in the cotton industry had fallen because of the high rate of unemployment that had prevailed in it year after year. In these circumstances, it was evident that the industry would not get or hold the labour it needed without a substantial improvement in wages even though its output were to fall a long way short of what it had been in the bad times before 1939.[51]

The Dundee jute industry, too, suffered; a lack of raw jute to process coincided with a lack of women workers. In 1946 their number was one-third of what it had been in 1931. An article in the *New Statesman* entitled 'Gynopolis' reported in 1946:

A jute employer, now looking for women's labour, said that women had been 'spoiled' in wartime industry with 'Workers' Playtime' and 'that sort of rubbish'. Another assured me that, if there were only more consumer goods to buy, the women 'would come tumbling back'. But a public official, whose job it is to know, said, 'Don't you believe it. Women who have got out of jute won't go back into it unless their families are going hungry again; and Dundee is balancing its new industries to see that won't happen.'

The same journalist mentioned local employers' worries that their work force of women might wither away in search of a better home life with fewer children to support:

Give the men a decent pay-packet which 'a gill on the road home' won't hurt; give the women a decent home and the chance to bring up a family, and will there be those 29,000 workers for Dundee's five-year plan? . . . The number of juveniles entering Dundee industry this year is a third less than ten years ago, because, as a public official said, 'Factory workers made a deliberate choice of labour.'[52]

Yet in areas where industry had no demands for female labour, women in search of work met with very different comments. Wales,

134

for example, was not included in the 1947 production drive at all, and here a women, turned down for jobs because she was married, wrote:

There is no tradition of female labour in South Wales, and especially now that there are ex-servicemen without employment, the prejudice against retaining married women in occupations is very strong. Scarcely a week passes without some indignant ratepayer writing to the postbag about pin-money women, and appealing for the dismissal of married women workers so that ex-servicemen may have their jobs, 'and thus become satisfied citizens'.[53]

Women's labour organisations and the demand for nurseries

The 1947 production drive for the increased labour of married women in certain industries did not, in the end, have the effect of meeting women's needs for childcare provisions. The ways in which these needs were formulated by the women's unions changed over the immediate postwar years, away from an emphasis on the need for *all* women to have access to community-based nurseries, to a justification of nurseries in terms of the requirements of specific industries for specific labour. The real exigencies of economic and political change between 1945 and the early 1950s entered into the expressions of union hopes, narrowing them. Shifts in the political history of the union-based women's organisations show the diffi-culties of assuming a close association between industrial and human needs.

For instance, the wartime and postwar conferences of the Repre-sentatives of Unions Catering for Women Workers paid great atten-tion to the need for full nursery provisions to enable married women workers to stay in industry after the war. At the same time, their value as a community service which should be broadly available was insisted on. In 1946 several speakers (including delegates from the progressive Trades Councils in Manchester, Salford and Birmingham) attacked the transfer of responsibility for nursery financing from central government to local government, because local authorities were claiming that they could not afford the cost of running them.[54] The next year the same conference agreed resolutions put forward by Miss Ault (Tobacco Workers) and Miss Chipchase (Railway Clerks) demanding that day nurseries should 'be open for everybody's use' and should be properly maintained and increased. Miss Chipchase commented that housewives were also entitled to have some mental relief while they were doing their job, since their occupation was 'just as much a job' as if they were working in a factory, shop or office.[55]

Speakers at the 1948 conference of Representatives of Unions Catering for Women Workers were less interested in metaphors of the housewife as worker, and more concerned with the postwar recruitment drive: if the government wished to recruit more married women to industry, then it must make it possible for local authorities to provide nurseries, by restoring the 100 per cent grant it had allowed them during the war. What in practice was happening, though, was the opening of factory nurseries and mill nurseries in the wool and cotton districts; and union delegates were anxious about the registration and inspection of these to ensure that they came up to local authority standards. One speaker was confident that the needs of production would bring about adequate childcare facilities: 'The Lancashire cotton industry was so dependent on women that the battle of the "balance of payments" was largely in their hands.'[56]

The 1949 conference continued these hopes that the demands of the economy could be a springboard for the industrial emancipation of women: 'Conference, being convinced that the operation of a full socialist programme was dependent upon the mobilisation of every available pair of hands in industry, placed on record the view that the adoption of the principle of the 'Rate for the Job' would go a long way towards encouraging many women to return to industry'.[57]

But the demands of production were at the same time causing a contraction in childcare provisions: the 1949 Conference was informed that, 'The building of new nursery schools could only be sanctioned where the Minister of Education was satisfied, after consultation with the Minister of Labour, that such work was required to assist the employment of married women in industry.'[58] By 1950, this restriction of nurseries to adjuncts of production, and not social means of responding to the needs of mothers and children, marked a complete break with the sentiments of 1945–6. The TUC General Council's support for nurseries became limited to 'areas where a case for them has been made out'.[59] Throughout 1948 and 1949 more mill and factory nurseries opened in Lancashire and the East and West Ridings. Through the early 1950s these employer-controlled provisions drew (deservedly or undeservedly) criticisms from many quarters, including attacks on women industrial workers as heartless child-dumpers. *Picture Post* demonstrates this change: it radically reversed its campaign for more and better nurseries as part of a postwar new deal 'for the ordinary family'. In 1956, by which time the magazine had admittedly sunk to a low point, it ran a feature on 'Children of Women Who Work'. The women were mill-workers; the children described as miserable in their factory nursery for long hours where, it said, the only glimpse of colour was provided by the oranges in the greengrocer's over the road. The mothers were destroying their children's emotional wellbeing for the sake of luxuries, it claimed: 'Is it *really* necessary in this Welfare State for women to go out to work, or do they do it for the ice cream and the TV?'[60] Women who went out to work became shameful. The possibilities of shorter hours, of improvements in nurseries, were no longer mentionable.

The fact that the postwar recruitment drive sought out not female labour power in general, but only certain kinds, in particular geographically restricted industries, did not work towards any all-round increase of childcare. On the contrary, it made the association of nurseries with limited employment all the more rigorous. The 1947 production drive only reemphasised the spirit of the war nurseries: childcare *while* and *where* women's labour was needed. The basing of postwar nurseries increasingly in mills and factories underlined the instrumental nature of their existence. No broadly emancipating moves towards what the Trades Union Council had used to call the 'social recognition' of childcare accompanied the cries for female labour. Nurseries, the business more and more of private employers, were increasingly tied in with the fluctuating needs of those employers, and less and less to any conception of social need.

The latter category had anyway been captured, in the immediate postwar years, by a rhetoric which spoke – depending on its political persuasion – of the needs of the nation or of the community for more children. Some women's organisations were better placed than the 'female' unions to avoid the restricting of discussion about childcare to the fluctuating demands of industry: the Women's Co-operative Guild annual congresses had passed resolutions in favour of nursery schools throughout the 1930s, on grounds which included their capacity to 'avert anxiety' to mothers living in bad housing conditions. In the 1940s they agitated for more war nurseries. In 1937 some branches had proposed a campaign 'of practical politics': 'the value of motherhood in national life should receive recognition in the form of a state scheme for the endowment of Motherhood and Family Allowances, such scheme to provide for pensions to Married Mothers at fifty-five years of age for services rendered.'[61] This concern with the practical recognition of maternal need, which continued to be voiced by the Guild throughout the war years, spoke about women at home and better local services. The 1946 annual conference demanded the provision of more maternity homes, 'fees to be within the reach of all working-class people', more maternity and child welfare clinics, a national maternity service, and 'the continued maintenance of wartime nurseries until such time as it is possible to provide Nursery Schools adequate to the needs of the people'.[62] 'The needs of the people' were, in the aspirations of the Women's Co-operative Guild at this period, to be met through the universal provision of adequate local authority facilities: needs were seen, roughly speaking, as social and general, 'community-based' rather than tied into the demands of industry. Although the very breadth of this understanding of the nature of needs led to a risk of blurring it with other contemporary vague and empty rhetoric about 'the mother', it did avoid another danger: arguing for maternal need and the needs of production in the same breath.

The intentions of working women postwar: attributions and investigations

The conditions under which working women in the 1940s were provided with state childcare were unpromising indeed: the gross event of a world war, in which the demand for a labour force could temporarily override the sexual division of labour in a 'normal' economy. For women to have undermined the assumptions behind wartime nursery provision would, – if it were possible at all – have required a degree of organisation which the conditions of their employment and their history as employees militated against. Would the end of the war see a transformation of these conditions? It was clear that female employment would alter. But what were women's own desires here?

This exercised the imaginations of many observers and political groupings who looked beyond the celebrations of women as heroic contributors to the war effort. Various parties seized the chance to speak for an artificially unified constituency of 'women', whose apparent silence and hesitations they eagerly claimed to fill in.

The Communist Party, for instance, took up the question of women's postwar work in a 1945 leaflet entitled 'Woman's Place?' A photograph of a filler in a shell factory is captioned, 'What kind of work for her after the war?' and of a landgirl, 'Will she want to continue on the land?' Of a shipyard worker, 'Perhaps a typist before the war, now an expert welder. Will she want to return to the desk?' The Communist Party was optimistic about the advent of a new socialist morality: 'The country's ideas have had a good shake-up. "A man's job" and "woman's place" haven't the same meaning as before. Men and women are becoming comrades.'

This comradeliness, mainfested in part by male workers helping to unionise their sisters, was a theme to which the Party had committed itself in the course of the war. In 1943 it had published a series of leaflets to this end. 'I am Proud and Happy' by a 'Woman War Worker' explained how you could do factory work and be a mother too with enough planning: '. . . and so, you see, my four children, a part-time job and my political work can be crammed into sixteen hours a day'. Other leaflets recommended that women at work should keep a close eye on health standards especially: 'Food, cleanliness, common sense; who should know better how to tackle these problems than the good housewife turned factory worker?' The involvement of women in union work is, typically, cheered on in 'A Soldier writes to his Wife':

139

Freda, do you remember how you used to get mad if I stayed out late at a Union branch meeting or had a drink or so with some of the lads afterwards to talk over Union business? None of that spirit now. You women have seen pretty quickly how much a strong Union can mean to production. . . . Derek and Joan must be proud of their Shop Steward mother. So am I!

In 1945, the theme of cooperation at work was reiterated in Party leaflets: In 'Woman's Place', a chief woman shop steward at a Durham steel works was quoted: '. . . the men shop stewards gave us every help. . . . I will certainly take part in the shaping of the new world after the war. Thousands of other women feel the same as I do'. The introduction of equal pay at once, said the leaflet,

would have a tonic effect on women workers. It would be as if the government were to say. 'Well, girls, you've been at it for over four years. You've shown your ability. So now we're going to give you a tonic – the rate for the job. . . .' It will help to make sure that there is no question of cutting the rate for the men when they return from the Forces. And it will establish the status of women.

The Labour Party's main policy declaration for the 1945 election, *Let Us Face the Future*, did not mention postwar prospects for women workers, but referred to the virtually universal conviction that the birth rate was dangerously low: 'A healthy family life must be fully ensured and parenthood most not be penalised if the population of Britain is to be prevented from dwindling'.

The Conservative Party, too, issued a pamphlet in 1946 called 'Women and the Peace' which relied on 'the personal touch'. It followed the work and housework prospects of four women, with the message that each could achieve her individual wants, if only 'state regimentation' were resisted. Charting population trends, it pointed to what it took to be the necessity for women to have more children; child allowance, then on the point of being introduced by the Government, should be paid to the mother. Jobs for women were advocated, for 'work makes work' – 'Everyone who can work, must work, either to augment our national income, or to help run our national services'. The Conservative Women's Reform Group

140

pamphlet in 1946 said that the male anxiety about the wider employment of women would 'be groundless in a nation geared for full
employment in order to maintain its national income and reestablish
its wealth'.

The tenor, then, of the literature of the main political parties was
to encourage women as workers. There was not, in the immediate
postwar period, any assumption that a return of women workers en
masse to the home was either necessary or desirable. But at the same
time they often included references to the dangerously low birth rate
and the importance of maternity. Meanwhile, the impression of
many contemporary sociologists and journalists was that married
women would leave the labour market in droves of their own accord
anyway. The biographer Margaret Goldsmith wrote in *Women and
the Future*, (1946):

Many women, possibly the majority of married women, have not enjoyed
their new independence; they have been made miserable by the wartime
interruptions of family life. As a result, many married women, perhaps the
majority, fervently wish themselves back into their prewar home routine. A
number of wives to whom I have talked are so homesick for their prewar way
of life that they seem to have created in their imagination a glowing fantasy
of what this life was like. All the small yet grinding irritations of domesticity
are forgotten.[63]

Behind this, she speculated, lay 'fatigue' and 'the wish for change'
after years of industrial work. Mass-Observation's study of demobi-
lisation, *The Journey Home* (1946), also described the majority of
married women in war work as hoping to settle down quickly after
the war.

Ellen Wilkinson, the Labour MP for Jarrow, distinguished
between skilled and unskilled workers here: 'The woman who is
finding factory work hard physically longs for that return, but I have
not yet found the woman who has interesting and responsible work
who wants to give it up just to be wife and mother in a small house.'[64]
Caroline Haslett, as President of the Women's Engineering Society,
had a special interest in the fate of skilled workers. 'Many of us,' she
said in 1946,

are hopeful that the nation's industry and economy will be sufficiently strong after the war to permit of many skilled women workers being retained, particularly in view of the reconstruction which will be necessary to repair the destruction of war and the industries which will be reestablished. It is to be expected that with a bold planning policy there will be work for all.[65]

In general, then, unskilled women workers were expected to return home gladly, while skilled women's wants modified this impression. Such forecasting, however, rarely paid much attention to the details of working women's lives in terms of conditions or childcare provision. Postwar journalists and sociologists tended to accept the wishes attributed to women to return home as true, and to confirm, or lament this wish, but not to scrutinise the original attribution. Mass-Observation's poll of women workers in *The Journey Home* (1944), is an object lesson in the superficial reading of survey responses. It quoted a Gallup Poll which had suggested that three-fifths of women wanted to go on working postwar, but modified it thus with its own survey: forty-three per cent of women believed that after the war women should not do men's jobs; twenty-five per cent thought that they should; twenty-eight per cent, that it depended on postwar circumstances. On the basis of these figures, Mass-Observation concluded that the majority of women would want to return home rather than take away employment from returning men.[66] But the picture is at once less decisive if the ambiguities of 'depends on postwar circumstances' are taken into account, and if the supposition that those who support a family are always male is questioned. Further questions by Mass-Observation did break down the apparent smoothness of the elision between men returning from war and women returning home.

The small survey literature of the postwar period seems less sure which way married women might jump in their desires to work or not. And the assumption was that such desires anyway would be on the basis of pure will, unmuddied by considerations like who would look after the children. Geoffrey Thomas's 1944 survey for the Ministry of Reconstruction, for example, at first sight appears to confirm that women *were* in favour of going home and not competing for men's jobs. In Autumn 1943, twenty-nine per cent of his married women wanted to work full-time postwar, thirty-six per cent not at all, and ten per cent part-time; and while two-thirds of the married women not wanting to go on working gave 'enough to do at home' for their reason for getting out, more of these were childless married women than mothers. Many also felt that 'there would not be jobs when the men came back'. Yet those who specifically believed what Thomas quotes as 'mustn't do a man out of his job in peacetime' were only one per cent of all respondents – illustrating the difference between principle, and pragmatics dictated by expectation.[67]

Women's experience of war work anyway was that it was temporary. We have seen that this experience was written into the spirit as well as the implementation of kinds of work, nursery provisions and the rest. Women had worked in circumstances which reinforced this air of 'replacing men'. Anxieties about jobs for the returning men were perfectly reasonable – even though in practice most women were not directly ousting men, but working in employment created by the war. Nonetheless, Thomas's figures do suggest an apparently greater conservatism among women than considerations of nursery places or of male unemployment would enforce: it was younger married women without children who were the most eager to return home, apparently. ('Younger' means under thirty-five.) Younger married women thought that women should be at home, unless forced out to work through the need for extra money. Those who in 1943 were keenest on going on working, especially on a part-time basis if they could, were the older married women. What sense can be made of what looks like a more conservative set of attitudes among the younger workers? There is more information in Geoffrey Thomas's second survey, an offshoot of the 1947 production drive.[68]

Thomas estimated that one-third of all women were in full-time work. Most workers were older married women. The main factors putting off younger ones were marriage, children and economics. Nine-tenths of unoccupied women in July 1947 were married; most of them had previously been 'operatives' in manufacturing industries; these were the workers which the postwar production drive wanted back in industry. But Thomas commented, 'The majority of women thought that women should go out to work only if they can carry out their duties to their homes and families. It is clearly this sentiment, that a women's first duty is to her home, which leads to many women abandoning their work on marriage.' Why the apparent prevalence of this conviction among younger 'lower economic group' women in particular? For both the Thomas surveys make the point that it is marriage as such, and not children, which stops women from working. (For example, in July 1947 only just over one-third of childless married women were working; whereas married women with over-five-year-old children worked as frequently as did married women who had no children.)

The interlinking of 'sentiment' and brute fact – for example, no nurseries – was thought by Thomas himself to be significant: 'The real and familiar difficulties women face when they consider taking up work are reinforced by the sentiment that a woman's first duty is to her home and family. Both must be tackled if a recruitment policy is to be successful and one has a direct bearing on the other.'[69] Low wages, he suggested, were in need of improving, and day nurseries should be reintroduced. Three-quarters of Thomas's interviewees wanted part-time work, the opportunities for which he assessed as slight in 1947. He also pointed out that a large proportion of women in lower income groups were already out working; these, 'the major source of unskilled and semi-skilled labour, have been drawn upon to a high degree'. Could clerical workers, he asked, be persuaded into factory work? The opportunities of employment open to women with higher education were already restricted enough; but the disadvantages in factory work were great: 'The present level of women's wages is too low to provide a sufficient incentive for many of the women who are not working now to make a special attempt to overcome their difficulties . . . the disadvantages of working outweigh the advantages which it offers at present'.[70]

Younger women's lack of interest in waged work, then, was determined by more hard-headed grounds than a purely sentimental conservatism about a woman's proper place after marriage. What had such work to offer, except to the badly off for whom the marginal gain might be critical if they had children to support, or to older women in the habit of outside work who 'missed the company'?

Marriage, women and work postwar: expectations and movements

In 1939, about a third of all women between twenty and twenty-four in England were already married and war speeded up an established tendency towards an earlier age of marrying. Not only were more women marrying younger but also children were being born earlier, and childbearing was being concentrated in fewer years. If you had been working in factories through the war, the chance of leaving and having a family must have had strong attractions. If you had been at school during the war years, the prospect of work wasn't enticing; marriage as an alternative 'career' to industrial boredom and low pay would have had its attractions.

One suggestive account of young women's expectations is Pearl Jephcott's *Rising Twenty*, a study of about 100 working class girls between seventeen and twenty-one in 1945. They came from a Durham colliery area, from a large Northern manufacturing town, and from central London. Their choices of work were shop, office, or factory (tailoring, machining, sweet-making or light engineering). Expected to help in their family home, they felt they had little to do but 'mark time' until they could marry. One girl in 1945 recalled her work a few years earlier: 'I left my job at the toffee factory (which I got through the Labour) because I got the end of my finger taken off by the machine and then I was suspended through lack of sugar. I used to get 13s 6d at the factory but it was a standing job (no wonder I am skinny). . . . It is very monotonous.'[71] This girl, commented Pearl Jephcott, was 'one who would like to begin to raise a family soon and would be prepared to sacrifice her dancing and pictures in order to have children of her own. Her attitude is probably affected by the fact that she sees no prospect of rising in her present job and has no conception of any career apart from marriage.'[72]

These girls, several of whose mothers had worked in munitions, said that they saw little point in their work, and would only think about staying on after marriage if their husband's pay alone was not enough 'to get a good home together': Pearl Jephcott noted that,

A few of the older girls are definitely proud of the technical skill, for

145

example in welding or blind-making, that they have acquired, as distinct from the earning power that this had given them . . . others realise that all they have learned by the age of twenty is, perhaps, to use a power machine; and they feel vaguely, that, although the money they take is 'alright', the six years should have taught them something more.[73]

An indifference to trades unionism accompanied little exposure to it. Experience of wartime work had not helped; one girl in the war had gone to 'a tailoring job in- another factory where at seventeen she was pressing cloth from eight a.m. to six p.m. with a certain amount of overtime. She found the work tedious, disliked the constant standing and the fact that the room was in partial blackout.'[74] Early engagements had been hurried along by the atmosphere of war and departures overseas. There was always the hopeful determination that your life would be better than your mother's had been, especially if she had tried to combine the care of several children with a factory job during the war.

But whatever women's own wants or expectations, and indeed whatever the extent of opinion against married women working and against the 'double wage', or the feeling that a working wife implied her husband's humiliating incapacity to support her, increasing numbers of married women did work postwar. The conventional estimate is that postwar figures agree with projections made from the end of the 1930s about the 'natural', that is, non-war-interrupted, gradual rise in the employment of women. This included a high proportion of married women, since more women married after the war, and did so younger.

In December 1945, the number of women workers, including those in the Armed Forces, was over one million higher than in 1939; but by December 1946, it was less than three-quarters of a million higher. Exclusive of those in the Armed Forces and Auxiliary Services, the number of women workers was 5,094,000 in 1939 and 5,710,000 in December, 1946.[75]

In May 1947, the Ministry of Labour forecast that by 1951 over half a million women in the fifteen to thirty-nine age group would have left industrial jobs and that prewar patterns of employment would 'spontaneously' reassert themselves.[76] But in 1955, Titmuss looked

146

back over the postwar period and observed that between 1946 and May 1955 the number of married women in gainful employment rose by $2\frac{1}{4}$ million to $3\frac{1}{4}$ million, or nearly half of all women at work: the biggest source of recruitment in recent years had been married women over thirty years of age. These figures included both full- and part-time work. At the same time Titmuss commented that the older woman who had got her childbearing over would find herself shut out from training and from pensionable occupations:

Motherhood and date of birth disqualify her, while the unthinking and the unknowing may condemn her in moralising terms for seeking work outside the home. Few subjects are more surrounded with prejudice and moral platitudes than this; an approach which perhaps deepens the conflict for the women themselves about their roles as mothers, wives, and wage earners.[77]

This increase in the average age of working women had been slowly developing throughout the war. Between 1943 and 1947, despite the fall in the absolute numbers of all women working, the average age of workers rose and was higher again than it had been in 1939.[78]

Between 1939 and 1957, the number of employed women over the age of fifteen rose from approximately six million to nearly eight million. By 1948, 6,785,000 women were registered as working; over the next ten years, another 840,000 joined them. These were mostly married women, whose numbers increased both absolutely and relatively to all women workers: at the end of May 1950, forty per cent of the female work force was married, some 2,850,000 women: by 1956, the proportion had risen to fifty per cent – 3,720,000 women. The period between 1931 and 1951 also saw broad changes in women's occupations: an extra three quarters of a million clerks and typists, and a large rise in unskilled labour, including machine minding. These changes continued between 1948 and 1958, when the Ministry of Labour estimated that, out of the influx of married women, 'More than a third have gone into distribution, and nearly a third into professional services. The only substantial decreases have been in domestic service, and, in the last three years, in textiles.'[79]

Some areas contributed more to the numerical growth of women workers: the largest increases were in the southern and eastern regions of England. Those who did continue to work outside the home, then, bringing the numbers up to what was held to be no more than a 'normal' increase on the 1931 census figures, were mostly women whose children were older or independent of them, or who were childless or widowed. But still a good fifth did have children of school age or younger (under fourteen) by the start of the 1950s. In 1944 Geoffrey Thomas had estimated that the highest postwar demand for work would come from women between the ages of thirty-five and forty-five, and that especially in the absence of part-time work and nurseries, married women under thirty-five would be the first to go.[80] This turned out to be a fair prediction. In 1948, he had reckoned that nearly a million women might be willing to take up outside work if wages were improved and nurseries provided with flexible hours, better shopping arrangements, and more and cheaper laundries.[81] Most of that extra million had, in fact, joined the labour force by the late fifties: but the recruitment of these women, in need of money, was not due to the provision of the social conditions recommended after the war to enable mothers to work; it came about in their absence, and in a climate of increasing hostility to mothers working outside the home at all.

Indifference to the complexity of work choices is one legacy of the postwar period; for sociological works of the 1950s and 1960s offer dazzlingly simple readings of the apparent postwar return to the home. Work like Geoffrey Thomas's surveys is cited selectively as objective contemporary evidence that women left paid employment because they did not want to work, period. The ambiguities of both the questionnaires and the responses are untouched. It is taken for granted that this research shows that women were glad to become housewives and mothers and resumed these positions in a drift of pure freedom. There's no suggestion that they operated in anything other than a vacuum of will alone; no suggestion that to refuse to be interested in long hours of (almost always) full-time work at low rates and low skill with no childcare provision is a rational refusal. That so many younger married women after the war did seem to want to get home and stay there is taken in the 1950s as proof of an absolute lack of interest in any work, under any terms, and as a confirmation of the naturalness of a longing to remain in a 'separate sphere'; and 'the experience of the war' is taken as evidence of essential truths about social organisation and the sexual division of labour.

There is a problem of how to interpret all this from the standpoint of post-1968 socialism and feminism: a dilemma of which expository path to follow. How far does one want to rewrite the apparent conservatism of women's statements quoted in Thomas's surveys, like 'a woman's first duty is to her husband and family', by taking a rational tack instead? By arguing, for example, that women who were already expected to be wholly responsible for housework and children couldn't be expected to want to take on paid work too, in circumstances which would have led to exhaustion – that life at home really was more enticing anyway, a lesser evil? There seem, looking for instance at the brief 1947 drive to get women back as 'operatives', to be enough 'material' reasons, like long monotonous hours of poorly paid work, to explain the seeming indifference of women, younger ones especially, to this prospect. And one can invoke 'material' reasons too for women's gradual return to the labour market – for instance financial need or the desire for company. But though the 'materialist' tack is useful to counter 1940s war-heroine literature and 1950s writings about the free choosers of hearth and home, it still has severe limitations as a mode of explanation. To indicate why this is so will need some preliminary discussion about a short but intensive period, from roughly 1941 to 1947, when ambitions about 'freeing mothers', and alarms about the birth rate were held together in a precarious balance.

CHAPTER 6

Postwar Pronatalism

The hero of Graham Greene's 1943 novel, *The Ministry of Fear*, encounters a dark front organisation disguised as a charity, and the following exchange ensues:

> *'What exactly is the cause?'*
> *'Comforts for free mothers – I mean mothers of the free nations.'*[1]

This reply comes from a supporter of the Mothers of the Free Nations fund. I'll abandon Greene's internationalist ironies here; but I'll keep hold of the phrase, 'the free mothers' to put it to use in a different set of ironies and political obscurities.

In asking whether the employment of married and unmarried women in the last war, including a proportion of mothers in both groups, made any differences to suppositions about 'women's place', we're entering a dense tangle of labour requirements, shifts in state suppositions about the family and the care of children, the nature of terms like popularisation, propaganda, ideology, and wants and needs. Did the reinstatement of the ideal of the women at home with the child simply seal over a surface which had been only superficially scarred by the peculiarities of the war economy? One way into this thicket is to ask to what extent 'the free mothers' are an impossibility, a contradiction in terms, not only practically (the double burden of work in and out of the home) but also from the aspect of political theory. For women as mothers and potential mothers sit firmly within the illusory unity of the category of 'the

150

family' – illusory in the sense that 'the family' is a complex object whose members possess different and sometimes antagonistic capacities and powers, and where money usually maps onto gender as well as age. There is no straightforward single recipient, 'the family', of family welfare measures. The lot of working mothers in wartime and after points up the incoherence built into social policy addresses to 'the family' which speak as if the interests and needs of women, men and children were always harmoniously unified. Mothers who work strain these assumptions of unity. 'The free mothers' of the 1940s were pinned down by that very status, both as war workers and after the war, in ways which were ultimately damaging from any liberationist or even egalitarian perspective.

Yet this rhetorical limiting took place against a myriad programmatic pronouncements, by a wide sweep of parties and interests, about freeing mothers, including by means of nurseries, from the intolerable drudgery of unrelieved childcare. But these 'free mothers' were to be released only into a more relaxed and wholehearted support of the family – freed into having more children. Both during the war and most strikingly just after it, the reproductive woman at the heart of family policy was surrounded by the language of pronatalism. By pronatalism, I mean that despondency and alarm over the low birth rate, both past and as anticipated by demographers, which took the solution to the problem to be encouraging women to have more children; four per family was a widely agreed target. Both this anxiety and this proposal for its remedy (as distinct from any economic analysis) had been building up throughout the 1930s and became more generally diffused towards the end of the war.

Pronatalist thinking generated a great deal of language about 'the mother', not all of which was decisively conservative, and much of which believed itself to be progressive. It filled bits of the world with sound, while the birth rate crept quietly upwards. But the ubiquity of this official nerviness about the falling population cannot in itself, without more evidence, be assumed to have affected women's reproductive behaviour one way or another. Rhetoric doesn't make women have more children through the sheer power of the word – the word narrowly conceived. Its presence matters, though, to put

151

it mildly, and has to be assessed, irrespective of whether it 'works' in the most detectable sense. This has to do with the general difficulty of how we understand the acting of 'bad language' in the world; how it enters into and also forms – in Raymond Williams' phrase – 'structures of feeling'.

How, exactly, are we to grasp the full force of what can be loosely referred to as 'a climate of pronatalist opinion'? If we do not understand its impact in terms of its demonstrable effects (most obviously, fluctuations of the birth rate) or if we can't detect any such hard effects, how then do we make sense of its overall presence? Some might conclude – wrongly – that British pronatalism in the 1930s and 1940s was a lot of noise which hurt nobody. This conclusion could be reinforced by the fact that pronatalism itself was no smooth unity, but a ragged orchestration of differing origins. Certainly the mere presence in the world of certain ways of speaking and writing guarantees nothing. Yet to stop at merely noting the pervasiveness of a particular discourse is to stop too soon. I do not know how best to make sense of the vast conceptual gaps between the equally uninviting options of either just hailing the existence of a discourse, or only assessing its quantifiable effects. But understanding pronatalism demands thought about this. Here I edge towards a comment on a particular instance of pronatalism: that damage was caused by the timing of British postwar pronatalism, in that for a brief period it sounded as if it spoke to the same needs for the 'protection of motherhood' about which various women's labour organisations had been agitating for decades. But the sources of pronatalist anxiety were different, and transient. The temporary coincidence of verbal object – the mother – in the diction of population policies, of social-democratic 'progressiveness', and of women's labour organisations brought about an emphasis on the mother as real worker in the home, equal or indeed greater in 'value' than the waged woman worker. In all this, the mother who did go out to work, and who consequently had especial needs, became an impossibility, regarded by no-one. The possibility of speaking politically about women's *needs* became obscured by a passing rhetoric of their maternal *function*.

This suggestion is a hesitant one: to talk about rhetoric as having 'effects' needs some conception of just where the effects are to be detected, and how. Simply to say about postwar pronatalism, 'yes, such language was reactionary, but we can demonstrate that it didn't affect women's behaviour one way or another,' only fights shy of the problems. But to move towards them is hard: how can we understand the spread of a particular rhetoric in relation to the more narrowly political discourses of the period? Can we accurately identify a dominant 'ideological' language, and then discover whether more limited forms of political speech engage head on with it, or exist quietly in its shade, or adopt its intonations? A political language possessed of any sensitivity but indifferent to such a socially overshadowing rhetoric as that of postwar pronatalism in Britain would be unlikely: then it's a matter of assessing the reasons for the *silences* of liberal, socialist, and feminist speech towards it; or what critical distances they took from it.

There is evidence of covert cynicism and some suspension of belief among respondents to sociological enquiries; but these traces of reserve can't alone guarantee resistance. An ideology is not reassuringly without 'effects' simply because it isn't wholeheartedly subscribed to. My sense of it is that, although in immediately postwar Britain there are few traces of *direct* unease with pronatalism in the formal expressions of women's labour organisations – rather, some understandable determination to exploit a climate for what it might usefully yield – the effects of this unease are elsewhere altogether, and are less susceptible to being read off from conference and branch reports. Instead they are oblique: in the field of political speech as silence, absence of challenge, indirection. Because portrayals of postwar pronatalism were largely in key with other, apparently anodyne presentations of family, home and nation, it was easier for them to get away unchallenged. Their impact lies in what was not said: as if they had acted to cover over a space, make certain objections unable to be raised or articulated. But a rhetoric could only ever have this power if accidentally allowed it by a previous set of failures: failures, in this case of postwar Britain, of radical analyses of the family, the nation, the state and the sexual division of labour. 'Good reasons' can be found for these absences, certainly. But that's a different point.

An important question is that of possible sources for the metaphor of the mother as worker, which held such sway in 1945–6 and had such a dulling presence in the formulations of political organisations, including women's labour organisations. For its implications were rarely refined to expose its contradictions. My point is not that mothers aren't workers in the obvious sense – far from it – but rather that a strong separation, albeit at the level of language alone, between mothers (who are assumed to be always married and always at home) and women (who are assumed to be periodically at work) is both artificial and politically dangerous. Artificial, in that it overlooks the real drifts of the labour market (as it did in postwar Britain); and dangerous, in that it asserts 'motherhood' as a self-evident value, but at the same time works directly against any admission of the real needs of women with children. Doing this, it confirms the most conservative understandings of gender, family, work. It contributes, too, to the 'stages' idea of women's work – that women's lives are stratified into a spell of paid work, followed by motherhood, then maybe reentry into the labour market. But this presumption of neatly autonomous strata runs against fact; for the layers are constantly flooded into each other; the histories, pressures and needs of one shape and determine the others, and make the theoretical 'choice' to return to work utterly impossible in practice.

Post-1968 feminism has grown up with a depiction of a mass return of women to the home after 1945, engineered by governmental deployment of maternal deprivation theories. This depiction misleads not only in that it assumes a collusion between the state and psychology; the movements of the labour market, too, were not so simply homeward-bound. It also colours our understanding of the 'state' in relation to 'the family', so as to preserve a falsely unitary sense of both: for in an analysis of what went on between labour requirements, welfare, governmental departments and women's work or the lack of it, neither a unified state nor an undifferentiated family can usefully be assumed.

In the case of wartime nursery provision, for instance, the 'state' fragments into internal government politics, dissensions between the Ministries of Health, Education, and Labour, reactions to pressures from industrialists, and splits between central and local

154

government authorities. As for 'the family' of immediately postwar family policy, the fiscal man and the reproductive woman and the stock of children compose a multiple target; there is no symmetry between the man as wage earner and the woman as mother. Analogous, then, to other questions thrown up by the transitions of the war and postwar years (like, under what political conditions could forms of education in motherhood *not* appear reactionary?) is the question of the language in which a truly progressive family policy could voice itself. Would it refer to the family as such, and take it as the true unit of society; or would it instead shake family members apart, and speak about the needs and clashes of needs between children and parents, women and men?

The mother in 1945 stood side by side with her children in her own spotlight of planning and welfare. But how enlightened an illumination was this focus, after all?

Pronatalism, right or left

George Orwell's essay, *The English People*, was written in May 1944 as a text for a Collins series, 'Britain in Pictures'.

The philoprogenitive instinct will probably return when fairly large families are already the rule, but the first steps towards this must be economic ones. Half-hearted family allowances will not do the trick, especially when there is a severe housing shortage, as there is now. . . . Any government, by a few strokes of the pen, could make childlessness as unbearable an economic burden as a big family is now: but no government has chosen to do so, because of the ignorant idea that a bigger population means more unemployed. Far more drastically than anyone has proposed hitherto, taxation will have to be graded so as to encourage childbearing and to save women with young children from being obliged to work outside the home. And this involves readjustment of rents, better public service in the matter of nursery schools and playing grounds, and the building of bigger and more convenient houses. . . . The economic adjustments must come first, but a change of outlook is also needed. In the England of the last thirty years it has seemed all too natural that blocks of flats should refuse tenants with children, that parks and squares should be railed off to keep the children out of them, that abortion, theoretically illegal, should be looked on as a peccadillo, and that the main aim of commercial advertising should be to popularise the idea of 'having a good time' and staying young as long as possible. Even the cult of animals, fostered by the newspapers, has probably done its bit towards reducing the birth rate. Nor have the public authorities seriously interested themselves in this question until very recently. Britain today has a million and a half less children than in 1914, and a million and a half more dogs. Yet even now, when the government designs a prefabricated house, it produces a house with only two bedrooms – with room, that is to say, for two children at the most. When one considers the history of the years between the wars, it is perhaps surprising that the birth rate has not dropped more catastrophically than it has. But it is not likely to rise to the replacement level until those in power, as well as the ordinary people in the street, come to feel that children matter more than money.[2]

This quotation is an exact compendium of attitudes which one can find throughout a wide selection of British periodicals, articles, books and broadcasts in the 1940s.

Population-fall anxiety acted as a backdrop to all proclamations and speculations on women, work, the nation and the family, throughout the war. (This bears out, to some degree, Orwell's own earlier remark: 'Progress and reaction are ceasing to have anything to do with party labels'.)[3] At the end of the war pronatalist feeling became both more diffused and more emphatic. It is this which helps, for instance, to make sense of the apparent contradiction that nurseries were closed at the end of the war, and at the same time hailed as key elements of social progress in party politics overall. The climate of universal pronatalism bathed all pronouncements on 'welfare' in a certain tint. It's not necessarily that what appears pink is, if you look at it more closely, really blue; that all postwar birth rate alarm can be taken as undifferentiated reaction as we look back from thirty years on, with the hindsight of information about European fascist eugenics. I'd say, still bearing Orwell in mind, that it's instead a case of Pronatalism, Right or Left. We are faced with the task of disentangling 'reactionary' from 'progressive' pronatalist sentiment; and of understanding what meanings these terms may be given.

The Royal Commission on Population was established in 1944 but did not report until 1949, while the papers of its supporting committees – Statistics, Economics, Biological and Medical – were not ready until 1950, by which time some of their suppositions and demographical information had become outdated. The brief of the Royal Commission on Population was

To examine the facts relating to the present population trends in Great Britain: to investigate the causes of these trends and to consider their probable consequences; to consider what measures, if any, should be taken in the national interest to influence the future trend of population; and to make recommendations.[4]

After five years' deliberations, the Commission concluded that a series of broad social reforms to aid families were vital if the population were not to sink below replacement level.

The report of the Statistics Committee of the Royal Commission on Population mentioned 'the striking and largely unexpected increase in the number of births which took place in Great Britain after 1941'.[5] The Statistics Committee itself was going against the tide of the rest of the Royal Commission on Population by being uncertain whether there was really a serious deficiency in the size of families. The absence of a 1941 census presumably helped to fix unmodified the projections on earlier evidence. The interwar years and the 1940s saw what one demographer has described as 'a considerable literature of immoderate dismay'[6] which rested its assumptions on the low birth rates of the 1930s and from there made predictions which fell notably short of subsequent 'achievements'. (The sum, for example, of the legitimate and illegitimate birth rates in 1933 was 743,360: this rose through the rest of the 1930s to fall to a low point of 668,834 in 1941. From there it moved up to 847,419 in 1944, a figure not equalled since 1923, and went on to rise, though unevenly, to 994,173 in 1947, continuing to increase until the mid-1960s.)[7]

Most demographers of the 1930s and 1940s had worked on the supposition that marital patterns and age-specific mortality would stay as they were, whereas in practice the continued decrease in the age of marrying, together with earlier childbearing, threw out their

157

predictions of a virtually dying population. The most moderate reaction to what was taken almost universally to be a crisis in the birth rate was voiced by the Economics Committee of the Royal Commission. It concluded that, despite popular assumptions, stationary (as opposed to increasing) numbers had economic advantages – a point it backed away from, though, by adding that economics was not everything and that 'British traditions, manners and ideas' in the world had to be borne in mind.[8] Immigration was thus not a desirable means of keeping the population at replacement level as it would in effect 'reduce the proportion of homebred stock in the population'. And, it reported that, even allowing for increases in the number of marriages, 'the fertility rates of the immediate prewar years are too low to sustain a stationary population, and would lead, if maintained, to one that would continuously decline by something like twenty per cent in each successive generation'.[9]

In brief, 'the case for reasonable and well-considered measures to mitigate the burden of parenthood is fully made out on economic and social grounds'.[10] At the same time, such 'measures to aid parents and to improve the care of children will strike at one of the main causes of poverty and malnutrition'.[11] This was the double edge of postwar pronatalism, here in its least alarmist form. While the general target was taken to be at least three and desirably four children per family, this was advocated in a context of social reform. Some of these reforms even materialised, although it's arguable that they would have done so without the pronatalist giftwrapping.

Democracy in obstetric help, for instance, surfaced at the level of official reports: the 1946 *Survey of Childbearing in Great Britain*, by a joint committee of the Royal College of Obstetricians and Gynaecologists and the Population Investigation Committee, referred to class differences in the obtainability of analgesics and anaesthetics in childbirth. Access to these was had by only one-third of the wives of manual workers, but by two-thirds of the wives of professional and salaried workers. Removing such a lack of parity (partly by issuing midwives with Minnit gas and air machines) fitted well with both the democratising aspirations of the prospective National Health Service, and the fact that the decline in family size (in working-class families particularly) to one or two children was causing alarm. A

concern for the 'quality' of the wished-for increase in the population mixed well with egalitarianism and the 1945 speech of social
democracy. Thus the supplying of contraceptives and the dissemination of contraceptive information no more ran counter to
pronatalist aims than did the improvement of maternity and infant
medical care; as pronatalists themselves pointed out, contraception
furthered such aims by ensuring the 'sensible spacing' of births and
encouraging parental 'responsibility'. A 'levelling up' in access to
contraceptive methods and advice, by encouraging clinics to deal
with the normally healthy married, not just the medically at risk,
served both educative, pro-quality ends and the social-democratic
spirit. The *Report on Reproductive Wastage of the Biological and Medical
Committee* (meaning still births, infant perinatal mortality and
abortion rates) to the Royal Commission on Population thus held
that it should become a duty of the National Health Service, once
established, to advise married enquirers on contraception.[12]

While, on the available demographic evidence (which had not
caught up with the facts of a birth rate which was beginning to rise) it
seemed reasonable to almost all political tendencies to express
anxiety about the low birth rate – and both Labour and Conservative programmes did so – not restricting British access to contraception was recognised as important. For *we* were not Germans. The
1949 *Population Report* again distanced itself carefully from what it
understood as reactionary pronatalism.

Concern over the trend of population has led to attempts in some countries,
e.g. Germany and Italy, in recent times to narrow the range of women's
interests and to 'bring women back into the home'. Such a policy not only
runs against the democratic conception of individual freedom, but in Great
Britain it would be a rebuking of the tide.[13]

Only harm, it considered, could come from refusing contraceptive
education and provision. In similar vein the Fabian evidence to the
Royal Commission on Population of 1945 recommended 'we should
have no dealing whatever with obscurantism or denial of facilities',
although it held that 'it is indisputable that the persistent decline in
the birth rate is largely due to contraceptive measures'.[14] In 1943
anxiety was pressing enough for *Picture Post* to run a piece entitled,

'Why Women Don't Have Babies', by Anne Scott James,[15] who rejected what she called 'the reactionary methods tried out by Germany and Italy', and advocated more nursery schools as part of a package of comforts for mothers of the free nations. Fascism and the refusal of access to birth control were well associated in the general imagination from the early 1940s on.

The contraceptive habits newly acquired by the working class were criticised in some quarters, however. The notion that a good example should be set by the upper middle classes, the guardians of racial quality, was stressed by more right-wing pronatalist writers, who also queried the advisability of the spread of any more contraceptive knowledge. 'Apathy' and a lack of 'morale' and faith in the future were pulled in as explanations for the contraceptive habits of the working class. Mass-Observation's *Britain and her Birth-rate* also goes in for this line of enquiry.[16] Eva Hubback's *The Population of Britain* is less cautious about voicing the dangers of more efficient contraceptive use, 'This would, by preventing unwanted pregnancies, result in a fall of the birth rate far greater than is usually anticipated'.[17] Although she thought that local health authorities should give advice, especially to 'those who need it most', the real business was to encourage 'a more courageous and robust faith in life among those who do not want more children owing to a defeatist attitude'.[18]

E. Lewis-Faning's *Report on an Enquiry into Family Limitation*, a large survey done for the Royal Commission on Population, asked over 11,000 women about their contraceptive practices and child-bearing aims. Apart from 'housing difficulties', he reported 'uncertainty due to the war' as determining the use of contraception, in the more recent marriages especially.[19] On the other hand, at the end of the war, 'materialist' accounts of the seemingly low birth rate turned only on the housing shortage. Debating the Housing (Temporary Accommodation) Bill in the Commons in September 1944, Mr Cocks (Broxtowe) said, typically tying up birth control with housing restrictions,

The Government say they need larger families and have made an appeal to the country for larger families. By erecting these houses [he meant the temporary steel bungalows which preceded the later 'prefabs'] they are more likely to stop childbirth altogether, and instead of calling them Portal bungalows they should be dedicated to Dr Marie Stopes.[20]

Others were fonder of rejecting such 'economistic' accounts in favour of theories of spiritual despair ranging from mild anomie to a profound national world-weariness; and some combination of practical and spiritual encouragements to women to reproduce was recommended by the common-sensical of all parties. Roy Harrod, a source of strikingly idiosyncratic rightist recommendations to more than one 'family' commission, wrote, 'Even if a spiritual *Aufklärung* were capable of having a marked effect on reproduction, it would not be within the power of the public authority to bring it about.' Instead, 'a moral impression' would be best made by 'early parliamentary action on the material plane'.[21] With a different set of practical plans in mind, the Royal Commission on Population settled for pragmatics too. Armed, by the end of the 1940s, with evidence which started to suggest that at least nonmanual workers were demonstrating 'a reaction against the small family' (as indeed turned out to be the case), they were hesitant about its significance. 'Stimulating the desire for children' would, they reckoned, still be necessary, and any recovery in the birth rate would in any event be a slow business needing official encouragement. Therefore, they wrote, practical steps should be taken to make motherhood a more attractive business

We believe that the instinctive desire for a family and the realisation of its lasting satisfactions may be relied upon, given reasonable social conditions, to ensure that families will be of sufficient size to replace the population from one generation to another. The problem is to create those social conditions on the assumption of a further spread of the practice of deliberate family limitation.[22]

How were 'social conditions' to be created? As with attitudes to contraception, the analysis of the 'social' left plenty of room for degrees of egalitarianism, or the lack of it. The Royal Commission on Population itself had hopes for nurseries, nursery schools, play centres and laundries to ease the lot of the mother. The Fabian recommendations to ensure family growth – 'the general aim must

161

be to secure that reproduction takes place at the age and rate which breeds the best biological stocks' – included free access for all to obstetric improvements, contraceptive advice, and nurseries for 'occasional relief'. Equal educational opportunities were essential too. 'We regard the perpetuation of such differential advantage [private education] as socially indefensible and as detrimental to the raising of the birth rate,' they said, on the standard note of the particular version of egalitarian democracy which prevailed imme-diately after the war.[23] While they held that the move to larger families should happen in a period 'which should be the shortest compatible with the need for providing the physical, social and economic circumstances in which women might reasonably be asked to bear children and preferably not longer than ten years', they advised no breeder/non-breeder split.[24] There was 'the desirability of preventing any marked difference in the fertility of different social groups'. Healthy immigrants would help the population problems, and would be 'best suited' if European: 'the eugenics of immigration cannot be overstressed', and 'sound stock' was essential for the national good.[25] Pronatalism, egalitarianism, social-democratic and racialist speech were all held together.

While women en masse were to be asked to have more children, the particularities of what it ever in practice *means* to 'choose' a pregnancy were rarely queried, and the question of who decided on the form and use of contraception was passed over silently. Even the most liberal social-democratic writing on the accepted population problem, exemplified in Richard and Kathleen Titmuss's *Parents' Revolt*, assumed that childbearing decisions were made by 'the parents' as a unitary force; the unlikely figure of the always rational, jointly deciding couple was rhetorically covered by the use of 'man':

From an enforced inarticulateness in the nineteenth century, man, by the use of birth control, vents his sense of frustration in the twentieth century by striking against parenthood. . . . The people of Britain have shown in an unmistakable way by their refusal to reproduce that the existing social and economic order just will not do. But this revolution in reproduction is a silent one. When will the ordinary man cease to be silent? It is time he spoke, for the hour is getting late and the future of the nation depends on him.[26]

The intermittent debate about the introduction of family allowances in the 1940s sat fairly close to contemporary pronatalism. Here, too, there was careful dissociation of England from unpleasant practices in fascist Europe. Both Titmuss and Beveridge, in his *Some Experiences of Economic Control in Wartime* (1940), discounted pronatalism's inspiring the family allowance system, to emphasise its social-democratic, ameliorative aspect. Unlike European programmes, Beveridge said, the British one aimed to alleviate poverty, not to raise the birth rate. The sources of family allowances are indeed, interesting and elaborate; they can by no means simply be seen as originating in socialist impulses alone. One of the last acts of the coalition government in 1945 was to put through the Family Allowances Act. It gave the *mother* (after Eleanor Rathbone's fight) 5s. a week for the second child.

Despite the efforts of the various campaigners for the introduction of family allowances to dissociate them from pronatalism, they were perceived by their recipients with some cynicism. This comes out in the Home Intelligence reports quoted by Paul Addison in *The Road to 1945* – 'There will be a catch,' said people who were expecting the family allowance to be knocked off their income tax allowance for children again.[27] And those quoted in Mass-Observation's *Britain and her Birth-rate* (1945) had little faith in the usefulness of 5s. Slater and Woodside's *Patterns of Marriage*, based on interviews done in 1943 and 1946 with working people in hospital for both 'neurotic' and physical illnesses, reports that

almost all thought of them [family allowances] as an effort to boost the birth rate rather than as an amelioration of hardship for the more prolific. They were taken as an inducement, a bribe, a payment – and a very inadequate one: 'the wife said *she* wasn't going to have a baby for five bob a week.' 'I'd like to see *them* keep a baby on five shillings.' No-one thought that the allowances would have any effect in encouraging fertility generally or that they would influence their own decision. They were judged in relation to their own income and standard and the real cost of a child.[28]

Irrespective, then, of the motives of the various campaigners, what these working-class families were alert to was the fact that the debate was pitched in a setting of pronatalism. And, Beveridge and Titmuss notwithstanding, some versions of the campaign were, quite accurately, seen to be more than coincidentally fixed there.

For instance, Eva Hubback, long concerned with family reforms and equal rights campaigns, took over the Family Endowment Society after the death of Eleanor Rathbone. Criticising the low rates offered in the 1945 Family Allowances Act, she wrote that such 'paltry increases . . . cannot by any stretch of the imagination be expected to stimulate the birth rate – except perhaps for those who may be so much on the margin of financial doubt as to whether to have another child that it takes very little to push them over'.[29] If allowances were to be introduced for first children, this innovation 'might do much to reduce the gap between marriage and the child's birth. Not that childbirth at an earlier age can in itself change the small-family pattern, but it may well prevent the stereotyping of a way of life without children'.[30]

Nonetheless, sustaining a purely instrumental approach to the question of encouraging family growth was at odds with the suppositions which the self-consciously progressive held. Although the Fabian evidence to the Royal Commission on Population quoted a 1939 Fabian Research group pamphlet[31] – 'It seems that the bulk of the working-class population can secure an income above the bare subsistence level only by limiting their family to two children at the most' – they were opposed to what they termed a narrow economism. A pro-child spirit had to be positively infused into the community, and thus the happiness of parenthood stressed by practical improvements plus an upgrading in its status.

Similarly pursuing a 'progressive' policy of working on all fronts at once, a PEP (Political and Economic Planning) broadsheet, *Planning*, in 1946 hoped for a levelling up of maternity provisions, accompanied by a change of heart: 'If parenthood is to be encouraged, the maternity services must take account of maternal psychology, no less than of maternal mortality, and of social as well as of medical needs'.[32] The tremendous weight attached to the problem of rejuvenating 'morale' was by no means the property of the right-wing pronatalist writers; and the degree of conservatism can often be gauged by the spirit in which 'morale' was understood – whether as susceptible to being raised by practical improvements in the social conditions for having children, or whether in a rhetoric of nationalism alone. G.D.H. Cole came down on 'morale' as the 'most significant determinant on the birth rate'; noting the upswing in marriages and births after 1940, he concluded that all turned 'on whether the people of this country feel on the whole hopeful or pessimistic about the future'.[33] The 'progressive' approach at the end of the war was defined by whether you took the line that material improvements could flesh out 'morale' effectively, to raise the country's spirit after its demoralisation by war. But progressiveness was committed to the importance of a shift of sensibility, too. Pearl Jephcott, a socialist sociologist, wrote about her alarm over the 'fashion' for smaller families among the working-class girls she interviewed. Though many of them remembered the continual exhaustion of their own mothers who had had large families, she thought that more intangible and nonmaterial causes were at work:

Despite all this, these girls on the whole give one the impression that it is something more subtle than the pictures, or lack of money, or being tied, that has influenced them; something which is allied to the fact that they are not fundamentally happy enough themselves to say, 'Life is O.K. Let's give it to plenty of other people.'[34]

As one looks through this war and postwar literature of pronatalism, it becomes a matter of trying to understand fine shades of relations: how it was that the family allowances programme, for instance, far from being captured by the Left in a way unambiguous from the perspective of socialism, in fact demands a closer comparative scrutiny. The equal pay debate was also flying in the wind of birth-rate anxiety. The Fabian Women's Group submitted evidence to the Royal Commission on Equal Pay in 1944; they argued that the introduction of equal pay would not have a 'dysgenic effect' on the birth rate. Women would not be tempted to flee marriage and maternity for the attractions of an equal wage – if mothers were recognised, and maternity no longer entailed 'being a slave to a broken sink or a decayed and obsolete coal range'. In this they followed the position adopted by the Standing Joint Conference of Working Women's Organisations on the social need to value the work of mothers in the home adequately and treat them as 'workers' too. The Fabian Women's group had to argue on all sides at once:

> We do not . . . accept the assumption . . . that the desire for children and for home-making has become so weak among British women that the introduction of reasonable rates of pay would cause a stampede away from the home; but we do not hold that sweating the mass of wage-earning women is a sensible or civilised way of persuading them to have children.[35]

The Royal Commission on Equal Pay (1944–6) was appointed officially, in the words of its own Preface, to 'examine the existing relationship between the remuneration of men and women in the public services, in industry and in other fields of employment: to consider the social, economic and financial implications of the claim to equal pay for equal work, and to report'. It is a strikingly detailed but tentative document; a survey of the existing relations between the pay of both sexes in many occupations, and an examination of the likely consequences and implications of equal pay for equal work. The Commissioners in effect backed a policy of equal pay in the civil service, teaching and local government, but not in industry and commerce; in this they relied on a philosophy that exact justice between individuals would run counter to the claims of economic progress. But there is a vigorous memorandum of dissent to this from three Commissioners – Dame Anne Loughlin, Dr Janet Vaughan and Miss Lucy Nettlefold – who objected to the majority view that the lower efficiency of women accounted for their lower wages. The dissenters claimed that unequal pay was itself an important element in maintaining unequal opportunity. The members of the Royal Commission on Equal Pay themselves speculated about the effects of equal pay on the birth rate, but felt that on that point they could reach 'not only conjectural, but meagre' conclusions. The Communist Party's evidence to the Commission dismissed such anxiety as pointless, and indicated the rising of the birth rate during the war, which had been a time of high and better-paid employment for women. The socialist economist Joan Robinson in her submission argued that since women's earnings and careers would be disturbed by childbirth and bringing up children, men would continue to earn more on average. There was no 'economic justification for adding artificial handicaps to the natural one'. And, she wrote, 'cheap labour tends to be wasted, like salt on the side of a dinner plate'.[36]

Cheap labour was women's labour. Some conservative opinion, on the other hand, was prepared to submit that there were 'social causes [meaning reasons for keeping] unequal pay'; one of which, in Roy Harrod's evidence, was 'to secure that motherhood as a vocation is not too unattractive financially compared with work in the professions, industry, or trade'.[37] The Commissioners themselves commented:

Ignoring the fluctuations due to war, the spread of feminist ideas has operated in recent decades both to enhance the demand for women's labour and to expand the supply. . . . If, now, an upward revaluation of the occupied women's standard of living were to coincide with a withdrawal of women from the market in response to a swing of social opinion in favour of motherhood and home life, such an improvement of standard might prove to be maintainable . . . even in the absence of a further rise in the intensity of the demand for women's labour.[38]

The arguments over the introduction of equal pay immediately after the war were, like those for family allowances and the provision of contraception, at least shaded with pronatalist thought. I want now to concentrate on 'the mother' as an intense focus of pronatalism.

'The mother' in postwar social policies

The welter of proposed improvements in the lot of the postwar mother and the family is quite dazzling at first glimpse. Immediately after the war, 'comforts for free mothers' continued to be widely touted by social theorists within a general social-democratic or liberal drift which crossed party boundaries. On the question of the mother, who was not a social democrat?

There is a huge literature, concentrated in 1945 and 1946, which argues for nurseries, after-school play centres, rest homes for tired housewives, family tickets on trains, official neighbourhood baby-sitters, holidays on the social services for poorer families, proper access for all to good gynaecological and obstetric help, a revolution in domestic architecture towards streamlined rational kitchens and a good number of bedrooms, more communal restaurants and laundries. Eva Hubback's suggestions in *The Population of Britain* included marriage guidance clinics, more adult education classes which would teach 'hygiene, family relationships, child management, and the domestic crafts', and 'education in family living' as part of the new school curriculum. Houses should be purpose-built for larger families of the future; women should be able to work part-time if they wished; the bar on women's working in certain professions after marriage should go; and training in civic values and 'citizenship' should be diffused through all educational levels. The recommendations of the 1946 *Survey of Childbearing in Great Britain* by the Royal College of Obstetricians and Gynaecologists also mentioned adult education in 'domestic relationships' and 'preparation for family life', as well as sex education and courses in household skills at school level. The 1949 Report of the Royal Commission on Population advocated a package of income tax reliefs, nurseries, improved house design, washing machines on the hire purchase system and a network of family holiday camps. The Fabian evidence to the 1945 Royal Commission on Population was also in favour of nursery schools, family travelling opportunities, education in citizenship and a system of effective financial aids to parents, including a marriage bonus 'to take the form of orders on shopkeepers for utility furniture and household equipment up to the specified amount'. Use should be made here, they wrote, of the Council of Industrial Design's new handbook.[39] Cash benefits for new mothers could be supplemented by baby things in kind, like prams. In 1948, Beveridge himself recommended 'holidays for housewives' and pointed to the example of the Lancashire Council of Social Services' home, the Brentwood Recuperative Centre for Mothers and Children. 'The housewife may at times be as much in need of rehabilitation to do her job as a crash-shocked airman or injured workman'.[40] Beveridge also approved of the 1945 Reilly plan which proposed 'a return to the village green' by making cooking and washing communal to ease the hard and isolated life of the housewife.[41]

Examples of these mixes of practical improvements, domestic innovations, and pronatalist devices could be multiplied indefinitely: it is the tight meshing of these elements which is so noticeable in retrospect. By 1945 the universal tone of social-democratic policy on the family had been so often invoked that its repetitions begin to look flattened and exhausted themselves, like the housewives' lives they sought to improve. (What happened to even Orwell's writing in the long extract quoted above is an indication of this.) From a perspective of thirty-odd years on, contemporary feminism tends to assume that 'the postwar rehabilitation of the family' really was a concerted drive to revive traditional values after the demoralisation of war, to reinstate the nuclear family after the closing of war nurseries and the return of women to the home. But books and articles of the period make it clear that 'the family' was a preoccupation all through the war; that anticipation of postwar social reforms had a wider base than the immediate cluster of excitement around the Beveridge report on *Social Insurance and Allied Services* in 1942; and that there was no imposed and concerted drive to reinstate the family 'from above' at the immediate end of the war. The Reconstruction Priorities Committee was set up in 1943, to pursue Beveridge's proposals: in November of that year, a new Cabinet Committee on Reconstruction was announced, with Lord Woolton as Minister. Surveys and investigations on postwar reconstruction had been well established earlier, however, including for instance, the Nuffield College Social Reconstruction Survey which was instituted in 1941. The 'social reforms' introduced by the Labour government in 1945 were in this sense a consolidation of what had been established under the Coalition government.

In 1940, Orwell had written,

There are wide gradations of income, but it is the same kind of life that is being lived at different levels in labour-saving flats or council houses, along the concrete roads and in the naked democracy of the swimming pools. It is a rather restless, cultureless life, centering aound tinned food, *Picture Post*, the radio and the internal combustion engine.[42]

But how accurate was this sense of a universal cultural flattening? My inclination now is to take 1945–7 as the moment of self-exhaustion of a particular social-democratic weighting on 'the family' which had been running through the war – as opposed to the more orthodox view that the pronouncements of 1945 were fresh moments of Labour family policy, a new end-of-the-war egalitarianism. In this light, that particularly intense concentration on the mother which got going in 1945–6 is a symptom of the impossibility of holding together, at the level of language, the doubtful unity of 'the family', once the end of the war had dissolved its rhetorical appeal. Orwell's fine phrase, 'the naked democracy of the swimming pool', ironically spins off from a rhetoric impossible to sustain for long after the war. The generality of 'the family', too, was less voiced after 1945.

For if you look for some uniform postwar movement to 'rehabilitate the family', it cannot be traced. Instead a series of specialised agencies, such as the new psychiatric social work, 'open up' only certain kinds of families to corrective inspection, like the revived category of the 'problem family'; look for the responsibility of family members for breakdowns in family functioning; and settle increasingly on the mothers. Not that 1945 was in any way unprecedented in its growing emphasis on the mother: rather that it marks one of many watersheds in the periodic invocations of the family. Postwar welfare penetrated the traditional 'privacy' of the family by speaking more and more to the assumed needs of separate family members.

One of the strongest attempts to hold together the unity of 'the family' before 1945 is evidenced, I'd think, through the many metaphors of the family as a cellular organism in the body politic of the state and the community. Family health was a building block in the edifice of national health, spiritual or physical. (That extraordinary book writen in 1943 by a woman doctor and a woman sociologist about a South London Health Centre, *The Peckham Experiment*, is one long metaphor of the family as a biological organism, a vital cell in the body of the national whole.)[43] The predominance of the vocabulary of 'citizenship' in 1945 to 1947, especially in Fabian writings, had a similar neutral wholeness to that which 'the family' possessed. The blank face of 'the citizen' possessed neither class nor gender: as a political notion it simply refused all those differences, social and sexual, in its aspirations for an egalitarian democracy. These 'the family' also concealed.

But the bundle of pronatalist and ameliorative elements in

postwar social policy on the family, taken together with the impossibility of sustaining a rhetoric of 'the family' as such after 1946, bring up a more solid possibility. That is, that 'family policy' is a contradiction: for the very good reason that the family does not exist as an entity. In so far as a 'family policy' has to do with children, and given that the bearing and rearing of children is by biology and custom respectively the province of women, then a main object of 'family policy' is women; the universally pronatalist climate of 1945–7 ensured that the true target of postwar social philosophy was the mother.

One of the clearest instances of this aiming at the mother is the manner in which the postwar retention of nurseries was argued. The very widespread pro-nursery sentiments of the late 1940s were perfectly congruent with familialism, enthusiasm for the family. Nurseries were advocated as key points for educating mothers through influence and precept, and as likely to raise the birth rate by lightening the burden of childrearing. Both conservatives and social democrats held that nurseries were an invaluable means for teaching 'mothercraft' to adolescent girls. The many postwar proposals for conveying first aid to tired mothers shaded into allegations of 'fecklessness' and incompetence, which could be remedied by on-the-spot instruction. 'Help' and 'training' were close neighbours in this literature, as in the tart comment in *Our Towns*, the result of investigations by the Hygiene Committee of the Women's Group on Public Welfare: 'We cannot afford not to have the nursery school: it seems to be the only agency capable of cutting the slum mind off at its root and building the whole child while yet there is time.'[44]

Advocacy of nurseries as adjuncts to motherhood training was adopted not only by the classically conservative but also by Fabian humanists: early in the war a Fabian pamphlet had argued that the Ministry of Health must make more adequate plans for nurseries, since there the mother would learn about 'nutrition, cleanliness, and correct physical education. . . . She will at once make use of this knowledge in her own home'.[45] In 1945 the Fabians again recommended the judicious use of nurseries for democratising ends: 'to provide the freedom from family cares which the well-to-do mother provides for herself'.[46] The main argument, however, was not egalitarian, but pronatalist; or more accurately, egalitarianism about the family was already part of pronatalism at this point. Mothers were to be freed by the provision of nurseries as a precaution against personal and 'therefore' family breakdowns: but they were to be freed for having more children.

The pronatalist use-value of nurseries was a platform common to the relatively progressive and the more conservative. The strong support of the 1949 Royal Commission on Population for nursery provisions has already been mentioned; its writers saw nurseries as vital to combat the chances of family size slipping under replacement level.

There arises among responsible and intelligent women of all classes an acute sense of conflict between having children and leading what they regard as a tolerable life . . . services should be developed so as to cater as much for the needs of mothers with young children for occasional help and relief in normal circumstances as for help in emergencies . . . even children under two may suffer no harm from an occasional spell of a few hours in a day nursery . . . The general aim should be to reduce the work and worry of mothers with young children.[47]

That nurseries, by reducing domestic strains, would make having babies more tolerable was claimed somewhat desperately by those whose first interest was not in population figures, but in saving nursery education. 'Motherhood must be made less of a drudgery and anxiety, if we are to secure the birth rate figures on which our national welfare and status depends,' ran a letter to *The Times* from a nursery movement supporter.[48]

And state-provided childcare could cement marriages, since it would ease the tensions caused by overcrowding. Nursery demands fed into housing demands very neatly. For instance, in the House of Commons adjournment motion on the fate of the wartime nurseries, in March 1945, pro-nursery Members of Parliament argued that if they were retained, housing, 'the basis of responsible, healthy family life', would be made more bearable where it was bad. Nurseries would save the birth rate and marriage by taking the stress off the wife: the husband need no longer 'escape' to the pub or politics – 'one is as bad as the other if it splits the home'.[49] That a vigorous nurseries programme would create 'happy homes' in a demoralised postwar population was claimed by Labour and Tory members alike: the one significant variation was the Labour plea on the grounds of class parity of access to childcare – for the rich could buy nannies. A 1945 deputation of professional nursery workers and others to the Ministries of Health and Labour similarly appealed to the need to avoid family collapse through overcrowding: 'emergency in housing is an emergency in family life,' and nurseries could do invaluable help in relieving the overpressed mother'.[50] The Ministry of Health's own brief remarked on

a feeling in many parts of the House that wartime nurseries should not simply be closed when their justification as an aid to war production ended, but that they should be continued, at least while housing and other wartime difficulties added to the burdens on the housewife.[51]

None of these considerations brought about a national network of postwar nurseries. The Government's interest in social need was merely rhetorical. It was not, in the end, swayed into action. Acute questions of childcare provision and other reforms central to the lives of women and children were decisively captured by a language in which the figure of the Mother was continuously produced as both cause and object of all these reforming movements.

It can be argued – and was argued at the time – that real progress was made out of all this: access to contraceptive and obstetric services was improved and democratised to some extent; children in care received fresh consideration; family allowances were introduced. These were gains in line with the long-voiced demands of women's labour organisations and were significant advances, however imperfect and flawed their implementation. G.D.H. Cole observed about the new social security plans:

The opinion of today credits women and children with individual rights and claims of their own. It is not so ready as its forerunners to say that the sins of the fathers shall be visited upon the children, or even upon the mother, or so sure that family life thrives best when women and children were offered up as victims to its sanctity.[52]

It was widely assumed by contemporary socialists and social

democrats that serious humanitarian advances had been begun by postwar family policies, even if the material gains were in practice slight – as with family allowances, the principle was respected, while the five shillings a week was derided. This position, though, as the Women's Co-operative Guild's resolution mentions, depended on some conviction about the longer-term possibilities of a progressive capitalism. And although social policy developments did in some lights treat women and children as separate family members, women were mothers within and with reference to the family, socially and economically. Although mothers were indeed addressed in their own right, this was not in itself any guarantee of a political advance, even if it held the promise of practical gains. There's a crucial difference between invoking 'the mother' and speaking about the practical needs of women with children: the first is a rhetoric of function and static position, the second discusses sexual-social difference in a way which doesn't fix it under the appearance of eternity. To say this is perfectly compatible with acknowledging that some real, if circumscribed, aims were achieved in the lives of women with children. But postwar pronatalist opinion did not of itself produce such gains – even if it acted as a spur, they had other and older origins. And pronatalist speech imposed a double edge on the expression of these limited social gains, for it was always at risk of falling back into instrumentality.

The risks of the metaphor of the mother as worker in the home in a climate of pronatalism are doubtless clearer in retrospect, as are its temptations. After the war, a redescription of the housewife as worker deserving special safeguards occurred on several fronts. Beveridge took it up himself in his *Voluntary Action: A Report on Methods of Social Advance*.[53] Some nursery supporters suggested that the working conditions of mothers could be improved by an entitlement to one day off a week. The raising of the housewife's status and the recognition of the essential nature of her work could be enshrined in legislating for a half share in her husband's salary. This was advocated by Edward Hulton in articles like 'Wages for Wives' in *Picture Post*[54] and by Edith Summerskill in Parliament[55]: she was quoted in 1943 as attributing the decline in family size to women's 'revolt' against their lack of any legal right to share the male wage.

174

That 'housewives and mothers' – the two so often named in the same breath that they might have been one hyphenated occupational category – did 'real and vital work' became a cliché of 1945 and 1946. The architects of reasoned kitchens were fond of it, the Fabian homage to the community and the ideals of citizenship relied on it, and its currency was such that its manifestation in certain kinds of feminist literature was unsurprising.

Postwar feminism, social democracy, and the rhetoric of the mother

The evidence of the Fabian Society to the Royal Commission on Population is a vivid instance of one incarnation of feminism within familialism – the mother-worker. It understood feminism as contributing to the spirit of participatory democracy, and to that humanisation of the lives of wives and mothers which inducted them into the community. Women need no longer be subjected to that 'narrowing of the women's horizon which is caused by childbearing and childrearing'. The woman who was

tied to the house at weekends or in the evenings by the need to look after young children is deprived of those opportunities for recreation in company with her husband which form a normal part of the married life of childless couples. This is a severe hardship which affects the quality of married life.[56]

For although parenthood must always entail sacrifice, 'it would be neither possible nor desirable to relieve them [parents] from the care of their offspring'; 'the community' must share the burden of its parents. Motherhood was an important job:

It is hardly necessary perhaps to state that a mother's first duty is to her children and her home, and that, except in cases of sheer necessity, a mother should not undertake outside work unless she can ensure proper care for her children. During the war, this principle has been lost sight of, and although women with children under fourteen have not been forced to work, they have been given every encouragement through the Government's provision of wartime nurseries, school care clubs, etc.[57]

Although such provisions, they wrote, had only 'catered for a

175

minority' of children of working mothers, 'official sanction' had been given during the war to mothers who

in too many cases allowed responsibility for their children to take second place. Teachers know, if the public does not know, the great amount of child neglect that is the result of mothers working full time on munitions. Unfortunately our government never stated that in war as in peace a mother's first duty is to her children, so that it is all the more to the credit of those mothers – eighty-five per cent – who have resisted the temptation to combine two full-time jobs under impossible conditions.[58]

Nevertheless, they continued, marriage alone was no justification for abstention from work. Not only that, but 'a woman, like a man, has a duty to the community to work to the full extent of her capacities all her working life and . . . the exercise of her special function of maternity cannot occupy her full-time for more than a portion of it'.[59] More part-time jobs should therefore be available, and jobs in which the experience of maternity afforded a positive advantage – teaching and welfare work. The democratisation of marriage, according to Fabian futurology, would accompany the spread of part-time work for mothers:

The mothers who choose to spend their whole time in looking after the children when they are small – which is what the majority of mothers will always do – must realise that they should give part-time service to the community when the children are older. If society solves the problem of how they are going to get help in their job of caring for the children when small, they must in turn help to get some tasks to put meaning into their lives when the children are gone. A democratic society cannot tolerate parasites, and married women who are not pulling their weight should be recognised as parasites.[60]

In sum, it continues, mothers should be freed to go out – but with their husbands, and in order to strengthen their marriages. They should be wholehearted full-time mothers, yet be ready to resign from work for the sake of 'the community'. They should be aided by social and economic reforms, but so that they could more easily have more and better children. The Fabian ideal of the 'new marriage' was 'teamwork' between husband and wife: Fabian feminism tended to look back, half bored and half scandalised, at the lamentable separatism of its mothers' generation. In place of that 'sex antagonism', it hoped that the new husbands and wives would constitute a marital team: this was analogous to the Communist Party's leaflets recommending parity on the shop floor – 'The country's ideas have had a good shake-up. . . . Men and women are becoming comrades'. The truly significant social unit in the Fabianism of this period was the family: women ought to have breaks and holidays, but these 'need to be thought of in terms of the family and not from the viewpoint of the individual member of the family group'. In short, 'what is really involved is a new set of values which will allow women to take their proper place in society, as mothers, workers and citizens'.[61]

In the aspirations of 1945 progressivism, women in production would work on the same terms as men: women at home – mothers – would pull their weight within 'the community', that de-classed terrain of pure sociability. Fabian social-democratic idealism, including its feminism, effectively collapsed sexual difference into a brisk citizenship, trampling over the solid intricacies of both class and gender; except in the case of maternity, where it fell in with the tenets of a broad pronatalism, liberally understood.

The responses of other self-declared feminist and women's labour organisations to the emphasis on 'the mother' and the anxieties about a dwindling British population were diverse, stemming in part from their different prewar political histories and forms of agitation. In these histories lie answers to the question which strikes post-1968 feminism: why was pronatalism not roundly and universally rejected *as such*, as inimical to the 'interests' of women?

Immediately after the war, there was no unified and dominant single feminist politics: not only in the sense in which there never is, but as evidenced by a proliferation of small groups whose objectives often coincided and so raise questions about why they did not, or could not, unite. There was no single stance of feminism in relation to women's labour organisations and political groupings: and no simple opposition of 'bourgeois feminism' to a feminism which understood women's work needs, either. The difficulty now is getting a sense of the relative weights and impact of the myriad groups which existed as diverse heirs of the feminist tradition at the end of the war. No one vigorous feminist platform was there to take up the half-revealed senses of unhappiness with the terms of women's wartime involvement, although some issues – most strikingly the Government's intentions to award a lower rate of compensation to women disabled through war injuries[62] – aroused an anger which might have inspired a coherent feminism in other conditions.

Instead, the literature of the many women's organisations gives the impression that feminism as a political philosophy was associated with the 'sex antagonism' of an older generation which had mercifully been outgrown: it was acceptable as an adjunct to achieving legislative and social 'equality' for women – for filling out the promises of social democracy between the sexes. The groups which, at the end of the war, stood for 'equality' concentrated on pursuing single issues, often through parliamentary lobbying, to the exclusion of a feminism with any spirit at the level of a broad theory. In so far as war conditions revived potential feminist thought, this was often held to be an ambiguous development: the socialist writer Margaret Goldsmith, in *Women at War* said,

The older women in Parliament and elsewhere have again become feminists, and feminism . . . is rearing its head again. Whether this indeed implies progress or retrogression is another matter . . . it seems a pity that the feminist issue has not been finally settled before 1939 or during the war. For the fact remains that 'feminism' will have a very real meaning until there is real equality between the sexes.[63]

Feminism as a philosophy was, at the end of the war, understood as only transitionally necessary: its function was to keep a vigilant check on the rate at which equality was being achieved.

Those groups, avowedly feminist or not, still extant in 1945 and dedicated to the pursuit of equality included the Married Women's Association, founded in 1938, which included a demand for the joint ownership of home and income in marriage, the National Women Citizen's Association, St Joan's Social and Political Alliance, a Catholic women's organisation for 'the practical application of the Christian principle of equality between the sexes', the Women for Westminster Movement, the Women's Freedom League, the Open

Door Council, the Six-Point Group, founded in 1918 to battle for equality on the six fronts of the political, occupational, moral, social, economic and legal, the National Union of Women Teachers, the Housewives' League, the National Association of Women Civil Servants, and the Association for Moral and Social Hygiene, founded in 1870 by Josephine Butler for the reform of the laws on prostitution. This list is far from exhaustive, and doesn't convey the high overlap in the aims of these organisations: the Status of Women Committee was formed after the war as an umbrella organisation for many of them. What's needed to clarify the history of British feminism is an account of the fragmentation of these groups, and starts are being made on this front.[64]

One wartime organisation attacked the sexually neutral category of 'the citizen', so dear to Fabians, by demanding that it should be implemented in a full, non-gender-discriminating way. The Women's Publicity Planning Association was formed in 1943 to back the Equal Citizenship (Blanket) Bill, the inspiration of Dorothy Evans, a feminist and former member of the Women's Social and Political Union. The idea was a once-and-for-all equal-opportunities sweep across the legislative board: hence 'Blanket'. A three-clause draft Bill, it aimed to make illegal all Parliamentary or Common Law Acts which contained any sex-based discrepancies: it included, for instance, the demands that income sharing between husband and wife be mandatory, and that factory 'protection' be extended to men too. It had the support of the Six-Point Group and of prominent 'progressives' like C.E.M. Joad; a demonstration for it took place in July 1944 in Trafalgar Square, overshadowed by 'rain and flybombs'. However, the death of Dorothy Evans, later that year, caused the Bill to collapse at a point when she had been trying to get it sponsored by one of the parliamentary parties.[65]

Many of the women's political organisations in the 1940s were small and relied heavily on the energies of their few members. Few said anything directly on postwar population anxieties: the perspective of 'equality' was, indeed, not theoretically broad enough to let them. There is one notable exception here, but it is something of a maverick: the one self-declaredly feminist group which did oppose pronatalism was the Open Door International for the Economic

Emancipation of the Women Worker, an organisation which was an assembly of national Councils. The British section was founded in 1926 by Elizabeth Abbott and Chrystal MacMillan: Elizabeth Abbott, closely involved with the Association for Moral and Social Hygiene, was also the joint author of a pamphlet, 'The Woman Citizen and Social Security', which argued against Beveridge's proposals for married women as being discriminatory.[66] The aims of the Open Door International and its Councils were:

To secure that a woman shall be free to work and protected as a worker on the same terms as a man, and that legislation and regulations dealing with conditions and hours, payment, entry and training shall be based upon the nature of the work and not upon the sex of the worker: and to secure for a woman, irrespective of marriage and childbirth, the right at all times to decide whether or not she shall engage in paid work and to ensure that no legislation or regulations shall deprive her of this right.

The first International Conference in 1938 had carried a resolution from Denmark deprecating pronatalism as against the interests of women in the labour market, 'both in dictator states like Germany and Italy and in democratic states'. 'Progressive' versions of pronatalism, as in Scandinavia, were

stated to serve not only the promotion of a higher fertility, but at the same time to secure better social and moral conditions of family life and the safeguarding of motherhood. In spite of these good intentions the danger is facing us. Old prejudices and traditional views are still prevailing in this domain, so closely connected with the most conservative elements of society, marriage and motherhood.[67]

The next International Conference in 1948 reiterated its opposition to pronatalist moves as being in effect attacks on working women: it noted

that in certain countries propaganda for an increased population has been and is being carried on in a manner which is tending to lead to an action against the work of married women outside their home: and that the woman is being increasingly looked on not as an independent personality, a complete human being but rather as a medium for the production of children. The work of the housewife and mother is being presented in such a way as to persuade many women, contrary often to their real wishes, to remain in the home and to consider it and it alone their 'proper place'. . . . Such propaganda holds immense dangers for women of every class, particularly as regards educational, vocational, professional and technical opportunities: it will also militate against proper apprenticeship.[68]

The Open Door's policy was to refuse the 'protection of motherhood' ('someone makes a proposal to restrict women's work and calls it "protection". And this protection becomes a fetish') as being in practice antagonistic to the needs of women workers, especially where it was tied into population alarms. Instead it wished to maintain the principle of equal protection for all workers regardless of gender – 'we must demand the protection of men and boys'. One British conference delegate made a gender-inverted polemic out of this:

one reason why the population problem is becoming such a danger to the position of women [is that] it brings with it the tendency to look for the wrong causes for the decline of the birth rate and to impose one-sided restrictions called 'protection' on women workers as they are the 'mothers of the race', without equally protecting the men, quite forgetting their function as fathers of the race![69]

Maternity, according to the Open Door International, ought not to be treated as a gender-specific incapacity, for in practice, special conditions for working childbearing women forced them to a low standard of life, low wage rates and low nutrition, and thereby defeated their own object: it ought instead to be dealt with by sickness benefit, common to both sexes as a cover for a temporary inability to work which was divorced from gender, and therefore not spread over the rest of life.

The Open Door groups, active though they were as critics (particularly of the International Labour Organisation's reports on working women) and as publicists, were without the weight of the women's labour organisations: they were subject at times, too, to internal tensions about their class composition and professional bias. One speaker at a conference, Annie Taylor, 'felt there was still a cleavage between the intellectual and the industrial woman worker, and a desire to teach the woman worker how to spend her money': a point contested by others, including Maud White who commented, 'those members with more leisure should seek to help, not to instruct industrial working women'.[70]

Women's labour organisations, on the other hand, seized on the postwar pronatalist moment differently: they used it to further their own long-established concern for the conditions of the working-class mother, rather than attacking its abstract promotion of maternity. In the teeth of complaints about the falling birth rate and the dereliction of maternal duties, the Standing Joint Committee of Working Women's Organisations said bitterly, in their evidence to the Royal Commission on Population,

> In a period when nearly every section of workers was enjoying improved conditions through trade union and Parliamentary action, those who were engaged in the biggest single occupation in the country – that of working housewife and mother – began to buy a little leisure with the tin-opener and birth control. If this has led to unfortunate results for the community, the community must bear its blame for the neglect of the home.[71]

Forced, in the 1930s, into arguments about whether an idle addiction to tinned salmon on the part of working-class wives contributed to their malnutrition and maternal morbidity,[72] organisations like the Standing Joint Committee of Working Women's Industrial Organisations had insistently defended the needs of housewives as mothers. The long battle of women's labour groupings for the practical 'protection of motherhood' – for improved maternity services, access to hospital treatment and doctors, and birth control advice – appeared to coincide with the demands of a broad postwar pronatalism for raising the status of motherhood, even though this coincidence was more verbal and rhetorical than political in its nature. The reaction of women's labour groupings such as the Women's Co-operative Guild, the Conferences of Unions Catering for Women Workers, and the Labour Party advisory committees, was on the whole to object to pronatalism just in so far as this took the form of criticisms of working women, but to argue for the real needs of mothers in the home. They publicised their knowledge of the poverty which attended the invisibility of working-class mothers, especially in the depressed areas where women continued to suffer the conditions documented in, for instance, Margery Spring-Rice's *Working-Class Wives* of 1939.

The Standing Joint Committee of Working Women's Organisations illustrates this strategy in action. Chaired just after the war, by Florence Hancock of the TUC's General Council, and with members from the Co-op Guild, the unions, the Labour Party and the Fabian Society, it accepted, as did everyone, the dangers of a shrinking population, but seized the time in its 1946 leaflets to insist that mothers would not have more children unless their working conditions were improved. This it repeated to the Royal Commission on Equal Pay, as well as to the Royal Commission on Population. In its own pamphlet, 'Reports on Population Problems and Postwar Organisation in Private Domestic Employment', it said that 'the real issue' over the birth rate 'was one of confidence' in peacetime social and economic conditions. Confidence necessitated higher children's allowances, housing for bigger families, electric washing machines; the Standing Joint Committee had forwarded a memo in 1943 to the Dudley committee on *The Design and Equipment of Postwar Houses*. Like many, it hoped for the continuation of the British Restaurant principle, for nursery schools to relieve the housing stress, for children beyond the school-leaving age to receive grants to be able to stay on. Nonetheless, it vigorously dissented from social-democratic orthodoxy and conservative thought on the matter of motherhood classes in schools: 'We deprecate suggestions that are sometimes put forward for instruction in Parentcraft in schools, or even for allotting a considerable part of the school curriculum to such subjects as Housewifery.'[73] The social services, it held, should make it possible for a woman to choose freely either to stay at home with her family or to work – but not under economic compulsion. Both the male wage and female labour should be recognised as contributing to the home and so joint ownership should follow; maternity grants, labour-saving devices, leisure chances would together raise women's status. For the woman in the home 'is doing work which has a social value as great as that of much of the work done outside'.

This is where the Standing Joint Committee of Working

Women's Organisations withdrew from what it understood feminism to be:

Some of the earlier feminist propaganda, with its emphasis on equality in fields of work previously closed to women merely on grounds of sex, tended to perpetuate the idea that the work of a home and children is of less importance than work outside the home, a less eligible career than most others, and may have helped to influence some women against motherhood. This attitude was found chiefly in middle-class and professional groups and is probably less usual today than it was twenty-five years ago. Our working women's organisations have never accepted it, and, while insisting on the right of women to follow the work of their choice, they have worked for many years for a better status for the work of the wife and mother in the home.[74]

The trouble was that once 'feminism' became associated by women's labour organisations like the Standing Joint Committee of Working Women's Organisations with the single, childless and professionally ambitious bourgeoisie (however good the reasons for this association seemed to be) then feminism could not be used in the fight for better conditions for working-class mothers. And in the absence of a loud and visible confrontation by self-declared feminists *with* postwar pronatalism, the ground of concern for the mother was most publicly captured *by* pronatalism. Women's labour organisations were faced with the task of insisting on the differences between their old history of trying to improve the lives of working women and mothers, and the newer twists in postwar pronatalism. Class parity, democracy and humaneness were the most obvious grounds of appeal. But these concepts alone could not generate the bases for criticising the entrenched rhetoric of the family and the supposition of a rigid sexual division of labour which were part of pronatalism. Only a critical feminist political philosophy could have generated this impulse, and that was not, apparently, historically available.

Such an absence made it all the more possible for the verbal formulations of an intended socialist 'protection of motherhood' to coincide with pronatalist writings. Where women's labour organisations did polemically employ the housewife/worker analogy, there was the risk of obscuring the complicated needs of those women with children who did waged work, whether through need or choice. The effect of the universal stress on the Mother was to create two irreconcilable parties: the housewife-mother and the woman worker. The latter was implicitly desexed by the absence of any discussion after the war about childcare provision other than that which, turning on the needs of the industrial productivity drive, was apt to wither away as the demands of industry changed. Working women with children became an invisible category, overlooked from virtually all perspectives.

The simple assertion that mothers as such are workers, too, is always empty in that form. However radical a defence of the lives of working women it aims at, it is nevertheless prone to deeply conservative uses, especially at points when pronatalist alarm seeks to 'preserve the family' and 'protect motherhood' in a way which marks off 'the mother' as a separate species-being. On the other hand, it would be mistaken to stop at the assumption that an emphasis on the needs of mothers is irretrievably and solely reactionary because it serves to reinstate the Mother. It may well do this, and in 1945 it did. But 'needs', however transitional, are solid enough; if you as a woman are solely responsible for the household shopping, then you as a waged worker need time to do it. British pronatalism never in fact delivered the planned packages of relief to tired mothers, in or out of paid work. Had these packages arrived (and compare the situation of Germany in the 1930s, where pronatalist policies *were* enacted) they could have been exploited whatever their ideological provenance. For instance, if you need and are allotted a nursery place at a time when they are scarce, you rapidly take it, whether or not you get it on the grounds of being a 'deviant mother'. Needs are both real and highly subject to being 'ideologically' met: and the recipients' spirit of greeting provisions may well be far removed from the bestowers' aims.

Assessing the conservatism of social policies raises questions about what fixes social 'roles', and what erodes them. One way of putting the question about the period in Britain between 1945 and 1948 is to ask whether we are concerned with a potential transition, via the envisaged large-scale employment of women with children, to the dissolution of motherhood as a role, a profession in itself – a fresh twist on Engels' supposition in his *Origins of the Family* that women's entry into production would entail their emancipation. Or rather are we concerned with the advent of the mother as worker with exaggeratedly special needs, which thereby confirm her as the Mother and facilitate her easy disposability from the labour market?

This generates a further speculation: under what conditions might the employment of mothers act to loosen the category of 'being a mother' – instead of sharpening the distinction between housewife-mother and working woman to the detriment of both? Possible answers to that are: only if the employment of all women were universal, only in an economy in a rare state of desperation, long-term desperation, for any native labour (Soviet Russia at certain points comes to mind); or else that mirage of a society so profoundly committed to egalitarianism that it would pay for the social provisions needed, and furnish revisions about the sexual division of labour too. Short of these conditions, the employment in practice of only some women with children, and their ghettoisation on the labour market, can serve to maintain a deep and often damaging gulf between working women and mothers – a gulf subject to unpleasant shifts in real or imputed class alignment.

This is chillingly exemplified in a book influential among British progressives: Alva Myrdal's *Nation and Family* of 1945. Admired for its Swedish clear-headedness by several English pronatalists, including Eva Hubback, it is a great text for those addicted to conspiracy theories. It suggests that those women with low wages and several children should be 'enabled' to stay at home, supported by deliberately revived archaic opinion:

For these cases, typified in the charwoman, all the old reactionary concerns about the conflict between motherhood and wage earning ought to be mobilised . . . the greater the ability to pay for domestic work and the more personally desired the job is, the less opposition there ought to be to women combining their work with motherhood.[75]

Careers were for the well off. The situation in which, all other things remaining unchanged, only *some* mothers work lends itself with a fatal facility to the depiction of socially approved career women who buy their childcare, versus unskilled wage slaves who should, at best, be paid off to go home and be 'real mothers'. And when 'the way forward' for working mothers is caught, as was much feminist progressiveness of the 1940s, in the tendency to a rhetoric of 'marriage as teamwork', then the new approved family becomes exemplary for the new democracy. Alva Myrdal commented that pronatalist interests were best served by a reversal of the tactic of demanding the right to work for married women: instead, 'defending the right of the working woman to marry and have children becomes a protection of, and not a threat to family values.'[76] Greater official tolerance of the employment of married women would, she wrote, serve to discourage abortions and illegitimacy (when pregnancy would no longer entail loss of jobs) and extramarital affairs (since it would be possible to be openly married, and continue in paid work). The phenomenon of married women working, far from destroying the family, 'ultimately serves the truly conservative goals of protecting the formal marriage rites and facilitating childbearing for a growing group of women.'[77]

In an intelligently run social democracy, according to this writer, the goals of comradely marriages, employment for those who could afford it because they could buy private childcare and a higher birth rate could thus be harmoniously reconciled. This is a fair representation of the ambitions of English Fabian-directed social democracy immediately after the war. What was left unvoiced was any consideration of shifting the balance of the sexual division of labour in the home. Nor was class mentioned. Although smoothed out into the uniform blandness of 'the community' or 'society', the fact was that badly paid, unskilled working-class women were to be encouraged into full-time housewifery, while only better-paid women, who could afford to buy the services of others, would be sanctioned as part-time workers. That this was also an effective class division went unsaid. The 1946 Equal Pay Commission did not recommend the introduction of equal pay for manual workers, although the aim of the 1947 production drive was the recruitment of unskilled and semi-skilled women workers, including those with children into industry. As an effect of the ambitions of the social democrats of the family, certain mothers would be free to work and others would be free not to work: in the hopes of the Ministry of Labour, working-class mothers

187

would resume or go on working without any fresh provision of means, like nurseries, to help them do so.

It is this climate which makes intelligible the bland tone of Bowlby's popular writings, which never voice the matter of social class. Class had already been rendered invisible in writings about work and maternity from the end of the war onwards. On the question of whether the wartime employment of married women contributed to the advance of women as workers, the particular combination of the universal postwar pronatalism plus the undifferentiating tones of social democracy was deadly. For women were, rhetorically, both over-personified as mothers and desexed as workers. There was little to meet the practical needs of working mothers, although women with children did indeed gradually go out to unskilled and semiskilled light industrial work more and more. All this fitted in very well with the actual conditions and forms of women's work during the war years, where everything accentuated the sense of 'for the duration only'. Far from war work serving to revolutionise women's employment on any serious level, it was itself characterised as an exceptional and valiant effort, from which women could thankfully sink away in peacetime.

Psychology, history and reconstructions: problems

The process of redescription of the wartime 'experiences' got well underway by the mid-1950s. Sociological commentaries stated that women had freely withdrawn from paid work, despite the fact that such a withdrawal was neither 'free' nor neatly occurring anyway. Popular psychological writings, drawing on the supposed evidence of war nurseries, evoked the dangers of separating mothers and children while claiming that the experiences of war had proved a vindication of the emotional health of unified family life.[78] But references to the 'evidence' of evacuation and nurseries constituted a misleading history. Despite the hopes and retrospective claims made for the didactic value of the war experiences of mothers and children, the literature on it was limited. Appeals to the authority of the 'lessons of war' in fact hook up, as we have seen, with the established prewar body of European and American psychoanalytic work on the dangers of institutionalising children in orphanages and hospitals.[79] But the claim of the 1950s is for the irreducible evidence, derived from the 'facts' of the war years, of the dangers of women going out to work.

On the surface, the postwar literature of family sociopsychology that purports to draw on the experience of the war implies a series of smooth and rational transitions from psychological 'knowledge' to the practices of welfare policies, as if 'the state' acted on the family according to the dictates of child and maternal psychology, which had itself drawn on the evidence of the war years. But what actually happened was a constant mutual appealing from history to psychology and back, which resulted in a web of cross-reference. To take this as genuinely indicative of anything independently accurate would be misleading: what is needed instead is a means of understanding the construction and effects of that web.

The complication here is that the density of representations which we set about stripping down is, at the same time, both our inheritance from the 1950s and the means by which we form the questions which we turn back on the 1940s. For instance, in the question of the relation of the state to women and children, my approach was determined by attributions which it then turned out to be necessary to query. The legacy of a politics of socialism and feminism out of the late 1960s and 1970s is a set of suppositions about the standing of the state vis-à-vis the family – the idea, for example, that the postwar government used Bowlby's theory of 'maternal deprivation' to get British women out of their jobs and back into their kitchens. This received but inaccurate history, which has fuelled so much indignation among feminists over the collusion of science and state at the expense of women, has strengthened a picture of 'ideology' as more or less deliberately generated by the state – one which seemed able to claim the experiences of 1945 to 1947 as evidence for itself. The political attitudes which inspired that indignant curiosity were themselves necessarily founded on the same attributions which the 1950s had made about the 1940s, even if they were inverted in political tone. Undoing those attributions meant pulling apart some of the political axioms which had determined the questions in the first place: notably the assumption that you could start with a 'state' which 'acted on the family' from above in a straightforward manner.

One move, tempting to make in reaction to the inaccuracies of attributions about 'the experience of the war' and what it showed about 'the need for family life', is to use the same evidence for opposite ends. So, for example, one could take women's responses to the surveys for the Ministry of Reconstruction and Labour (mentioned in chapter 5) and reinterpret them, rereading them so as to make them 'really' speak as one would prefer, picking up ambiguities and hesitations in women's replies and thus recapturing them for one's own side, drawing them across the line to rejoin 'us' where they really always were. This enticing enterprise can be helped along, too, by a seemingly 'materialist' method of working – that is, by answering questions about why, for instance, many younger women cheerfully anticipated abandoning work for marriage, by pointing out all the practical conditions which surrounded their anticipation. One could describe the uninviting nature of the available work, the low degree of skill and unionisation, and the weight of the prospect of untrained years in the factory, offset by hope in the saving grace of marriage. Or one could even sidestep by commenting that really after all women did not withdraw from work anyway.

This sort of 'materialist' tack is a necessary one; some version of it is an essential starting point, but only if it is used in full recognition of its risks and limits. The anxiety I've felt about using it to undermine the surface obviousness of a response from 1945 like, 'I shan't want to work when I'm married,' lies in the inadequacy of its approach to the question of why and how people produce particular formulations about what they want (the considerations which, for example, the Italian historian Luisa Passerini discusses in her 'Work, Ideology and Consensus under Italian Fascism'); attitudes, behaviour, language, 'a sense of identity' and how these are susceptible to coercion.[80]

In the absence of a solution to these considerations, I've sensed my work oscillating between two explanatory models: the one of saying, 'Women really did want to work, they did want nurseries; if we read the responses to these flat questionnaires correctly, we can surely decipher these wishes; or we can uncover the buried evidence of meetings, demonstrations and petitions to reveal their wants.' And the second of saying, 'Well, no wonder women were, on the whole, indifferent: what else, given these political conditions and these circumstances of work, could these women have done in 1945?' Both these explanatory models carry a certain amount of truth: but the truth can't comfortably be thus divided without being at risk of tearing apart. And it does seem to be divided; not because it's not possible to reconcile these paradigms in the abstract, but because in practice they stand for and attract other attitudes.

On the one hand, the attempt to uncover real wishes can slip into presuming a clear and well-formed set of wants – of a 'progressive' cast at that – so that the struggle is to read correctly responses from the past, between the lines even, and give them a framework in which they can speak out unambiguously; as in the supposition that if you could only put the right questions to women industrial workers in 1945 about their work aims, then they would speak truly, demonstrating through their dissatisfactions their latent socialist consciousness. But the trouble with the attempt to lay bare the red heart of truth beneath the discolourations and encrustations of thirty-odd years on, is that it assumes a clear space out of which voices can speak – as if, that is, ascertaining 'consciousness' stopped at scraping off history. That is not, of course, to discredit what people say as such, or to imply that considering the expression of wants is pointless. The difficulty is that needs and wants are never pure and undetermined in such a way that they could be fully revealed, to shine out with an absolute clarity, by stripping away a patina of historical postscripts and rewritings.

But, on the other hand, some kinds of materialist explanation which skip the search for the nature of true need in favour of pragmatic accounts of the apparent conservatism of people's behaviour have serious deficiencies too. Explanations of the form, 'what else under these actually obtaining circumstances could people have done', are essential but incomplete, because they have nothing to say about desires, hesitations, cynicism, or self-conceptions on the part of the historical actors. Because of this silence, even explicitly and polemically socialist forms of this materialist approach invite in neighbours they wouldn't care for. The theory of collusion, for instance

– exemplified at its simplest in 'women collude in their own oppression' – presents explanatory shortcuts of a dangerously psychologising kind. It's this kind of theory which can rush in with the air of filling the gaps left in those pragmatic materialist accounts which fight shy of considering why people 'act against their own interest'.

Versions of this collusion idea are occasionally raised as a refusal of the 'heroinisation' of women and as an insistence that women will only step into history if allowed to be fully marked by their culpability, which then has to be accounted for. The Italian Marxist writer, Marie-Antonietta Macciocchi, does this in her 'Female Sexuality in Fascist Ideology',[81] where she treats the question of a seemingly gender-privileged 'consent' to fascism by Italian women. It might be thought that these suppositions could be contested by a materialist account, yet most materialisms tacitly support them by keeping quiet themselves about the fuller complexities of human actions: for instance, socialist versions of the 'home as refuge from the harsh world' school of apologetics might describe periods of retrenchment and the conservatising of daily life, as in post-Bolshevik Russia or National Socialist Germany, as inevitable given the rigorous material conditions of the time. Doing so, they are, with the best of intentions, and with the sanction of Trotsky in *The Revolution Betrayed*,[82] acting as kindly variants of collusion theory. They seek to let people off from the charge of having 'reactionary' desires to go back to the warm privacy of the home, by redescribing them as materially based. For accusation, materialism is substituted, and an imaginative and sensitive materialism at that.

But the generosity of materialist pragmatics here is premature: its kindness can serve to mask the possibilities of real dissent, real resistances, voiced or not, on the part of those whose behaviour it seeks to excuse. It forgets that desires can be contradictory; and forgets, too, that 'the home' can hardly constitute a refuge for those who were always there, as providers and housekeepers and childcarers, at the heart of it anyway. It has nothing new to say to the problem of an apparent 'consent' to a reactionary social order. Instead it merely *writes all over it* – it covers it with elaborate descriptions of the historical details of how people acted. Ignoring the problems of why they acted, it leaves the way open for theories of collusion to be tacked, not inharmoniously, on.

I can only suggest that, to a materialist-realist explanation of seemingly conservative drifts in domestic organisation, two further steps could replace the home-as-refuge treatment. The first would be the refusal to take 'the family' as a unitary object for investigation. The second would be an attempt to examine the exact nature of the gaps at particular times, between, say,

> psychology: social policy
> social policy: social practices
> propaganda: people's behaviour
> policies: their enactment: people's acceptance.

Each of the colons in this sample list marks a point where derivation is conventionally claimed or assumed: policy flowing into practice, for example. But social practice cannot necessarily be read off from social policy, or even social consent from social practice. The whole range of speeches, articles, broadcasts to 'the family' does not guarantee any acceptance on, let alone a full complicity with, such notions of the part of their targets. Pronatalist rhetoric may flourish, and the birth rate may rise; but the former may not have brought about the latter.

'The feminine sex,' wrote Alva Myrdal, 'is a social problem.'[83] The dilemma is that of understanding social-sexual difference in 'progressive' or conservative ways: as transitionally produced and so susceptible to change; or as essential, guaranteed for all time. Human needs, too, can be understood as the volatile products of a complexity of production, speech, desires, consumption; or as the fixed products of social roles which generate them. One effect of the fixing and freezing of the Mother as a social category is to create an inflexible notion of needs as well to accompany this social role. So a double social-sexual fixity is set up.

There is no clear theory of need available to us. The insistence on the historically produced nature of needs in Marx is neither specific to Marxism nor enough to constitute a theory. I've said that people's needs obviously can't be revealed by a simple process of historical unveiling, while elsewhere I've talked about the 'real needs' of mothers myself. I take it that it's necessary both to stress the non-self-evident nature of need and the intricacies of its determinants, and also to act politically as if needs could be met, or at least met halfway.[84] The benign if traditionally unimaginative face of 'socialist planning', is, at the least, preferable to its known alternatives, however much its objects will always tend to be in excess of it and slip away.

And, once on the terrain of family policies, socialist feminism will have to search for an understanding of need; this cannot be fully supplied by a kind of Fabian sociological thermometer for measuring, for example, the needs of mothers for nurseries. Nor, though, can needs be given transcendentally, to be fulfilled under some hypothetical communism of plenitude. For human needs may not be witnesses to the demands of some eternal human nature – but nor can they be expected to settle down to some final satisfiable form under a transformed mode of production. Yet once that unsatisfactory vision is rejected as exemplifying the 'sterility' of Marxism, the wish for something better, for some truly humane yet still specifically socialist good-heartedness, may well light on the old search for a 'socialist psychology'. But this is a doubtful goal; psychology cannot stand as a self-evident home of the humane (or for that matter the inhumane) fit to be translated into socialism by receiving new objectives, but otherwise keeping much as it is.

Such worries about what needs *are* does not mean that nothing can be done. For instance, even though it is true that arguing for adequate childcare as one obvious way of meeting the needs of mothers does suppose an orthodox division of labour, in which responsibility for children is the province of women and not of men, nevertheless this division is what, by and large, actually obtains. Recognition of that in no way commits you to supposing that the care of children is fixed eternally as female. What conclusions, of use for qualifying that supposition, might the narrative of the postwar government, of psychological theories and and their languages yield?

Because the task of illuminating 'the needs of mothers' starts out with gender at its most decisive and inescapable point – the biological capacity to bear children – there's the danger that it may

194

fall back into a conservative restating and confirming of social-sexual difference as timeless too. This would entail making the needs of mothers into fixed properties of 'motherhood' as a social function: I believe this is what happened in postwar Britain. Understanding social-sexual difference entails being alert to the real effects of existing differences, which must be acknowledged as effects – instead of being prematurely absorbed into neutral categories like 'citizenship'. Such categories, because they are systematically indifferent to gender, guarantee a return of that dominant order, the masculine, about which they are silent.[85] And, on the other hand, taking social-sexual difference as something essential and to be celebrated can be equally misconceived – whether from the standpoint of the chauvinistic 'vive la différence', or of certain versions of feminism.

In the last war, women as workers and women as reproductive social beings were understood in the most conservative ways. Women's war work, even in presentations of their collective heroic capacities, was work done by *women*, marked through and through by the gender of its performers, and consequently by the especial temporariness of the work of women who were mothers.

In some obvious ways, all this weighting on gender is unsurprising. Only at an exceptional point of demand for all possible labour – the war economy – were all women, regardless of their reproductive status, made publicly visible as workers. But what could abstractly have been the moment to seize and push through the logic of sexual difference – through to the proper provision of child-care facilities and working conditions – was concretely impossible. Everything about the employment of married women in industry militated against their being taken seriously as real workers: by 1945 the dominant rhetoric held out an opposition between the mother and the woman worker.

The postwar collapse of the war nurseries only underlined the 'special nature' of temporary concessions to working mothers. The coincidence of pronatalism with the end of the war intensified the 'facts' that all women were mothers or potential mothers, that all women were marriage-prone, that no-one had children who was not married. Hence two marginal presences: the spinster, an isolated

195

professional woman who might utterly legitimately work and who deserved equal pay; and the unmarried mother, who resurfaces in the psychosociology of the early 1950s as 'pathologically disturbed'. While it was 'transitionally' necessary to insist on better conditions of housing and money in which to have children in 1945, the coincidence of this with the prominent rhetoric of the 'value of motherhood' blurred the needs of mothers with the essence of maternity in a way fatal for any real approach to the meeting of need.

This universal concentration on a synthetically conceived mother did everything to secure a psychology which also had a life as a loose, yet deeply pervasive social philosophy – a philosophy whose influences remain. One of its legacies has been a transparently conservative account of motherhood, contested by women's liberation. My conviction is that, over and beyond this, there can be no version of 'motherhood' *as such* which can be deployed to construct a radical politics. The apparent validation of 'motherhood' by a particular psychoanalytic tendency, Kleinian or other, cannot be hailed as a guarantee of that tendency's kinship to feminism, in the name of respecting female creativity, or female 'power'. Great intricacies are wrapped up in the bland package labelled 'motherhood'; stubborn and delicate histories, wants and attributions are concealed in it. To overlook these and to let a strong separation between women and mothers set in again would only repeat the unhappy developments which these chapters have outlined.

Notes

Chapter 2   Developmental Psychology, Biology and the Social

1. Politzer, *La Crise de la psychologie contemporaine*, p. 150.
2. Marx, Introduction to the *Grundrisse*, pp. 83, 84, 85.
3. See Marx, *Grundrisse*, pp. 496, 485.
4. See Schaffer, *The Growth of Sociability*, pp. 81–105, for his discussion of 'The Familiarization Process'.
5. Trevarthen and Murray, 'The Nature of an Infant's Ecology'.
6. Ainsworth, Bell and Stayton, 'Infant-Mother Attachment and Social Development', pp. 99–135.
7. Friedlander, 'Receptive Language Development in Infant Issues and Problems', pp. 7–15.
8. Harré, 'Conditions for a Social Psychology of Childhood', pp. 245–62; Shotter, 'The Development of Personal Powers', pp. 215–44.
9. Berger and Luckmann, *The Social Construction of Reality*.
10. Shotter, 'What Is It to Be Human?', pp. 53–71, 68.
11. Compare the discussion by R. S. Peters on 'The Aims of Education – A Conceptual Inquiry', *The Philosophy of Education*, pp. 11–57.
12. Hampshire, *Thought and Action*, p. 99.
13. Schaffer, *The Growth of Sociability*, p. 107.
14. *Ibid.*, pp. 13–14.
15. *Ibid.*, p. 18.
16. *Ibid.*, p. 19.
17. *Ibid.*, p. 33.
18. *Ibid.*, pp. 37–8.

19. *Ibid.*, p. 14. His reference here is to William James's remark in *Principles of Psychology*, USA, 1890: 'The baby, assailed by eyes, ears, nose, skin and entrails all at once, feels it all as one great booming, buzzing confusion'.

20. Fantz's papers include (see Bibliography) 'The origin of form perception', 'Visual perception from birth as shown by pattern selectivity' and 'Pattern discrimination and selective attention as determinants of perceptual development from birth'.

21. See discussion in Schaffer, *op. cit.*, pp. 43–8.

22. See, for example, Gewirtz, 'Deprivation and Satiation of Social Stimuli as Determinants of their Reinforcing Efficacy' and 'Mechanisms of Social Learning: Some Roles of Stimulation and Behavior in Early Human Development'.

23. See, for example, the contributions to *Before Speech: the Beginning of Interpersonal Communication*, ed. M. Bullowa, including Trevarthen, pp. 321–47, and Chappell and Sander, pp. 89–109.

24. Trevarthen and Murray, *op. cit.*

25. See Bruner, 'The Ontogenesis of Speech Acts' and 'From Communication to Language: A Psychological Perspective'. For the idea of communicative competence, see Ainsworth and Bell, 'Mother-Infant Interaction and the Development of Competence'.

26. See Hughes *et al.*, *Nurseries Now: a Fair Deal for Parents and Children*; and the Oxford PreSchool Research Project Series, including Bruner, *Under Five in Britain*.

27. Sève, *Man in Marxist Theory and the Psychology of Personality*, pp. 9–60, (37).

28. See Werskey, *The Visible College*, for an account of British Marxist scientists before the last war.

29. Zavodovsky, 'The "Physical" and the "Biological" in the process of organic evolution', pp. 69–94, 70, and the introduction to the second edition of *Science at the Crossroads*, P. G. Werskey.

30. Zavodovsky, p. 76.

31. *Ibid.*, p. 77.

32. *Ibid.*, p. 80.

33. See also Piaget, *Biology and Knowledge*, chap. 3, p. 70, for a call to a different 'multi-disciplinary' method.

34. Rose, H. and Rose, S., 'Ideology in Neurobiology'.

35. *Ibid.*

36. Merleau-Ponty, *The Phenomenology of Perception*; McMurray, *Persons in Relation*.

37. Kate Soper has formulated a similar concept of 'social biology' in her chapter 'Marxism, Materialism and Biology', *Issues in Marxist Philosophy*.

38. See Merleau-Ponty, *op. cit.*, especially chapters 5 and 6.

39. Althusser, *For Marx*, p. 243.

40. Balibar, in Althusser and Balibar, 'The Elements of the Structure and their History', *Reading Capital*, pp. 247–53.

41. Brim and Wheeler, *Socialisation after Childhood*, p. 5.

42. Becker, *The Birth and Death of Meaning*, pp. 127–30.

43. This is discussed by Julia Kristeva in *La Révolution du langage poètique*, p. 114.

44. The main contribution here has been Juliet Mitchell's *Psychoanalysis and Feminism*; and see the continuing debates in periodicals like *Screen, m/f, Gay Left*.

45. See Castel's *Le Psychanalysme: l'ordre psychanalytique et le pouvoir* for a critique of French clinical practices; and the review of Castel's book by Colin Gordon in *Ideology and Consciousness*, 2, 1977, pp. 109–27.

46. See Reich, *What is Class Consciousness?* and *The Mass Psychology of Fascism*.

47. Juliet Mitchell's chapters on Reich, in *Psychoanalysis and Feminism*, pp. 137–223, are useful. For a recent attempt to analyse the 'appeal' of fascism, see Marie-Antonietta Macciocchi, 'Female Sexuality in Fascist Ideology' and the critique of this article by Jane Caplan.

48. See Reich, *Dialectical Materialism and Psychoanalysis* and Bernfeld, 'Psychoanalysis and Socialism'.

49. Reich, *Selected Sexpol Essays 1934–37*, p. 123.

50. Fromm, *The Crisis of Psychoanalysis*, p. 154.

51. Politzer, *La Crise de la psychologie contemporaine*; Sève, *Marxisme et théorie de la personnalité*.

52. Timpanaro, *On Materialism*, p. 58.

53. See review articles on Timpanaro by Raymond Williams in *New Left Review*, and by Kate Soper in *Radical Philosophy*; and see chapters in *Issues in Marxist Philosophy*, vol. 2. *Materialism*, edited by Mepham and Ruben.

54. Merleau-Ponty, *op. cit.*, p. 165.

Chapter 3   Child Psychologies in Europe and America

1.   Klein, *Envy and Gratitude*, p. 81.

2.   The point that empirical studies of infants were made before the last two decades of the nineteenth century is emphasised by Dennis, 'Historical Beginnings of Child Psychology'. Nonetheless, these are isolated 'examples' rather than any genre of work.

3.   Taine, *Mind*, pp. 252–7.

4.   Sully, *Cornhill Magazine*, pp. 539–54.

5.   Sully, *Studies of Childhood*, p. 18.

6.   *Ibid.*, pp. 16–17.

7.   Preyer, *Mental Development in the Child*, p. xix.

8.   *Ibid.*, pp. xv–xvi.

9.   *Ibid.*, pp. xvii-xviii.

10.   Including *Specielle Physiologie des Embryo*, a part of which is translated by Coghill as 'Embryonic Motility and Sensitivity'.

11.   Preyer, *op. cit.*, p. 29.

12.   Sully, *Outlines of Psychology*, pp. 1–17.

13.   Lewes, *Mind*, pp. 278–9. *Mind*, true to its own byline, carried frequent discussions on the relations between psychology and philosophy: for example, an 1883 editorial, 'Psychology and Philosophy' by Croom Robertson, debated the English versus the Kantian epistemological traditions as they bore on this question.

14.   But see Sully, *Outlines of Psychology*, p. 70, for a critical note to Galton's work on twins.

15.   Galton, *English Men of Science*, pp. 12–13.

16.   *Ibid.*, p. 16.

17.   *Ibid.*, pp. 258–9.

18.   Galton, *Hereditary Genius*, p. 343.

19.   Roback in the *Journal of Applied Psychology* stressed the intimate link between a profession like medicine and social reform movements; and, as an analogy in his critique of Munsterberg, points out that 'whatever benefits the working man should reap by the efforts of psychology to perfect the industrial efficiency system, the advantage accruing to him would be indirect, while the employer is gaining a net profit out of the psychologist's findings and management'.

20. By Kirkpatrick, 1903, reviewed, in *Mind*, vol. xiii, pp. 569–71 by Edgar.

21. *Mind*, vol. xiii, p. 569.

22. *Mind*, vol. xiii, p. 570.

23. Kirkpatrick, *Fundamentals of Child Study*, p. 10.

24. Baldwin, *Mental Development in the Child and the Race*, p. 365.

25. Baldwin, *Social and Ethical Interpretations in Mental Development*, p. 24.

26. *Ibid.*, p. 18.

27. *Ibid.*, pp. 21–2: 'The only way to get a solid basis for social theory based on human want or desire, is to work out first a descriptive and genetic psychology of desire in its social aspects; and . . . the only way to get an adequate psychological view of the rise and development of desire in its social aspects is by a patient tracing of the conditions of social environment in which the child and the race have lived and which they have grown up to reflect'.

28. Stern, *Psychology of Early Childhood*, p. 12.

29. *Ibid.*, p. 9, and see pp. 14, 38.

30. *Ibid.*, p. 14.

31. *Ibid.*, p. 37.

32. *Ibid.*, p. 33.

33. *Ibid.*, pp. 33–4.

34. See Jay, *The Dialectical Imagination*, chap. 1.

35. *Ibid.*, p. 219.

36. *Ibid.*, pp. 103–6, p. 227, and see Adorno, 'Social Science and Sociological Tendencies in Psychoanalysis', and 'Sociology and Psychology', p. 95.

37. Horkheimer, *Critical Theory*, p. 109.

38. *Ibid.*, p. 128.

39. Laplanche and Pontalis, *The Language of Psychoanalysis*, p. 139.

40. Sigmund Freud, 'Analysis of a Phobia in a Five-Year-Old Boy', p. 5.

41. See Kern, 'Freud and the Birth of Child Psychiatry', pp. 360–68.

42. Charcot, *Leçons sur les maladies du système nerveux*.

43. See Ernest Jones, *The Life and Work of Sigmund Freud*, pp. 342–9.

44. See Quen, 'Asylum Psychiatry, Neurology, Social Work and Mental Hygiene', p. 10.

45. Watson, 'Psychology as the Behaviourist Views It', p. 169.

46. Gesell and Thompson, *Infant Behaviour*, p. 333.
47. See Bibliography for these writers.
48. Róheim, *Psychoanalysis and the Social Sciences*, p. 7.
49. See Bibliography for these articles: their authors are, respectively, Silberpfennig, La Barre, Kris and Leites, Sterba, and Gorer.
50. Kris and Leites, 'Trends in Twentieth-Century Propaganda', p. 408.
51. Freud, *Moses and Monotheism*, pp. 99–100.
52. In Róheim, *Psychoanalysis and the Social Sciences*, pp. 9–33.
53. Sève, *Man in Marxist Theory and the Psychology of Personality*, pp. 231–53.
54. Kardiner, *The Individual and His Society*, p. 372.
55. *Ibid.*, p. 387.
56. *Ibid.*, pp. 126–34, for a discussion of 'basic personality structure'.
57. See Linton, *The Study of Man* and *The Cultural Background of Personality*.
58. Kluckhohn and Leighton, 'Some Aspects of Navaho Infancy and Early Childhood', pp. 40–41.
59. Kluckhohn and Leighton, 'Some Aspects', p. 41.
60. *Ibid.*, p. 67.
61. *Ibid.*, pp. 85–6.
62. Erikson, 'Childhood and Tradition in Two American-Indian Tribes', pp. 319–20.
63. *Ibid.*, p. 321.
64. *Ibid.*, pp. 323–4.
65. *Ibid.*, p. 327.
66. *Ibid.*, p. 337.
67. *Ibid.*, p. 344.
68. *Ibid.*, p. 350.
69. *Ibid.*, p. 350.
70. See Russell Jacoby, *Social Amnesia*, for a critical history of 'conformist psychology' in America.
71. Erikson, 'Childhood and Tradition', p. 350.
72. Hartmann, 'Ich-Psychologie und Anpassungsprobleme', p. 128.
73. Mead, 'Research on Primitive Children', p. 735.
74. See account by Rosalind Coward, 'On the Universality of the Oedipus Complex'.

75. Mead, 'Research on Primitive Children', p. 742.

76. Mead, *Childhood in Contemporary Cultures*, p. vii.

77. Hartmann, 'Psychoanalysis and Developmental Psychology', p. 17.

78. See, for example, Margaret Fries, 'An Integrated Health Plan'.

79. Hartmann and Kris, 'The Genetic Approach in Psychoanalysis', p. 13.

80. Anna Freud, *The Psycho-Analytic Treatment of Children*, pp. 3–52.

81. *Ibid.*, Preface, p. x.

82. *Ibid.*, p. 55.

83. *Ibid.*, p. 36.

84. *Ibid.*, p. 42.

85. *Ibid.*, p. 52.

86. Sigmund Freud, *The Ego and the Id*, p. 3.

87. See Laplanche and Pontalis, *op. cit.*, pp. 282–7.

88. Klein, 'The Development of a Child', pp. 1–53, and see discussion in 'Explanatory Notes' to *Love, Guilt, and Reparation*, p. 420.

89. Klein, 'Early Stages of the Oedipus Conflict', p. 186.

90. *Ibid.*, pp. 187–8.

91. Klein, 'The Early Development of Conscience in the Child', p. 257.

92. Klein, 'On Observing the Behaviour of Young Infants', p. 244.

93. Laplanche and Pontalis, *op. cit.*, pp. 314–19.

94. Klein, 'On Observing the Behaviour of Young Infants', p. 242.

95. Klein, *Envy and Gratitude*, p. 14, p. 81.

96. *Ibid.*, p. 15.

97. *Ibid.*, p. 82.

98. *Ibid.*, p. 83.

99. *Ibid.*, p. 3.

100. See the references to Abrahams in Jones, *The Life and Work of Sigmund Freud*.

101. Jones, *The Life and Work of Sigmund Freud*, p. 576, pp. 586–7.

102. Anna Freud, *The Psycho-Analytic Treatment of Children*, Preface, p. ix.

103. Glover, 'Examination of the Klein System of Child Psychology', p. 90.

104. *Ibid.*, pp. 116–17.

105. *Ibid.*, p. 91.

106. *Ibid.*, p. 92.

107.   Kris, 'Development and Problems of Child Psychology', p. 30.

108.   Hartmann, *op. cit.*, p. 17.

Chapter 4   The 'Popularisation' of Psychoanalysis and Psychology in Britain

1.   Reich, *Dialectical Materialism and Psychoanalysis*, p. 52.

2.   Forrester, *Language and the Origins of Psychoanalysis*, p. 91.

3.   Bowlby, 'Psychoanalysis and Child Care', p. 56.

4.   Winnicott, 'A Personal View of the Kleinian Contribution', p. 171.

5.   *Ibid.*, p. 172.

6.   Winnicott, 'Appetite and Emotional Disorder', p. 51.

7.   Winnicott, 'A Personal View of the Kleinian Contribution', pp. 175, 178.

8.   *Ibid.*, p. 177.

9.   Winnicott, 'On the Contribution of Direct Child Observation to Psychoanalysis', p. 111.

10.   *Ibid.*, p. 114.

11.   Winnicott, 'A Personal View of the Kleinian Contribution', p. 177.

12.   Winnicott, 'The Theory of the Parent-Infant Relationship', p. 39.

13.   Winnicott, 'Classification: Is There a Psychoanalytic Contribution to Psychiatric Classification?', p. 126.

14.   Winnicott, 'A Personal View of the Kleinian Contribution', p. 114.

15.   Winnicott, 'Psychoanalysis and the Sense of Guilt', p. 25.

16.   Mitchell, *Psychoanalysis and Feminism*, pp. 228–9.

17.   Including *Intellectual Growth in Young Children* (1930) and *The Social Development of Children* (1933).

18.   Ribble, *The Rights of Infants*, p. 141.

19.   *Ibid.*, p. 100.

20.   *Ibid.*, p. 144.

21.   Winnicott, 'What About Father?', p. 12.

22.   *Ibid.*, p. 2.

23.   *Ibid.*, p. 12.

24.   Winnicott, 'Why Do Babies Cry?', p. 6.

25.   *Ibid.*, p. 7.

26.   *Ibid.*, p. 16.

27.   Winnicott, 'Their Standards and Yours', pp. 13–14.

28. Winnicott, 'The Deprived Mother', p. 64.

29. *Ibid.*, p. 67.

30. For instance, Barbara Law, 'The Homesick Child' and Susan Isaacs, 'The Uprooted Child'.

31. Mitchell, *op. cit.*, p. 229.

32. *Ibid.*, p. 231.

33. As in, 'The Influence of Early Environment in the Development of Neurosis and Neurotic Character'. And see Freud's family references in *New Introductory Lectures*, 1933.

34. These include Barbara Wootton, 'Theories of the Effects of Maternal Separation or Deprivation', *Social Science and Social Pathology*, and Michael Rutter, *Maternal Deprivation Reassessed*.

35. See, for instance, Lee Comer's *Wedlocked Women*, and Elizabeth Wilson, *Women and the Welfare State*, for a critical approach to this supposition, pp. 64–5.

36. Bowlby and Durbin, *War and Democracy*, p. 3.

37. *Ibid.*, p. 36.

38. *Ibid.*, pp. 51–2.

39. *Ibid.*, p. 149. See also p. 133, 'The Persecution of German Jews by National Socialists Now Belongs to History'.

40. Bowlby, *Personality and Mental Illness*, pp. 190, 194.

41. Bowlby, 'The Influence of Early Environment in the Development of Neurosis and Neurotic Character', p. 154.

42. *Ibid.*, p. 155.

43. *Ibid.*, p. 178.

44. See Laing, *The Divided Self*, and Laing and Esterson, *Sanity, Madness and the Family;* also Laplanche and Pontalis, *The Language of Psychoanalysis*, p. 160. For an appraisal and critique of Laing's work see *R. D. Laing* by Andrew Collier.

45. Bowlby, 'The Influence of Early Environment', p. 175.

46. *Ibid.*, p. 177.

47. Bowlby, 'The Problem of the Young Child', *The New Era*, p. 62.

48. *Ibid.*, p. 60.

49. *Ibid.*, p. 62.

50. Rickman, *The New Era*, p. 53.

51. *Ibid.*, p. 54.

52. Bowlby, *Evacuation Survey*, p. 189.

53. *Ibid.*, p. 190.

54. See notes 34 and 35 above.

55. In *International Journal of Psycho-Analysis*, vol. xxv, 1944, pp. 19–53, 107–28.

56. Bowlby, *Forty-Four Juvenile Thieves*, Preface, not paginated.

57. *Ibid.*, p. 55.

58. Bowlby, *Maternal Care and Mental Health*, Preface, p. 6.

59. Bowlby, *Maternal Care*, pp. 15–62.

60. *Ibid.*, p. 6.

61. *Ibid.*, p. 46.

62. Compare, for example, Wilhelm Preyer's work on embryology and sensitivity at the foetal period, discussed in Chapter 1 above.

63. Bowlby, *Maternal Care*, pp. 13–14.

64. *Ibid.*, p. 59.

65. *Ibid.*, p. 61.

66. *Ibid.*, p. 62.

67. *Ibid.*, p. 68.

68. *Ibid.*, p. 68.

69. *Ibid.*, p. 69.

70. *Ibid.*, p. 71.

71. See Rosemary Dinnage, 'John Bowlby', *New Society*, 10 May 1979.

72. Bowlby, *Child Care and The Growth of Love*, p. 61.

73. See the discussion by Laplanche and Pontalis, *The Language of Psycho-analysis*, pp. 214–17.

74. Bowlby, *Discussions on Child Development*, p. 182.

75. *New Society*, 10 May 1979, pp. 323–5.

76. Bowlby, *Discussions on Child Development*, pp. 26–7.

77. *Ibid.*, p. 185.

78. Bowlby, 'The Nature of the Child's Tie to His Mother', p 358.

79. Freud, 'Instincts and their Vicissitudes', p. 124.

80. Bowlby, 'The Nature of the Child's Tie', p. 361.

81. *Ibid.*, p. 364.

82. *Ibid.*, p. 364.

83. *Ibid.*, p. 365.

84. *Ibid.*, p. 365.

85. *Ibid.*, p. 369.

86. Robert Hinde, 'Changes in Responsiveness to a Constant

Stimulus', *British Journal of Animal Behaviour*, 2, pp. 41–5.

87. Bowlby, 'The Nature of the Child's Tie', p. 367.

88. Bowlby, *Psychoanalysis and Contemporary Thought*, p. 39.

89. *Ibid.*, p. 48.

90. Including 'Processes of Mourning' (1961) in *International Journal of Psycho-Analysis*, vol. 42, pp. 317–40.

91. See Wootton, *Social Science and Social Pathology*, p. 145.

92. *Ibid.*, pp. 151–2, 155.

93. See Juliet Mitchell, *op. cit.*, p. 295.

94. In the BBC radio series, 'The Formative Years'.

Chapter 5 Policies on War Nurseries: the Labour Market for Women

1.   *British Medical Journal*, 8 January 1944, vol. I, p. 50. Unsigned editorial, 'War in the Nursery'.

2.   World Health Organisation, Expert Committee on Mental Health, Report on the Second Session, p. 16.

3.   For the Medical Women's Federation reports, see the *British Medical Journal*, 17 August 1946, p. 217; and see M. McLaughlin, 'The Physical Health of Children Attending Day Nurseries', August 1946, pp. 591–4. See also *The Lancet*, October 1946, H. F. Menzies, 'Children in Day Nurseries', pp. 499–501, and H. Mackay, 'The Proper Place for Children', 3 July 1943, p. 21.

4.   Ferguson and Fitzgerald, *Studies in the Social Services*, p. 211.

5.   H. F. Menzies, 'Children in Day Nurseries', *The Lancet*, 5 October 1946, p. 499.

6.   H. Mackay, 'The Proper Place for Children', *The Lancet*, 3 July 1943, p. 21.

7.   See discussion in previous chapter; and see John Bowlby, *Maternal Care and Mental Health*, pp. 15–51.

8.   *British Medical Journal*, unsigned editorial, 'Loneliness in Infancy', 19 September 1942, vol. II, pp. 345.

9.   Marguerite Hughes, 'Mothers and Woman Power in Relation to Nurseries, Foster Mothers and Daily Minders', *Mother and Child*, August 1942, pp. 91–5.

10. *British Medical Journal*, 8 January 1944, vol. 1, p. 50.

11. Edited by Padley and Cole, and containing a contribution on 'Psychological Aspects' by John Bowlby.

12. Bruce, *The Coming of the Welfare State*, p. 270.

13. Burlingham and Freud, *Infants Without Families*, 1965 edition, pp. vii–ix.

14. Burlingham and Freud, *Infants Without Families*, (1944) p. vi.

15. World Health Organisation, Expert Committee on Mental Health, Report on Second Session, p. 16.

16. See Ferguson and Fitzgerald, *op cit.*, pp. 16–17.

17. See the files of the Ministry of Health in the Public Record Office – 'Arrangements for the Provision of Wartime Nurseries, 1941–42', PRO/MH 55/695.

18. See Ferguson and Fitzgerald *op. cit.*, p. 186.

19. PRO/MH 55/695.

20. See the files of the Ministry of Health in the Public Record Office, Kew; 'The Children of War Workers', 1941–42, PRO/MH 55/884.

21. 'Arrangements for the Provision of Wartime Day Nurseries 1941–42', PRO/MH 55/695.

22. PRO/MH 55/695.

23. Deputation on Nursery Provisions to the Ministers of Health and Education, PRO/HM 55/803.

24. Hansard, Commons Debates, *406*, column 1970, and columns 1356, 1966–7: Commons Debates, *408*, columns 368–9 and 2425–50.

25. The London Women's Parliament was linked with the London Council of the People's Convention and the Anglo-Russian solidarity campaign. It held three sessions from 1941–2, and sent a draft Bill on women's industrial conditions to Bevin, and composed others on nursing and civil defence training and conditions. It aimed to be a joint platform of women from factories, trade unions, political parties, housewives' groups, cooperative groups, and tenants' groups: between 1941 and 1942 it published three reports on its sessions, before apparently ceasing to function.

26. See discussions in the Reports of the Annual Conference of Representatives of Unions Catering for Women Workers, 1946 through to 1950: and see *Planning*, xv, no. 285, Employment of Women, 23 July 1948.

27. PRO/MH 55/803.

28. H. M. D. Parker, *Manpower*, pp. 482, 491, Tables 1b and vii of Statistical Appendix.

29. G. Thomas, 'Women at Work'.

30. E. Bowen, *The Heat of the Day*, p. 142.

31. Mass-Observation, *People in Production*, pp. 165–6.

32. *Ibid.*, pp. 134–5.

33. P. Inman, *Labour in the Munitions Industry*, pp. 352–67.

34. Mass-Observation, *People in Production*, p. 131.

35. Ministry of Labour, 'Women in Shipbuilding'.

36. Mass-Observation, *People in Production*, p. 189.

37. *Ibid.*, p. 232.

38. Absenteeism literature includes S. Wyatt *et al.*, *A Study of Certified Sickness Absence Among Women in Industry*, Medical Research Council, London 1945; *Why is She Away? The Problem of Sickness Among Women in Industry*, Industrial Health Research Board of the Medical Research Council, London, 1945; *A Study of Women in War Work in Four Factories*, Medical Research Council, London, 1945; *The War and Women's Employment*, International Labour Organisation, Montreal 1946.

39. Mass-Observation, *People in Production*, p. 230.

40. G. D. H. Cole, *The Intelligent Man's Guide to the Post-War World*, p. 586.

41. Mass-Observation, *People in Production*, p. 129.

42. See discussion of average wages in P. Inman, *Labour in the Munitions Industries*, and in the Labour Research Department pamphlet, 'Women in War Jobs'.

43. *Picture Post*, 30 March 1940, and 11 March 1944.

44. Labour Research Department, 'Women in War Jobs'.

45. National Conference of Women called by H. M. Government, Royal Albert Hall, 28 September 1943, Report of Proceedings, HMSO London 1943.

46. Quoted in Vera Douie, *The Lesser Half*, pp. 97–8.

47. *Ministry of Labour Gazette*, June 1947, p. 183.

48. Geoffrey Thomas, 'Women and Industry: an inquiry into the problem of recruiting women for industry, carried out for the Ministries of Labour and National Service', Social Survey Reports 104.

49.   *Ministry of Labour Gazette*, January 1948, p. 2.

50.   G. D. H. Cole, *op. cit.*, p. 586.

51.   *Ibid.*, p. 587.

52.   *New Statesman*, 16 November 1946.

53.   *New Statesman*, 3 May 1947.

54.   Report of the 16th Annual Conference of Representatives of Unions Catering for Women Workers, 1946, pp. 32–3.

55.   Report of the 17th Annual Conference of R. U. C. W. W., 1947, p. 39.

56.   Report of the 18th Annual Conference of R. U. C. W. W., pp. 38–9.

57.   Report of the 19th Annual Conference of R. U. C. W. W., p. 2.

58.   *Ibid.*, p. 4.

59.   Report of the 20th Annual Conference of R. U. C. W. W., p. 5.

60.   Article by Venetia Murray in *Picture Post*, 7 January 1956.

61.   Report of Annual Congress of the Women's Co-operative Guild, London 1937, p. 16.

62.   Report of 63rd Annual Congress of the Women's Co-operative Guild, London 1946, p. 29.

63.   M. Goldsmith, *Women and the Future*, p. 15.

64.   M. Goldsmith, *Women at War*, p. 190.

65.   Cited in Goldsmith, M., *Women at War*, p. 200.

66.   Mass-Observation, *The Journey Home*, p. 64.

67.   G. Thomas, 'Women at Work'.

68.   G. Thomas, 'Women and Industry'.

69.   *Ibid.*

70.   *Ibid.*

71.   P. Jephcott, *Rising Twenty*, p. 24.

72.   *Ibid.*, p. 82.

73.   *Ibid.*, p. 120.

74.   *Ibid.*, p. 52.

75.   G. D. H. Cole, *op. cit.*, p. 434.

76.   *Ministry of Labour Gazette*, May 1947, p. 142.

77.   Richard Titmuss, *Essays on 'The Welfare State'*, pp. 102–3.

78.   *Planning*, vol. xv, no. 285, 23 July 1948.

79.   *Ministry of Labour Gazette*, March 1958, p. 97.

80.   G. Thomas, 'Women at Work: the attitudes of working women

toward postwar employment and some related problems', Wartime Social Survey Reg 1.3, London 1944. Thomas's estimate is the same as that derived from the Registration of Employment Order by the Ministry of Labour.

81. G. Thomas, 'Women and Industry', 1948.

Chapter 6   Postwar Pronatalism

1. Graham Greene, *The Ministry of Fear*, p. 12.

2. George Orwell, *The Collected Essays, Journalism and Letters*, vol. 3, 'As I Please', 1943, pp. 49–50.

3. George Orwell, *The Collected Essays*, vol. 2, 'My Country Right or Left', 1940–43, p. 112.

4. Royal Commission on Population Report, p. 1.

5. Report and Selected Papers of the Statistics Committee, Papers of the Royal Commission on Population, vol. 11, p. 2.

6. Rosalind Mitchison, *British Population Change Since 1860*, pp. 82–3.

7. From 'Annual Live Births, Great Britain, 1855–1947', on p. 206 of Statistics Committee Report to the Royal Commission of Population: *see table on following page (212)*.

8. Economics Committee of the Royal Commission, Report, Papers of the Royal Commission on Population, vol. 3, p. 52.

9. *Ibid.*, p. 53

10. *Ibid.*, p. 57.

11. *Ibid.*, p. 61.

12. Reports of the Biological and Medical Committee to the Royal Commission on Population, vol. 4, p. 25.

13. Report of the Royal Commission on Population, p. 159.

14. Fabian Society, *Population and the People, A National Policy*, p. 9.

15. *Picture Post*, 13 November 1943.

16. Mass-Observation, *Britain and her Birth-rate*, p. 198.

17. Eva M. Hubback, *The Population of Britain*, p. 107.

18. *Ibid,*, p. 277.

19. E. Lewis-Faning, *Report on an Enquiry into Family Limitation and its Influence on Human Fertility during the Past Fifty Years*, Papers of the Royal Commission on Population, vol. 1, p. 21.

Statistics Committee Report to the Royal Commission of Population:

	Legitimate	*Illegitimate*	*Total*
1930	706,728	36,632	743,360
1933	635,587	31,372	666,959
1935	655,802	30,882	686,684
1938	678,003	31,828	709,831
1940	645,799	30,724	676,523
1941	631,872	36,962	668,834
1944	784,699	62,720	847,419
1945	695,995	70,874	766,869
1946	864,302	60,823	925,125
1947	941,259	52,914	994,173
1961			965,000
1963–4			1000,000
(from O. P. Censuses and Surveys)			
1971–2			862,000
1976–7			655,300

20. Hansard, 26 September 1944, Commons Debates.
21. Memoranda presented to the Royal Commission, Papers of the Royal Commission on Population, vol. 5, p. 85.
22. Report of the Royal Commission on Population, p. 160.
23. Fabian Society, *Population and the People, A National Policy*, p. 34.
24. *Ibid.*, p. 44.
25. *Ibid.*, pp. 48–50.
26. Richard and Kathleen Titmuss, *Parents' Revolt: A Study of the Declining Birth-rate in Acquisitive Societies*, p. 123.
27. Paul Addison, *The Road to 1945*, p. 247.
28. E. Slater and M. Woodside, *Patterns of Marriage*, p. 189.
29. Eva M. Hubback, *op. cit.*, pp. 92, 94.
30. *Ibid.*, p. 94.
31. Louis Ginsburg, 'Parenthood and Poverty', p. 36.
32. *Planning*, 'A Complete Maternity Service', no. 204, 31 January 1946.

33. G. D. H. Cole, *The Intelligent Man's Guide*, p. 442.

34. Pearl Jephcott, *Rising Twenty*, p. 86.

35. Fabian Women's Group, Minutes of Evidence taken before the Royal Commission on Equal Pay, Appendix xi–xix, p. 184.

36. Joan Robinson, Evidence taken before the Royal Commission on Equal Pay, Appendices ix and x, pp. 107–8.

37. Roy Harrod, Evidence taken before the Royal Commission on Equal Pay, p. 92.

38. Royal Commission on Equal Pay, pp. 118–19.

39. Fabian Society, *Population and the People, A National Policy*, p. 14.

40. Sir William Beveridge, *Voluntary Action: A Report on Methods of Social Advance*, pp. 264–5.

41. Lawrence Wolfe, *The Reilly Plan: A New Way of Life*.

42. George Orwell, 'The Lion and the Unicorn', *The Collected Essays*, vol. 2, p. 98.

43. Innes H. Pearse and Lucy H. Crocker, *The Peckham Experiment: A Study in the Living Structure of Society*.

44. Women's Hygiene Committee of the Women's Group on Public Welfare, *Our Towns: A Close-up*, p. 105.

45. Dr B. Stross, *Nursery Education*.

46. Fabian Society, *Population and the People, A National Policy*, p. 32.

47. Report of the Royal Commission on Population, pp. 181, 184–5, 187.

48. Sir Drummond Shiels, letter to *The Times*, 23 December 1944.

49. Hansard, Commons Debate, 9 March 1945, vol. 408, columns 2425–50.

50. 1945 Deputation to the Ministers of Health and Education on Nursery Provisions, PRO/MH 55/803.

51. PRO/MH 55/803.

52. G. D. H. Cole, *op. cit.*, p. 542.

53. Sir William Beveridge, *Voluntary Action: A Report on Methods of Social Advance*, p. 264.

54. *Picture Post*, 15 February 1944.

55. Hansard, Commons Debate, May 1943, vol. 389, column 643 and November 1943, vol. 393, column 675.

56. Fabian Society, *Population and the People, A National Policy*, p. 18.

57. *Ibid.*, p. 22.

213

58. *Ibid.*, p. 22.

59. *Ibid.*, p. 22.

60. *Ibid.*, p. 25.

61. *Ibid.*, p. 25.

62. For parliamentary debates on equal compensation to civilian women for war injuries, see Mrs Tate (Frome) in Hansard, Commons Debates, 1942–3, vol. 385, columns 750–828.

63. Margaret Goldsmith, *Women at War*, p. 181.

64. David Doughan, *Lobbying for Liberation, British Feminism 1918–1968*.

65. The Six-Point Group, *Dorothy Evans and the Six-Point Group*, p. 18.

66. Elizabeth Abbott and Katharine Bompas, 'The Woman Citizen and Social Security, A Criticism of the Proposals made in the Beveridge Report as They Affect Women'.

67. The Open Door International for the Economic Emancipation of the Woman Worker, Conference Report, 1938, p. 21.

68. Open Door International, Conference Report, 1948, p. 10.

69. Open Door International, Conference Report, 1938, p. 26.

70. Open Door International, Conference Report, 1938, p. 46.

71. Report of Royal Commission on Population, pp. 147–8.

72. See, for instance, the Report of the Maternal Mortality Committee, *Maternal Mortality*.

73. Standing Joint Committee of Working Women's Organisations, 'Reports on Population Problems and Postwar Organisation of Private Domestic Employment'.

74. *Ibid.*

75. Alva Myrdal, *Nation and Family*, p. 121.

76. *Ibid.*, p. 121.

77. *Ibid.*, p. 418.

78. M. Bruce, *The Coming of the Welfare State*, p. 270.

79. René Spitz, 'Hospitalism'; an 'Inquiry into the Genesis of Psychiatric Conditions in Early Childhood', *The Psychoanalytic Study of the Child*, vol. 1, pp. 53–74.

80. Luisa Passerini, 'Work, Ideology and Consensus under Italian Fascism', pp. 82–109.

81. Marie-Antonietta Macciocchi, 'Female Sexuality in Fascist Ideology', *Feminist Review*, 1, and critical introduction by Jane Caplan in the same volume.

82. Leon Trotsky, *The Revolution Betrayed*, pp. 140–41.
83. Alva Myrdal, *op. cit.*, p. 418.
84. See Kate Soper, *On Human Needs*.
85. For a discussion of sexual difference in psychoanalytic theory, see Stephen Heath, 'Difference', *Screen*, 19, no. 3.

Documents Used

Maternal Mortality Committee Report, London 1934.

Ministry of Health file, Public Record Office, Kew: PRO/MH 55/803. '1945 Deputation to the Ministers of Health and Education on Nursery Provisions'. PRO/MH 55/884 'The Children of War Workers'. PRO/MH 55/695 'Arrangements for the Provision of Wartime Day Nurseries, 1941–42'.

National Conference of Women called by H. M. Government, 28 September 1943: Report of Proceedings. HMSO, London, 1943.

Proceedings from the International Society for the Study of Behaviour Development, (unpublished), 3rd Biennial Conference, Guildford, 13–17 July 1975.

Reports of the Conferences of Open Door International for the Economic Emancipation of the Woman Worker, London, 1938, 1948.

Reports and Evidence to the Royal Commission on Equal Pay. HMSO, London, 1944–6.

Wartime Social Survey and Social Survey Reports: Central Office of Information, London.

Women's Co-Operative Guild: Reports of Annual Congresses of the Women's Co-Operative Guild, 1937–46.

Unions Catering for Women Workers: Reports of the Annual Conferences of Representatives of Unions Catering for Women Workers, 1946–50.

Bibliography

Abbott, Elizabeth, and Bompas, Katharine, 'The Woman Citizen and Social Security, A Criticism of the Proposals made in the Beveridge Report as They Affect Women' (pamphlet), London, 1943.

Abraham, Karl, 'Das Erleiden sexueller Traumen als Form infantiler Sexualbetätigung', 1907, translated as 'The Experiencing of Sexual Traumas as a Form of Sexual Activity' in *Selected Papers on Psychoanalysis*, pp. 47–63, London, 1927, 1942.

Abraham, Karl, 'The First Pre-Genital Stage of the Libido', 1916, *Selected Papers on Psychoanalysis*, London, 1927, 1942, pp. 248–79.

Abraham, Karl, 'The Influence of Oral Erotism on Character Formation', *Selected Papers on Psychoanalysis*, London, 1927, 1942.

Addison, Paul, *The Road to 1945*, London, 1975.

Adorno, Theodor W., 'Social Science and Sociological Tendencies in Psychoanalysis', 1946, unpublished in English, German version in *Sociologia II: Reden und Vortrage*, ed. M. Horkheimer and T. W. Adorno, Frankfurt, 1962.

Adorno, Theodor W., 'Sociology and Psychology', Part 2, *New Left Review*, 47, January–February 1968, p. 95.

Aichhorn, August, *Verwahrloste Jugend*, Vienna, 1925, translated as *Wayward Youth*, New York, 1935, London, 1936.

Ainsworth, M., Bell, D. S., and Stayton, D. J., 'Infant-Mother Attachment and Social Development', *The Integration of a Child into a Social World*, ed. M. P. M. Richards, Cambridge University Press, 1974.

Ainsworth, Mary D. S., and Bell, Sylvia M., 'Mother-Infant Interaction and the Development of Competence', *The Growth of Competence*, ed. K. Connolly and J. Bruner, London, 1974, pp. 97–118.

Althusser, Louis, *For Marx*, London, 1962.

Althusser, Louis, and Balibar, Etienne, *Reading Capital*, London, 1970.

Bakwin, R. M., and Bakwin, H., *Psychological Care During Infancy and Childhood*, New York, 1942.

Baldwin, J. M., *Mental Development in the Child and the Race*, New York, 1895.

Baldwin, J. M., *Social and Ethical Interpretations in Mental Development*, New York, 1897.

Balibar, Etienne, 'The Elements of the Structure and their History', *Reading Capital*, L. Althusser and E. Balibar, London, 1970, pp. 247–53.

BBC Radio, 'The Formative Years', (broadcast series 1968), BBC Publications 7404, London.

Becker, Ernest, *The Birth and Death of Meaning*, London and New York, 1962.

Bernfeld, Siegfried, 'Psychoanalysis and Socialism', 1925, translated and appended to W. Reich, *Dialectical Materialism and Psychoanalysis*, London, 1972.

Bernfeld, Siegfried, *Psychology of the Infant*, 1925, trans. R. Hurwitz, London and New York, 1929.

Bernfeld, Siegfried, *Sisyphus, or The Limits of Education*, trans. F. Lilage, Berkeley, Cal., 1973.

Berger, P. L., and Luckmann, T., *The Social Construction of Reality*, London, 1967.

Beveridge, Sir William, *Voluntary Action: A Report on Methods of Social Advance*, London, 1948.

Bowen, Elizabeth, *The Heat of the Day*, London, 1947.

Bowlby, John, and Durbin, E. F. M., 'Personal Aggressiveness and War', *War and Democracy*, Bowlby J., Durbin E., Thomas, I., *et al.*, London, 1938.

Bowlby, John, 'The Problem of the Young Child', *The New Era in Home and School*, vol. 21, no. 3, March 1940, pp. 59–64.

Bowlby, John, 'The Influence of Early Environment in the Development of Neurosis and Neurotic Character' in *International Journal of Psycho-Analysis*, vol. 21, 1940, p. 154.

Bowlby, John, *Personality and Mental Illness*, London, 1940.

Bowlby, John, 'Psychological Aspects', *Evacuation Survey: A Report to the*

Fabian Society, ed. R. Padley and M. Cole, London, 1940, pp. 186–96.

Bowlby, John, *Forty-Four Juvenile Thieves: Their Characters and Home-Life*, London, 1946. Also in *International Journal of Psycho-Analysis*, vol. xxv, 1944, pp. 19–53, 107–28.

Bowlby, John, *Maternal Care and Mental Health*, a report prepared on behalf of the World Health Organisation, Geneva, 1952.

Bowlby, John, *Child Care and the Growth of Love*, London, 1953, 1965.

Bowlby, John, 'Can I Leave My Baby?' (pamphlet), National Association for Mental Health, London, 1958.

Bowlby, John, 'The Nature of the Child's Tie to His Mother', *International Journal of Psycho-Analysis*, 38–9, 1958, pp. 350–72.

Bowlby, John, 'Psychoanalysis and Child Care', *Psychoanalysis and Contemporary Thought*, ed. J. D. Sutherland, London, 1958, pp. 33–57.

Bowlby, John, 'Processes of Mourning', *International Journal of Psycho-Analysis*, vol. 42, 1961, pp. 317–40.

Bowlby, John, 'The Formative Years, BBC Publications 7404. Talk on 'Security and Anxiety', London, 1968.

Bowlby, John, *Attachment and Loss*, vol. 1: *Attachment*, London, 1969. vol. 2: *Separation: Anxiety and Anger*, London, 1973. vol. 3: *Loss*, London, 1980.

Brazelton, T. B., Koslowski, B., Main, M., 'The Origins of Reciprocity: The Early Mother-Infant Interaction', *The Effect of the Infant on its Care-Giver*, ed. Lewis and Rosenblum, New York, 1974, pp. 49–76.

Brim, O. G., and Wheeler, S., (eds.) *Socialisation after Childhood: Two Essays*, New York, 1966.

British Medical Journal, (unsigned editorials), 'Loneliness in Infancy', vol. II, 19 September 1942, p. 345, and 'War in the Nursery', vol. I, 8 January 1944, p. 50.

Bruce, Maurice, *The Coming of the Welfare State*, London, 1961.

Bruner, J. S., 'The ontogenesis of speech acts', *Journal of Child Language*, 2, 1975, pp. 1–20.

Bruner, Jerome, 'From Communication to Language: a Psychological Perspective', *Cognition*, 1965, *3*, pp. 255–87.

Bruner, Jerome, *Under Five in Britain*, Oxford Pre-School Research Project Series: 1, London, 1980.

Bühler, Charlotte, *Sociologische und psychologische Studien über das erste Lebensjahr*, Berlin, 1972.

Bühler, Charlotte, 'The Social Behaviour of Children,' *A Handbook of Child Psychology*, ed. C. A. Murchison, Worcester, Mass; Clark, U. P.; London, OUP, 1933.

Bukharin, N. ed., *Science at the Crossroads*, Papers Presented to the International Congress of the History of Science and Technology, London, 1931 and 1971.

Burlingham, Dorothy, and Freud, Anna, *Infants Without Families: the Case For and Against Residential Nurseries*, New York and London, 1944, 1952, 1965.

Burlingham, Dorothy, and Freud, Anna, *Young Children in Wartime*, London, 1942.

Caplan, Jane, Introduction to 'Female Sexuality in Fascist Ideology', *Feminist Review*, 1, 1979, pp. 59–66.

Carmichael, C., ed., *Manual of Child Psychology*, New York, 1954.

Castel, Robert, *Le Psychanalysme: l'ordre psychanalytique et le pouvoir*, Paris, 1973.

Chappell, P. F., and Sander, L. W., 'Mutual regulation of neonatal-maternal interaction: context for the origins of communication', *Before Speech: the Beginning of Interpersonal Communication*, ed. M. Bullowa, pp. 89–109, CUP, 1979.

Charcot, Jean-Martin, *Leçons sur les maladies du système nerveux faites à la Salpêtrière*, Paris, 1887, trans. G. Sigerson, *Lectures on Diseases of the Nervous System*, 3 vols., London, 1877–89.

Cole, G. D. H., *The Intelligent Man's Guide to the Post-War World*, London, 1947.

Collier, Andrew, *R. D. Laing: the Philosophy and Politics of Psychotherapy*, Hassocks, 1977.

Comer, Lee, *Wedlocked Women*, Leeds, 1974.

Coward, Rosalind, 'On the Universality of the Oedipus Complex: Debates on Sexual Divisions in Psychoanalysis and Anthropology', *Critique of Anthropology*, Spring, 1980, *15*, vol. 4, pp. 3–28.

Croom Robertson, G., 'Psychology and Philosophy', *Mind*, vol. VIII, 1883, pp. 1–21.

Darwin, Charles, 'A Biographical Sketch of an Infant', *Mind*, vol. II, 1877, pp. 285–94.

Bibliography

Dennis, Wayne, 'Historical Beginnings of Child Psychology', *Psychological Bulletin*, vol. 46, New York, 1949, pp. 224–45.

Dinnage, Rosemary, 'John Bowlby', *New Society*, 10 May 1979, pp. 323–5.

Doughan, David, *Lobbying for Liberation, British Feminism, 1918–1968*, Fawcett Library, London, 1980.

Douie, Vera, *The Lesser Half*, London, 1943.

Edgar, J., Review of Kirkpatrick's *Fundamentals of Child Study*, *Mind*, 1904, vol. XIII, pp. 569–71.

Emminghaus, H., *Die psychischen Störungen des Kindesalters*, Tubingen, 1887.

Engels, Frederick, *Anti-Dühring*, 1878.

Engels, Frederick, *Dialectics of Nature*, 1878, first published 1925.

Engels, Frederick, *The Origin of the Family, Private Property, and the State*, 1884.

Erikson, Eric H., 'Observations on Sioux Education', *Journal of Psychology*, 7, 1939, pp. 101–56.

Erikson, Eric H., 'Childhood and Tradition in Two American-Indian Tribes', A. Freud ed., *The Psychoanalytic Study of the Child*, vol. 1, New York, 1945, pp. 319–50.

Erikson, Eric H., 'Observations of the Yurok: Childhood and World Image', *American Archaeology and Ethology*, 35, 1943, pp. 257–301.

Fabian Society, *Population and the People, A National Policy*, by a Committee of the Fabian Society under the chairmanship of Dr W. A. Robson, London, 1946.

Fabian Women's Group, Minutes of Evidence taken before the Royal Commission on Equal Pay, Appendix xi–xix, HMSO, London, 1945.

Fantz, R. L., 'The Origin of Form Perception', *Scientific American*, vol. 204, pp. 66–72, 1961.

Fantz, R. L., 'Visual Perception from Birth as Shown by Pattern Selectivity', *Annals of the New York Academy of Science*, vol. 118, pp. 793–814, 1965.

Fantz, R. L., 'Pattern Discrimination and Selective Attention as Determinants of Perceptual Development from Birth', in A. H. Kidd and J. C. Rivoire (eds.), *Perceptual Development in Children*, International Universities Press, 1966.

Feldmann, H., *De statu normale functionum corporis humani animadversiones quondam*, Bonn, 1833.

Ferguson, Sheila, and Fitzgerald, Hilde, *Studies in the Social Services: History of the Second World War*, HMSO, London, 1954.

Forrester, John, *Language and the Origins of Psychoanalysis*, London, 1980.

Foucault, Michel, *The Archaeology of Knowledge*, trans. A. M. Sheridan Smith, London, 1972.

Foucault, Michel, *Histoire de la sexualité*, vol. 1, *La Volonté de savoir*, Paris, 1976, trans. Robert Hardy, *The History of Sexuality: An Introduction*, London, 1979.

Freud, Anna, *The Psycho-Analytic Treatment of Children: Technical Lectures and Essays*, trans. N. Procter-Gregg, London, 1946.

Freud, Sigmund, 'Analysis of a Phobia in a Five-Year-Old Boy', 1903, Standard Edition, vol. X, London, 1955, p. 5.

Freud, Sigmund, *Introductory Lectures on Psychoanalysis*, Standard Edition, vol. XV–XVI, London, 1916–17.

Freud, Sigmund, *New Introductory Lectures on Psychoanalysis*, Standard Edition, vols. XXII, pp. 5–182, London, 1933.

Freud, Sigmund, 'Instincts and their Vicissitudes' (1915), Standard Edition, vol. 14, London 1957, pp. 114–140.

Freud, Sigmund, *Das Ich und das Es*, translated as *The Ego and the Id*, Standard Edition, vol. XIX, London, 1927, p. 3.

Freud, Sigmund, *Moses and Monotheism* (*Der Mann Moses und die monotheistische Religion*), trans. London, 1939, Standard Edition, vol. XXIII.

Freud, Sigmund, *Totem and Taboo*, Standard Edition, vol. XIII, London, 1950, p. 1.

Friedlander, B. Z., 'Receptive Language Development in Infancy: Issues and Problems', *Merrill-Palmer Quarterly*, 16, 1970, pp. 7–15.

Fries, Margaret, 'An Integrated Health Plan', *The Psychoanalytic Study of the Child*, ed. A. Freud, vol. 1, 1945.

Fries, Margaret, 'Interrelated Factors in Development. A Study of Pregnancy, Labor, Delivery, Lying-in Period and Childhood', *American Journal of Orthopsychiatry*, vol. VIII, October 1938, pp. 726–52.

Fries, Margaret, 'Mental Hygiene in Pregnancy, Delivery and the Puerperium', *Mental Hygiene*, vol. XXV, April 1941, pp. 222–36.

Fromm, Erich, 'The Method and Function of an Analytic Social Psychology' (1932), *The Crisis of Psychoanalysis*, London, 1971.

Galton, Francis, *Hereditary Genius*, London, 1869.

Galton, Francis, *English Men of Science: Their Nature and Nurture*, London, 1874.

Galton, Francis, 'Twins, as a Criterion of the Relative Powers of Nature and Nurture', *Journal of the Anthropological Institute*, 1875, *5*, pp. 324–9.

Gesell, A., *Infancy and Human Growth*, New York, 1928.

Gesell, A., *Studies in Child Development*, New York, 1948.

Gesell, A., *et al.*, *Biographies of Child Development: the Mental Growth Careers of Eighty-Four Infants and Children*, New York, 1939.

Gesell, A. L., and Illg, F. L., *The Child from Five to Ten*, New York, 1946.

Gesell, A. L., *The First Five Years of Life: a Guide to the Study of the Preschool Child*, London (USA pr.), 1941.

Gesell, A., and Thompson, H., *Infant Behaviour: its Genesis and Growth*, New York and London, 1934.

Gewirtz, J. L., 'Deprivation and Satiation of Social Stimuli as Determinants of Their Reinforcing Efficacy', *Minnesota Symposia on Child Psychology*, vol. I, Minneapolis, 1967, pp. 3–56.

Gewirtz, J. L., 'Mechanisms of Social Learning: Some Roles of Stimulation and Behavior in Early Human Development', pp. 57–213, *Handbook of Socialization Theory and Research*, ed. D. Goslin, Chicago, 1969.

Ginsburg, Louis, 'Parenthood and Poverty', Fabian Research Pamphlet, London, 1939.

Glover, Edward, 'Examination of the Klein System of Child Psychology', in *The Psychoanalytic Study of the Child*, vol. 1, 1945, pp. 75–118.

Goldsmith, Margaret, *Women and the Future*, London, 1946.

Goldsmith, Margaret, *Women at War*, London, 1943.

Gordon, Colin, 'The Unconscious of Psychoanalysis', *Ideology and Consciousness*, 2, Autumn 1977, pp. 109–27.

Gorer, Geoffrey, *Japanese Character Structure and Propaganda*, New Haven (mimeograph), 1942.

Greene, Graham, *The Ministry of Fear*, London, 1943.

Hall, Stanley, 'The Content of Children's Minds', *Princeton Review*, 11, 1883, pp. 249–72.

Hampshire, Stuart, *Thought and Action*, London, 1959.

Harré, R., 'Conditions for a Social Psychology of Childhood', *The Integration of a Child into a Social World*, ed. M. Richards, CUP, 1974, pp. 245–62.

Harrod, Roy, Evidence taken before the Royal Commission on Equal Pay, Appendices ix and x, HMSO, London, 1945.

Hartmann, Heinz, 'Ich-Psychologie und Anpassungsprobleme', *Internationale Zeitschrift für Psychoanalyse und Imago XXIV*, 1939 – discussed in Heinz Hartmann and Ernst Kris, 'Genetic Approach in Psychoanalysis', *The Psychoanalytic Study of the Child*, vol. 1, 1945.

Hartmann, Heinz, *et al.*, 'Comments on the Formation of Psychic Structure', *The Psycho-Analytic Study of the Child*, 1946, *2*, pp. 11–38.

Hartmann, Heinz, 'Psychoanalysis and Developmental Psychology', *The Psycho-Analytic Study of the Child*, vol. 1, 1950, pp. 7–17.

Hartmann, Heinz, and Kris, Ernst, 'The Genetic Approach in Psychoanalysis', in *The Psycho-Analytic Study of the Child*, vol. 1, 1945, pp. 11–30.

Heath, Stephen, 'Difference', *Screen*, 19, no. 3, Autumn 1978, pp. 51–112.

Hinde, R. A., 'Changes in Responsiveness to a Constant Stimulus', *British Journal of Animal Behaviour*, 2, 1954, pp. 41–5.

Horkheimer, M., *Studien über Autorität und Familie* (1936), translated as 'Authority in the Family', pp. 47–128, in *Critical Theory: Selected Essays*, trans. M. J. O'Connell, New York, 1972.

Hubback, Eva M., *The Population of Britain*, London, 1947.

Hughes, Dr Marguerite, 'Mothers and Woman Power in Relation to Nurseries, Foster Mothers and Daily Minders', in *Mother and Child*, August 1942, vol. XIII, no. 5, pp. 91–5.

Hughes, M., Mayall, B., Moss, P., Perry, J., Petrie, P. and Pinkerton, G., *Nurseries Now: a Fair Deal for Parents and Children*, Harmondsworth, 1970.

Inman, P., *Labour in the Munitions Industry*, HMSO, London, 1957.

Isaacs, Susan, ed., *The Cambridge Evacuation Survey*, London, 1941.

Isaacs, Susan, *The Nursery Years*, London, 1929, 1932.

Isaacs, Susan, *Intellectual Growth in Young Children*, London, 1930.

Isaacs, Susan, *Social Development of Children*, London, 1933.

Isaacs, Susan, 'The Uprooted Child', *The New Era*, March 1940, vol. 21. no. 3, pp. 54–9.

Jacoby, Russell, *Social Amnesia: A Critique of Conformist Psychology from Adler to Laing*, Boston, Mass, 1975 and Hassocks, 1977.

James, William, *Principles of Psychology*, New York, 1890.

Jay, Martin, *The Dialectical Imagination: A History of the Frankfurt School and the Institute of Social Research*, 1923–50, London, 1973.

Jephcott, Pearl, *Rising Twenty*, London, 1948.

Jones, Ernest, *The Life and Work of Sigmund Freud*, Harmondsworth, 1964.

Kardiner, Abram, *The Individual and His Society: The Psychoanalysis of Primitive Social Organisation*, New York, 1939.

Kern, Stephen, 'Freud and the Birth of Child Psychiatry', *Journal of the History of the Behavioural Sciences* (Vermont, US), vol. IX, no. 4, October 1973, pp. 360–68.

Kirkpatrick, E., *Fundamentals of Child Study*, New York, 1903.

Kléin, Melanie, 'The Development of a Child' (1919) is Part I of 'The Development of a Child' (1921), in *Love, Guilt and Reparation and Other Works 1921–1945*, London, 1975, pp. 1–53.

Klein, Melanie, 'The Early Development of Conscience in the Child', *Psychoanalysis Today*, ed. S. Lorand, New York, 1933, pp. 248–57.

Klein, Melanie, 'On Observing the Behaviour of Young Infants', *Developments in Psycho-Analysis*, by M. Klein, Paula Heimann, Susan Isaacs and Joan Rivière, London, 1952, pp. 237–70.

Klein, Melanie, *Envy and Gratitude*, London, 1957.

Klein, Melanie, 'Early Stages of the Oedipus Conflict' (1928), *Love, Guilt and Reparation and Other Works 1921–1945*, London, 1975, pp. 186–98.

Klein, Melanie, 'The Scope and Limits of Child Analysis', *The Psychoanalysis of Children*, trans. A. Strachey, London, 1975, pp. 279–82.

Kluckhohn, A., and Leighton, D. (1946), *The Navaho*, Cambridge, Mass., 1947.

Kluckhohn, C., and Leighton, D., *Children of the People*, Cambridge, Mass., 1947.

Kluckhohn, Clyde, 'Some Aspects of Navaho Infancy and Early Childhood', *Psychoanalysis and the Social Sciences*, vol. 1, 1947, pp. 37–86.

Kris, Ernst, 'Development and Problems of Child Psychology', *The Psychoanalytic Study of the Child*, vol. v, 1950, pp. 24–46.

Kris, Ernst, and Leites, Nathan, 'Trends in Twentieth-Century Propaganda', *Psychoanalysis and the Social Sciences*, vol. 1, 1947, pp. 393–409.

Kristeva, Julia, *La Révolution du langage poètique*, Paris, 1974.

Kussmaul, H., *Untersuchungen über das Seelenleben des neugeborenen Menschen*, Heidelberg and Leipzig, 1859.

La Barre, W., 'Some Observations on Character Structure in the Orient: 1. The Japanese', *Psychiatry*, vol. 8, 1945, pp. 319–42.

Labour Research Department, 'Women in War Jobs', London, 1942.

Laing, R. D., *The Divided Self*, London, 1960, 1965.

Laing, R. D., and Esterson, A., *Sanity, Madness and the Family: Families of Schizophrenics*, London, 1964.

Laplanche, J., and Pontalis, J. B., *The Language of Psychoanalysis* (1967), London, 1973.

Law, Barbara, 'The Homesick Child', *The New Era*, May 1940, vol. 21, no. 5, pp. 121–4.

Lewes, G. H., 'New Books: The Physical Basis of Mind', *Mind*, vol. 11, 1877, pp. 278–9.

Lewis-Faning, E., *Report on an Enquiry into Family Limitation and its Influence on Human Fertility during the Past Fifty Years*, Papers of the Royal Commission on Population, vol. 1, HMSO, London, 1949.

Linton, Ralph, *The Cultural Background of Personality*, New York, 1945, and London, 1947.

Linton, Ralph, *The Study of Man: an Introduction*, New York, 1936.

Macciocchi, Marie-Antonietta, 'Female Sexuality in Fascist Ideology', *Feminist Review*, I, 1979, pp. 67–82.

Mackay, H., 'The Proper Place for Children', in *The Lancet*, 3 July 1943, p. 21.

Marx, Karl, *Introduction to the Grundrisse: Foundations of the Critique of Political Economy* (1857), trans. M. Nicolaus, Harmondsworth, 1973.

Mass-Observation, *Britain and her Birth-rate*, London, 1945.

Mass-Observation, *The Journey Home*, London, 1944.

Mass-Observation, *People in Production*, London, 1942.

Maternal Mortality Committee Report, *Maternal Mortality*, London, 1934.

Maudsley, Henry, *Physiology and Pathology of the Mind*, London, 1867.

McLaughlin, M., 'The Physical Health of Children Attending Day Nurseries', *British Medical Journal*, August 1946, pp. 591–4.

McMurray, John, *Persons in Relation*, London, 1961.

Mead, Margaret, *Sex and Temperament in Three Primitive Societies*, London, 1935, repr. 1952.

Mead, Margaret, 'Research on Primitive Children', *Manual of Child Psychology*, ed. C. Carmichael, pp. 735–80, New York, 1954.

Mead, Margaret, *Childhood in Contemporary Cultures*, ed. M. Mead and M. Wolfenstein, Chicago, 1955.

Menzies, H. F., 'Children in Day Nurseries', *The Lancet*, 5 October 1946, pp. 499–501.

Mepham, J. and Ruben, D., *Issues in Marxist Philosophy*, vol. 1, *Dialectics and Method*; vol. 2, *Materialism*; vol. 3, *Epistemology, Science, Ideology*, Brighton, 1979.

Merleau-Ponty, Maurice, *The Phenomenology of Perception*, trans. Colin Smith, London, 1962.

Middlemore, Merell, *The Nursing Couple*, London, 1941.

Ministry of Health files, Public Record Office, PRO/MH 55/803: '1945 Deputation to the Ministers of Health and Education on Nursery Provisions'; PRO/MH 55/884, 'The Children of War Workers'; PRO/MH 55/695, 'Arrangements for the Provision of Wartime Day Nurseries, 1941–2'.

Ministry of Labour, 'Women in Shipbuilding', London, 1943.

Ministry of Labour Gazette, HMSO, London, June 1947, January 1948, March 1958.

Mitchell, Juliet, *Psychoanalysis and Feminism*, London, 1974.

Mitchison, Rosalind, *British Population Change Since 1860*, London, 1977.

Morgan, Patricia, *Child Care: Sense and Fable*, London, 1975.

Murray, Venetia, 'The Children of Women Who Work', *Picture Post*, vol. 70, 7 January 1956, pp. 7–8.

Myrdal, Alva, *Nation and Family*, London, 1945.

National Conference of Women called by H. M. Government, 28 September 1943: *Report of Proceedings*, HMSO, London, 1943.

National Council of Social Service, *The Neglected Child and his Family*, Oxford, 1948.

Open Door International for the Economic Emancipation of the Women Worker: *Conference Reports* 1938, 1948. London, 1938, 1948.

Orwell, George, *The Collected Essays, Journalism and Letters*, 3 vols, London 1970.

Padley, Richard, and Cole, Margaret, *Evacuation Survey: A Report to the Fabian Society*, London, 1940.

Parker, H. M. D., *Manpower: A Study of Wartime Policy and Administration*, HMSO, London, 1957.

Passerini, Luisa, 'Work, Ideology and Consensus under Italian Fascism', *History Workshop Journal*, 8, Autumn 1979, pp. 82–109.

Pearse, Innes H., and Crocker, Lucy H., *The Peckham Experiment: A Study in the Living Structure of Society*, London, 1943.

Peters, R. S., *The Philosophy of Education*, OUP, 1973.

Piaget, Jean, *Biology and Knowledge: An Essay on the Relations between Organic Regulations and Cognitive Processes*, Edinburgh University Press, 1971.

Planning (Political and Economic Planning), 'The Employment of Women', XV, no. 285, 23 July 1948.

Planning (Political and Economic Planning), 'A Complete Maternity Service', no. 204, 31 January 1946.

Polizter, Georges, *Critique des fondements de la psychologie*, Paris, 1929.

Politzer, Georges, *La Crise de la psychologie contemporaine*, Paris, 1947.

Preyer, Wilhelm, 'Psychogenesis', *Deutsche Rundschau*, 1880, vol. 23, pp. 198–221, trans. Maria Talbot, *Journal of Spec. Philosophy*, 1881, *15*, pp. 159–88.

Preyer, Wilhelm, *Die Seele des Kindes*, Leipzig, 1882, trans. H. W. Brown as *The Mind of the Child*, New York, 1888, 1889.

Preyer, W., *Specielle Physiologie des Embryo: Untersuchungen über die Lebenserscheinungen vor der Geburt*, Leipzig, 1885, part translated by Coghill, G. E., and Legner, W. K., as 'Embryo Motility and Sensitivity', *Monogram for the Society for Research on Child Development*, *2*, pp. 1–115.

Preyer, Wilhelm, *Die Geistige Entwicklung in der ersten Kindheit*, trans. H. W. Brown as *Mental Development in the Child*, New York, 1893 and London, 1894.

Quen, Jacques, M., 'Asylum Psychiatry, Neurology, Social Work and Mental Hygiene', *Journal of the History of the Behavioural Sciences*, January 1977, vol. 23, no. 1, pp. 3–11.

Reich, Wilhelm, *Dialectical Materialism and Psychoanalysis* (1929), trans. Socialist Reproduction, London, 1972.

Reich, Wilhelm, *What is Class Consciousness?* (1934), Socialist Reproduction, London, 1971.

Reich, Wilhelm, 'Dialectical Materialist Science Against Intellectual Dilettantism in the Socialist Movement', *Zeitschrift für politische Psychologie und Sexualökonomie*, vol. 4, *Verlag* für Sexualpolitik, Copenhagen, 1937, trans. *Sexpol Essays 1934–1937*, Socialist Reproduction, London, 1973, p. 123.

Reich, Wilhelm, *Selected Sexpol Essays, 1934–1937*, trans. Socialist Reproduction, London, 1974.

Reich, Wilhelm, *The Mass Psychology of Fascism*, trans. V. R. Carfagno, Harmondsworth, 1975.

Ribble, Margaretha A., *The Rights of Infants: Early Psychological Needs and their Satisfaction*, New York, 1943.

Rickman, J., ed., *On the Bringing Up of Children*, London, 1936.

Rickman, J., Foreword to 'Emotional Problems of the Evacuation', *The New Era*, vol. 21, no. 3, March 1940, pp. 53–4.

Roback, A. A., 'The Moral Issues involved in Applied Psychology', *Journal of Applied Psychology*, vol. 1, 1917 (US), pp. 239, 231–43.

Robinson, Joan, Evidence taken before the Royal Commission on Equal Pay, Appendices ix and x, HMSO, London, 1945.

Róheim, Geza, *The Origin and Function of Culture*, New York, 1943.

Róheim, Geza, 'The Psychoanalytic Interpretation of Culture', *International Journal of Psycho-Analysis*, 1941, *22*, pp. 147–69.

Róheim, Geza, 'Psychoanalysis and Anthropology', *Psychoanalysis and the Social Sciences*, vol. 1, London, 1947.

Róheim, Geza, ed., *Psychoanalysis and the Social Sciences*, vol. 1, London, 1947.

Rose, S. and H., 'Ideology in Neurobiology', *Cognition*, 2(4), 1974, pp. 479–502.

Royal Commission on Equal Pay, HMSO, Cmd. 6937, London, 1944–6.

Royal Commission on Population Report, HMSO, Cmd. 7695, London, 1949.

Royal Commission on Population Papers, vol. 3. Report of the Economics Committee, HMSO, London, 1950.

Royal Commission on Population Papers, vol. 3. Report of the Selected Papers of the Statistics Committee, HMSO, London, 1950.

Royal Commission on Population Papers, vol. 4. Reports of the Biological and Medical Committee, HMSO, London, 1944–9.

Royal Commission on Population Papers, vol. 5. Memoranda presented to the Royal Commission, HMSO, London, 1950.

Rutter, Michael, *Maternal Deprivation Reassessed*, Harmondsworth, 1972.

Schaffer, H. R., *The Growth of Sociability*, Harmondsworth, 1971.

Schaffer, H. R., ed., *The Origins of Human Social Relations*, London and New York, 1971.

Sève, Lucien, *Marxisme et théorie de la personnalité* (1968), Paris, 1974, trans. by J. McGreal as *Man in Marxist Theory and the Psychology of Personality*, Hassocks, 1978.

Shinn, M. W., *Notes on the Development of a Child*, University of California, Berkeley, US, 1893–9.

Shinn, M. W., *The Biography of a Baby*, Boston, 1900.

Shotter, John, 'The Development of Personal Powers', *The Integration of a Child into a Social World*, ed. M. Richards, pp. 215–44. CUP, 1974.

Shotter, John, 'What Is It to Be Human?', *Reconstructing Social Psychology*, ed. N. Armistead, Harmondsworth, 1974, pp. 53–71.

Sigismund, Berthold, *Kind und Welt: Vatern, Muttern, und Kinderfreunden gewidmet*, Braunschweig, 1856.

Silberpfennig, Judith, 'Psychological Aspects of Current Japanese and German Paradoxa', *Psychiatric Review*, 1945, pp. 74–86.

Six-Point Group, *Dorothy Evans and the Six-Point Group*, London, 1945.

Slater, E. and Woodside, M., *Patterns of Marriage*, London, 1951.

Soper, Kate, 'On Materialisms', *Radical Philosophy*, 15, Autumn 1976, pp. 14–20.

Soper, Kate, 'Marxism, Materialism and Biology', *Issues in Marxist Philosophy*, vol. 2, *Materialism*, pp. 61–97, Brighton, 1979.

Soper, Kate, *On Human Needs*, Brighton, 1981.

Spitz, René, 'Hospitalism: an Inquiry into the Genesis of Psychiatric Conditions in Early Childhood', *The Psychoanalytic Study of the Child*, 1, pp. 53–74.

Spitz, René, 'Anaclitic Depression', *The Psychoanalytic Study of the Child*, vol. II, 1946, pp. 313–42.

Spitzer, H. M., in consultation with Benedict, R. F., *Bibliography of Articles and Books Relating to Japanese Character*, Office of War Information, Washington, US, 1945.

Standing Joint Committee of Working Women's Organisations, 'Reports

Bibliography

on Population Problems and Postwar Organisation of Private Domestic Employment', London, 1946.

Sterba, Richard, 'Antisemitism and Negro Race-Riots in Detroit', *Psychoanalysis and the Social Sciences*, ed. Róheim, vol. 1, 1945, pp. 411–27.

Stern, William, *Psychology of Early Childhood*, trans. A. Barwell, London, 1st ed. 1914, 2nd ed. 1921, 3rd ed. 1923.

Stross, Dr B., *Nursery Education*, Fabian Tract Series, 255, London, 1941.

Sulloway, Frank J., *Freud, Biologist of the Mind: Beyond the Psychoanalytic Legend*, London, 1980.

Sully, James, 'Babies and Science', *Cornhill Magazine*, *43*, London, 1881, pp. 539–54.

Sully, James, *Outlines of Psychology*, London, 1894.

Sully, James, *Studies of Childhood*, London, 1895, 1903.

Taine, J., 'Notes sur l'acquisition de langage chez les enfants et dans l'espèce humaine', *Revue Philosophique*, *1*, 1976, pp. 3–23, trans. *Mind*, 2, pp. 252–7, 1877 as 'The Acquisition of Language by Children'.

Tanner, J. M. and Inhelder, B., eds., Discussions on Child Development, vols 1–4, vol. 1, *Proceedings of the 1st Meeting of the WHO Study Group on the Psychobiological Development of the Child: Geneva 1953*, London, 1956.

Thomas, Geoffrey, 'Women at Work: the attitudes of working women toward postwar employment and some related problems', Wartime Social Survey, Reg, 1.3, London, 1944.

Thomas, Geoffrey, 'Women and Industry: an inquiry into the problem of recruiting women for industry, carried out for the Ministries of Labour and National Service', Social Survey Reports, 104, Central Office of Information, London, 1948.

Tiedemann, H., 'Beobachtungen über die Entwicklung der Seelenfahrigkeiten bei Kindern', *Hessichen Beitrage zur Gelehrsamskeit und Kunst*, 2, pp. 313ff., 386ff., 1787, trans. *Journal Genetic Psychology*, 1927, *34*, pp. 205–30.

Timpanaro, Sebastiano, *On Materialism*, London, 1975, 1980.

Titmuss, Richard and Kathleen, *Parents' Revolt: A Study of the Declining Birth-rate in Acquisitive Societies*, London, 1942.

Titmuss, Richard, *Essays on 'The Welfare State'*, London, 1958.

Trevarthen, C., and Murray, L., 'The Nature of an Infant's Ecology', in Proceedings from the International Society for the Study of Behavioural

Development, 3rd Biennial Conference, Guildford, 13–17 July 1975 (unpublished).

Trevarthen, C., 'Communication and Co-operation in Early Infancy: a Description of Primary Intersubjectivity', in ed. M. Bullowa, *Before Speech: the Beginning of Interpersonal Communication*, CUP, 1979, pp. 321–47.

Trotsky, Leon, *The Revolution Betrayed*, London, 1937.

Unions Catering for Women Workers: *Reports of the Annual Conferences of Representatives of Unions Catering for Women Workers, 1946–1950.*

Watson, J. B., 'Psychology as the Behaviourist Views It', *Psychological Review*, vol. xx, May 1913, pp. 158–77.

Werskey, Gary, *The Visible College*, London, 1978.

Williams, Raymond, 'Problems of Materialism', *New Left Review*, no. 109, May–June 1978, pp. 3–17.

Wilson, Elizabeth, *Women and the Welfare State*, London, 1977.

Winnicott, D. W., 'Appetite and Emotional Disorder' (1936), *Collected Papers: Through Paediatrics to Psycho-Analysis*, London, 1958, pp. 33–51.

Winnicott, D. W., 'The Deprived Mother' (broadcast, 1939), in *The New Era in Home and School*, no. 21, March, 1940, and in *Getting to Know Your Baby*, London, 1944, and revised in *The Child and the Family: First Relationships*, London, 1957.

Winnicott, D. W., *Getting to Know Your Baby: Six Broadcast Talks*, including 'Getting to Know Your Baby', 'Their Standards and Yours', 'Why Do Babies Cry?', 'What About Father?', 'The Deprived Mother', London, 1944.

Winnicott, D. W., 'What About Father?', in *The New Era in Home and School*, vol. 26, no. 1, January 1945, also in *The Child and the Family: First Relationships*, London, 1957, and in *Getting To Know Your Baby*, London, 1944.

Winnicott, D. W., 'Psychoanalysis and the Sense of Guilt', *Psychoanalysis and Contemporary Thought*, ed. J. D. Sutherland, London, 1958, pp. 15–32.

Winnicott, D. W., 'Classification: Is There a Psychoanalytic Contribution to Psychiatric Classification?' (1959–64), *The Maturational Processes and the Facilitating Environment*, London, 1965, pp. 124–39.

Winnicott, D. W., 'On the Contribution of Direct Child Observation to Psychoanalysis', *The Maturational Processes and the Facilitating Environment: Studies in the Theory of Emotional Development*, London, 1965, pp. 109–14.

Winnicott, D. W., 'A Personal View of the Kleinian Contribution' (1962), *The Maturational Processes and the Facilitating Environment*, London 1965, pp. 171–8.

Winnicott, D. W., 'The Theory of the Parent-Infant Relationship' (1960), *The Maturational Processes and the Facilitating Environment*, London, 1965, pp. 37–55.

Winnicott, D. W., *The Child, the Family, and the Outside World*, London, 1964.

Wolf, K. M., 'Evacuation of Children in War Time – a Survey of the Literature, with Bibliography', *Psychoanalytic Study of the Child*, vol. 1, 1945, pp. 389–404.

Wolfe, Lawrence, *The Reilly Plan: A New Way of Life*, London, 1948.

Women's Co-Operative Guild: *Reports of Annual Congresses* of the Women's Co-Operative Guild, London, 1937–46.

Women's Hygiene Committee of the Women's Group on Public Welfare, *Our Towns; A Close-up*, London, 1943.

Wootton, Barbara, *Social Science and Social Pathology*, London, 1959.

World Health Organisation, 'Separation of the Pre-School Child from the Mother', Expert Committee on Mental Health: *Report on the Second Session*, pp. 14–19, Technical Report Series, no. 31, Geneva, 1951.

Zavodovsky, B., 'The "Physical" and the "Biological" in the Process of Organic Evolution', *Science at the Crossroads*, ed. N. Bukharin, London, 1931, 1971.

Index

Index